# AN INTRODUCTION TO MODERN EUROPEAN PHILOSOPHY

# An Introduction to Modern European Philosophy

Edited by

**Jenny Teichman**
*Fellow of New Hall*
*University of Cambridge*

and

**Graham White**
*Internationale Akademie für Philosophie*
*Liechtenstein*

St. Martin's Press     New York

St. Martin's Press, Scholarly and Reference Division,
175 Fifth Avenue, New York, N.Y. 10010

First published in the United States of America in 1995

Printed in Great Britain

ISBN 0–312–12853–3 (cloth)
ISBN 0–312–12855–X (paper)

Library of Congress Cataloging-in-Publication Data
An introduction to modern European philosophy / [edited by] Jenny
Teichman and Graham White.
p. cm.
Includes bibliographical references and index.
ISBN 0–312–12853–3 (cloth). — ISBN 0–312–12855–X (paper)
1. Philosophy—Introductions. 2. Philosophy, European.
3. Philosophy, Modern. I. Teichman, Jenny. II. White, Graham,
1957– .
BD21.I53 1995
190—dc20                                    95–14912

# Contents

LIST OF CONTRIBUTORS                                       vi

PREFACE                                                   vii

GLOSSARY                                                 viii

INSTEAD OF AN INTRODUCTION              G. White            1

REFLECTIONS ON THE PRESENT CONFLICT     G. White            4

G.W.F. HEGEL                            R. Stern           18

ARTHUR SCHOPENHAUER                     J. Teichman        38

SØREN KIERKEGAARD                       R. Stern           49

KARL MARX                               G. Howie           63

FRIEDRICH NIETZSCHE                     J. Teichman        76

EDMUND HUSSERL                          G. White           91

MARTIN HEIDEGGER                        G. White          105

JEAN-PAUL SARTRE                        J. Teichman       120

SIMONE DE BEAUVOIR                      G. Howie          132

JÜRGEN HABERMAS                         N. Davey          145

M. FOUCAULT ✓                           S. Christmas      162

1968 AND AFTER                          S. Plant          175

INDEX                                                     192

# List of Contributors

Simon Christmas, Gonville and Caius College, University of Cambridge, Cambridge, England.

Nicholas Davey, University College, Llandaff, University of Wales, Cardiff, Wales.

Gill Howie, Department of Philosophy, University of Liverpool, Liverpool, England.

Sadie Plant, Department of Cultural Studies, University of Birmingham, Birmingham, England.

Robert Stern, Department of Philosophy, University of Sheffield, Sheffield, England.

Jenny Teichman, New Hall, University of Cambridge, Cambridge, England.

Graham White, International Academy of Philosophy, Schaan, Liechtenstein.

# Preface

This book is an introduction to European philosophy for English-speaking readers. In the Introduction, one will find an exploration of the misunderstandings which arise from the notion that English philosophy is analytic, and therefore very dry and abstract, while European philosophy is non-analytic, and therefore more relevant to human concerns. The divide between analytic philosophy and continental philosophy is sometimes taken as self-evident. Yet logic, and linguistics, and the philosophy of mathematics – areas usually associated with Anglo-American philosophy – have not been neglected in Europe during the last two hundred years; on the contrary, great advances in these fields were made by Peano (an Italian), Frege (a German), Lukasiewicz (a Pole) and other Europeans.The works of these people, however, are probably too difficult to be useful as subject matter in an introductory text.

The philosophers we have chosen to discuss concerned themselves, on the whole, with less arcane matters. It has to be admitted, moreover, that philosophy in continental Europe during the last two centuries has been richer than English philosophy in ideas and theories about politics, history, religion, music and the nature of Western culture; matters which do not strictly speaking belong to philosophy itself, or not, at least, to its more technical side. For these reasons we believe that this text will be accessible to humanities undergraduates generally and not only to students of philosophy. And since each chapter is more or less self-contained, it will be possible for individual readers to begin by reading the ones which deal with their own particular concerns. Students of political theory and history will find the essays on Marx and Habermas especially significant, while theology students may want to start with Kierkegaard and Nietzsche. Psychology students will discover that Husserl's theory of knowledge incorporates ideas about the psychology of perception, and that de Beauvoir and Foucault both discuss the psychology as well as the ideology of sex. Schopenhauer's concept of the will embodies yet another aspect of psychology. Students of literature may find out how Sartre's philosophy of freedom is expounded in his novels. An account of the interaction between philosophy and politics in France is given in the last chapter. Finally, since almost every thinker represented herein had a theory about the fundamental nature of reality, the book as a whole comprises a brief history of two hundred years of metaphysics.

# Glossary

**Alienation** A Hegelian and Marxist concept, according to which certain entities, typically people and social institutions, develop by passing through stages, some of which involve dissolution and loss. These latter are states of alienation.

**Bracketing** See Epochē.

**Conventionalism** The doctrine that the connection between signs, language, etc., and what these stand for is a matter of arbitrary convention.

**Destruction** and **Deconstruction** Heideggerean Destruction is the view that certain key concepts (for example the Western concept of Being) are fundamentally muddled. To extricate ourselves from muddle, we have to analyse these concepts into their historical roots. Deconstruction is associated with Derrida, who has a theory about signification according to which all our concepts are unstable. The process of exposing the instability is called deconstruction.

**Dialectics** Generally used for a variety of philosophical methods which go beyond the capacities of merely formal logic. Used especially of the methods of Hegel and Marx.

**Epistemology** The theory of knowledge.

**Epochē** A term borrowed by Husserl from the philosophical sceptics of ancient Greece, and which means suspending judgement. It is a central principle of phenomenology that, in order to discover the truth about some things – for example the structure of reality – it is necessary to suspend judgement on others – for example the existence of material objects.

**Essentialism** The theory that things have fixed natures, from which their other properties, and their behaviour, can be inferred.

**Existentialism** A theory which arose in opposition to essentialism. It holds that individuals as such – especially human individuals – do not have essences or fixed natures.

**Fordism** and **post-Fordism** Terms relating to Henry Ford, who introduced large-scale assembly-line manufacturing procedures based on a "rational" division of labour and the regimentation of the work process. Post-Fordism refers to recent developments in manufacturing, made possible by new technology, which seem to escape from the Fordist paradigm.

**Gender Bias** A gender biased theory, outlook or doctrine uses gender-specific concepts in an unreflective way, and thereby reinforces the sexual status quo. To genderise a theory is to introduce gender-biased concepts.

**Gender Theory** Any theory involving a critical examination of the way in which gender-biased concepts affect thinking.

**Idealism** and **Realism** Idealism is the theory that reality consists of ideas and consciousness. Realism is a theory or group of theories according to which the world has real non-mental constituents.

**Ideology** A term which can be used neutrally or polemically. Neutrally it means a system of beliefs, especially those characteristic of a given society. In polemics, and particularly Marxist polemics, it means a false system of beliefs supporting the power structure of a given society.

**Identity Philosophy** The position that the basic constituents of reality are static and self-sufficient. Hegel invented the term to use polemically against the early Schelling.

**Logic** This has been defined as the "laws of thought", an expression which can be taken in more than one way. It can mean either a study of how people ought to reason, or of how they do in fact reason. Formal logic studies reasoning by presenting it in symbolic form. There is disagreement amongst logicians and other philosophers about whether all of human reasoning can be represented symbolically.

**Mereology** The formal theory of parts and wholes.

**Metaphysics** Refers either to the philosophical study of existence and knowledge, or to any general integrative discipline that ties the various parts of philosophy together.

**Modernism** and **Post-Modernism** Modernism is a group of theories which maintain that society is progressing towards a state of greater rationality and thereby a state of greater justice. Its proponents include Kant and J. S. Mill. Post-modernism is the view that the era in which modernism is valid is over.

**Ontology** Literally the study of being or existence; sometimes used as a synonym for metaphysics.

**Particular** See universal.

**Phenomenology** A group of philosophical methods which use introspection to study the structure of experience by imagining variations in its contents. The word was first used in this sense by Husserl, who invented the method.

**Post-Fordism** See Fordism.

**Post-Modernism** See Modernism.

**Praxis** A term which (especially in Marxism) means a combination of theory and action.

**Project** A long-range structure of plans and desires.

**Projection** Investing some external objects, for example other persons, with attributes which do not belong to them but which come from one's own mental life.

**Realism** See Idealism.

**Reification** The error of treating as things items which are not things – for example, relations, propositions, concepts (such as justice, patriarchy, etc.).

**Solipsism** The doctrine that the only reality is a single isolated consciousness, for example mine.

**Structuralism** A family of theories, associated with Saussure, which emphasises the importance of relations, rather than the nature of objects in isolation. Often associated with conventionalism.

**Superstructure** A Marxist concept referring to the non-material components of society, for example art, religion etc.

**Thrownness** A Heideggerean concept, referring to the fact that we find ourselves in a situation in the world which we did not choose and cannot fully grasp or control.

**Transcendent** To transcend a domain is to go beyond it. The transcendent is generally taken to be those realities which lie beyond what we can immediately know.

**Transcendental** A Kantian term which applies to subject and object, and to arguments. The transcendental object and subject, as distinct from merely empirical objects and subjects, are the two basic constituents of reality. A transcendental argument is one which starts from the conditions of possibility of a premise, rather than from the premise itself.

**Transcendental Idealism** The theory that the transcendental subject is prior to the transcendental object.

**Universal** and **Particular** A particular is an individual of some kind, for example a person, a chair, a table. The word universal is used either of a collection of similar real or imaginary particulars (for example horses, thoughts, volcanic eruptions, unicorns), or as a synonym for the words type, class, sort, kind.

# 1 Instead of an Introduction
## Graham White

Jan was not pleased: her ski trip started tomorrow, she had a complicated paper to write towards her Master's degree, and it looked as if she was going to have to stay up all night to finish it. Might as well start it, though. She looked at her desk, covered with old, boring, crumbly books about Western intellectual history in the late twentieth century. The period had never attracted her: two hundred years ago, and it seemed to be horrifyingly violent, physically as well as intellectually. Obscure, too; she had tried to start on the paper several times, but had always given up when she could not keep straight the names of the faction leaders. What was the title? Oh yes, "Describe some academic controversy of the late twentieth century". Finding an academic controversy had been easy enough; a quick search of the computer databases had turned up a squabble in Cambridge between one of the local professors and a French philosopher. Who were they? Jacques Mellor? No... ah, that was it, *Jacques* Derrida and *Hugh* Mellor. Problem number one, then: who were Derrida and Mellor? That had not taken very long to find out, although she could not seem to find a comprehensible description of what Derrida thought. Problem number two: what happened at Cambridge? Mellor and other Cambridge philosophers had tried to prevent Derrida from getting an honorary degree, she found out. Ah. A boring little academic squabble of the usual sort. What did British intellectuals think about it? A collection of reprints from magazines and newspapers soon gave the answer to that one: British intellectuals were, on the whole, extremely confused by the whole thing.

So why not just write all that down and hand it in? No... she could remember her supervisor's words, tearing her last effort to shreds. "Why, Jan, why? Keep asking yourself *that*. You say 'first X happened, then Y, then Z' – but you never explain *why* it all happened. You forget that they were real people that you're talking about. What got them worked up? What turned them on? Why did they do these things to each other? And don't just read textbooks – read the sources, find out what these people said in their own words. The textbooks are mostly wrong, you know." The professor was a wonderful historian, of course. But a perfectionist. And her deadline was approaching.

So how was she to answer the professor's questions? And particularly the big question that was lurking in the background: what was this squabble *really* about? Let's start with an easy question: how did the two parties think of each other? Well, the Cambridge faction thought of Derrida as a European philosopher, and they thought of themselves as English philosophers. But that didn't make any sense – when she looked up the intellectual predecessors of Cambridge thought of that period – Brentano, Tarski, Wittgenstein – she found out that they came from Austria and Poland. And how was it the other way round? Well, the French thought of the English as "positivists" – but that didn't make any sense either, because positivism had been invented in *France* by a man called Comte a couple of hundred years before that, and in any case the English just weren't positivists. She did find out – a wonderfully obscure fact, this would really impress her supervisor – that a few imitators of a Viennese movement called "logical positivism" had been active for a while in England about thirty years before the Derrida incident; but they seemed too early and too insignificant to matter. So all that was a dead end.

If the parties' own descriptions of the conflict don't make any sense, she thought, then maybe there were still good reasons for it; maybe they just had different styles of thought, different authorities, that sort of thing. So who did both sides consider as authorities? First, the Cambridge lot. They seemed to be very fond of logic. At least, they *said* they were. Jan felt a flicker of interest – after all, she wanted to one day write her doctoral thesis on the history of logic. "So let's have a look," she thought, "at some of this stuff. But no... what's that? They can't *still* be using first order predicate calculus? In 1990? I'm confused." The research for this paper was one incomprehensible fact after another. The Europeans were no more tractable: they said that their work was based on history and the human sciences. "So", Jan thought, "I'm taking nothing for granted – I'll look at some of the history that Derrida uses." Thus it was that she spent two hours tracing Derrida's opinions on "the Western metaphysical tradition" – first back to Heidegger's historical remarks, and then back from Heidegger to Brentano's historical works (a difficult one that, Heidegger never used footnotes) and back from Brentano to some other nineteenth century histories of philosophy. But this meant that, despite Derrida's appeals to history, many of the things he said were based on historical research that was not only, in his time, a hundred years out of date, but also known to be wrong when he was writing.

Four a.m. Anything to show for this? "I seem to have gone backwards. When I began, I thought I could tell a story. Now I can't even tell a story." She rested her head in her hands and tried to concentrate. "Maybe

I can still describe it in another way. Let's think – what was that I just heard in those philosophy of religion seminars? Myth and ritual? Plenty of that here, seems to me. Both sides making up myths about each other. And about themselves. Lots of ritual, too – those analytic philosophers, they weren't using logic to learn anything from it. They just used it to give authority to what they believed anyway. What do the sociologists call that? 'Legitimation'? That's it. And the French and the Germans, too: talking about history all the time, but most of them, they didn't want to know about the real history. They just wanted legitimation too."

The dawn was breaking when Jan finished the draft of her paper. It was good, though, she thought; difficult, but worth the effort. The professor had better be impressed. A good title, too: "Myth and Ritual: The Essential Irrationality of Late Twentieth Century Academic Debate".

# 2 Reflections on the Present Conflict
## Graham White

This book is an introduction to European philosophy for English-speaking readers. This is a neutral description, both of the subject matter and of the intended audience – but to be neutral covers up the unavoidable fact that the situation is, and for a long time has been, extremely polemical; European philosophy and Anglo-Saxon thought are supposed to be two opposing – and maybe irreconcilable – camps, and the authors of a book such as this cannot do to forget such circumstances. Whether one likes it or not, one is involved in the polemic.

But neither can one assume that the issues of the polemic are easy to comprehend. We may take sides, but we should not assume that we can describe accurately either our own side's position or that of the "enemy". Caricatures abound: for example, the picture of analytic philosophy, wedded to clarity and common sense, versus a deliberately obscure and irrational European philosophy. Or – from the other side – the picture of a mechanistic, "positivist" analytic philosophy, uncaring about life or art, opposed to a humanistically oriented, politically engaged philosophical tradition. These caricatures are gravely wrong, and almost impossible to pin down in any exact terms. Most attempts to describe the opposition in some non-geographic way come to grief. Consider, for example, the problem of "metaphysics". Forty years ago, when logical positivism flourished, analytical philosophers were against metaphysics – or at any rate quite a lot of them were. Now, however, it seems that many French philosophers deny the possibility of metaphysics – they think it has "come to an end" – whereas analytical philosophers are busily writing about the subject (see, for example, the works of Michael Dummett). One finds this sort of thing over and over again: hardly any term that one chooses will reliably demarcate one side from the other, but will change sides with bewildering rapidity.

The worst culprit here is the word 'positivism'; it has a fairly exact meaning – roughly speaking, a positivist is someone who believes that science should only correlate and describe observations, and should not talk about unobservable entities. The problem is, however, that many unlikely people turn out to be positivists in this sense (Goethe, for exam-

4

ple, had a fairly positivist philosophy of science, *avant le lettre*), whereas most people who are accused of being positivists are definitely not positivists: the majority of analytic philosophers are not positivist in the exact sense, and hardly any scientists are. Scientists really *believe* in quarks and genes and microbes and such like unobservables. So when someone gets called a "positivist", what does it usually mean? It mostly seems to get used, by people who are not analytic philosophers, of analytic philosophy, and usually about arguments which are technical, or which use some logical symbolism, or are in some similar way difficult for an outsider to comprehend. These may or may not be valid grounds for accusation, but using a term like 'positivist' in this context does nothing but mystify.

Things are even worse when politics enters the picture. It certainly is true that a good deal of French and German philosophy is rather more directly politicised than Anglo-Saxon philosophy, and there is, of course, nothing wrong with that: politics has, after all, a very wide scope, and there is nothing in our philosophical activity that could remove it somehow from the sphere of the political. But what is not good for philosophy (or, indeed, politics) is when the politicisation of philosophy happens – as it often does – by the construction of what one could call a politico-philosophical dictionary. By this I mean a list, with philosophical concepts on one side, and, on the other side, their supposedly fixed political meanings. Thus – to take some contemporary examples – essentialism is supposed to be right wing, constructivism is supposed to be left wing, realism is supposed to be right wing, and so on. This is a hindrance to thought and to good politics, because it assumes that the political significance of a given philosophical concept is somehow fixed and independent of subject matter or of the occasion of use. In any case, these alignments change sides every so often: nowadays realism is supposed to be right wing; about thirty years ago, realism was supposed to be left wing, and idealism right wing.

## What is an Introduction, Anyway?

The usual genre for an introduction to a book of this sort would be like this. One would firstly give a brief history of German philosophy since Kant (Fichte, Schelling, Hegel, and so on), then one would tell a continuing story on that basis, locating each of one's authors within that story. This would serve several purposes. Firstly, it would give each of one's authors a place in some meaningful pattern. Secondly, it would tell one what each of the authors was trying to do, since the story is the story of a group of thinkers each building on the results of the previous one and each aiming at some set of common goals. Thirdly, it would introduce quite a lot of useful terminology, since the terminology of European philosophy is, more or less, Hegelian.

It would also be misleading. There are several things wrong with the story. One is that it falsifies the history: there is no uninterrupted succession of Hegelianism in Europe from the early nineteenth century onwards. Hegel was not an undisputed philosophical leader in his own time (Schleiermacher had far larger audiences for his lectures), and was practically forgotten in Europe in the late nineteenth century: Brentano, writing at the turn of the century, could dismiss Hegel as someone "who is not to be taken seriously". At that time, there seem to have been far more Hegelians in Britain than in Europe; Bertrand Russell was one, for example. The philosophy of the *late* nineteenth century had its own problems and its own interests, which were not those of the early nineteenth century. The natural and social sciences had expanded to such an extent that it was no longer possible to envisage philosophy as a subject which would synthesise the results of all the particular sciences, as Hegel did, and the questions which late nineteenth century philosophy had to deal with were, firstly, those of the fragmentation of knowledge, and, secondly, the problems posed by a rather aggressive reductionism, which tried to explain almost everything in scientific, and particularly in biological, terms – Nietzsche was heavily influenced by this reductionism.

Secondly, the standard narrative introduction tends to describe the history in terms of philosophers' acknowledged influences. If philosopher A *says* he was influenced by B, one simply writes that A *was*, in fact, influenced by B. The problems with this approach are both negative and positive. Negatively, it leaves out a number of important philosophers who everyone is influenced by, but nobody cites: thus Bergson is a significant influence on the French, but hardly any of them mention him by name. Similarly, Brentano is an important influence on Husserl and Heidegger, but Heidegger hardly mentions him. One could go on: there is a long list of philosophers who are both interesting in their own right and because of their influence, but who have fallen through the net of the standard historiography – the neo-Kantians, Brentano's school, Scheler, Marcel, Blondel, Gilson.

The positive distortions are also considerable. The problem here is that, even though a philosopher claims to have been influenced by someone, this influence may rest upon a misunderstanding. This problem is particularly acute in the case of the French assimilations of German philosophy: it is well known that Heidegger protested against Sartre's interpretation of him, but it remains to be seen whether Derrida's purported Heideggereanism is any more accurate.

As well as these material difficulties with narrative history, there are certain formal difficulties, which mostly stem from the fact that narrative is linear. The ease with which significant figures are simply forgotten may well stem from this desire to tell a linear story. But there is more: the story is told in such a way that it is similarly a narrative and a philosophical argument. The step from A to B is presented in such a way as to make it seem that it is not just a historical event, but a logically rigorous deduction: if you accept A, then you have to accept B as well. Hegel's dialectic explicitly made this sort of double claim – that is, it claimed to be both a story and a logical argument – but, unless one is a doctrinaire Hegelian, there seems little reason to accept this sort of thing, especially in view of the recent criticisms of dialectic described in the last chapter of this book.

The other formal difficulty with narrative lies in the desire to present a story with a coherent cast of characters. The "characters" here, however, are not philosophers but their doctrines, and the picture is that one has a relatively fixed collection of philosophical ideas – "subject", "object", "self", "mind", "history", "being", and so on – which undergo various adventures in that philosophers have different ideas about them. This only works, however, if these ideas have a relatively stable meaning which allows them to be identified and reidentified as the same in various different philosophies: for some of them – "mind", for example – this is maybe possible, but for others – such as "subject" and "object" – it is extremely problematic, because, although philosophers may use the same words, they can mean radically different things by them.

But what remains if one discards the narrative? Not, surely, some sort of grand message, to the effect that European philosophy is the sole repository of human values, or that it is the only correct way to do philosophy, or that it represents some Great Tradition which has been abandoned by the Anglo-Saxon world, or that it is a kind of permanently oppositional thought that is the only appropriate expression of intellectual and political dissent – a singularly implausible claim, considering the sort of hierarchical intellectual establishments that European thought emanates from. Although European philosophy has been advocated in these terms, such an appeal would only be one of many dangerous caricatures about the relation between the two sorts of philosophy.

# Open Problems

So far, we have criticised two of the main approaches to writing about European philosophy for the English-speaking market. Both of these approaches, as we have seen, depend on mythology: they either invent fictitious opponents, or a fictitious past. We will try to say something more meaningful about European philosophy, attempting to capture common themes from the diverse philosophies presented in this book. One consequence will be that the distinction between European and analytic philosophy – which formerly seemed to be absolute – will turn out to be much less distinct: similarities abound, as well as differences. Here follows a survey of some common problems which concern both contemporary European, and also analytic, philosophy.

## *Foundationalism*

This is the idea that philosophy, or science, should be, or is, based on some set of privileged foundations, which are either better known, or more certain, or clearer, or temporally or logically prior to, the rest of philosophy, which is based on those foundations. Foundationalism comes in two varieties, justificatory and descriptive: the former claims that, in order to be rigorous, philosophy must be *based* on such foundations; the latter claims that one can *describe* various different systems of philosophy solely by describing the foundations, and then deducing the other important features of the various systems from one's description of the foundations.

There has been a great deal of argument recently about justificatory foundationalism, and it is hard to find anyone in the contemporary philosophical scene who is a justificatory foundationalist. Things are quite otherwise with descriptive foundationalism: there are many philosophers who take a strongly anti-foundationalist line as far as the justification of theories goes, but who are nevertheless foundationalist when they describe philosophical theories. Heidegger is such a philosopher: his arguments against justificatory foundationalism are well known, but he has an explicitly foundationalist position when it comes to description, since he holds that what is fundamental for describing and analysing somebody's thought is their ontology (roughly speaking, their views on what sort of things there are). Similarly, when Habermas describes Marxism as a variant of Hegel's philosophy of identity, he is using a descriptive terminology which dates back to the early nineteenth century (in this case, to Hegel's critique of the early Schelling), which is used extensively for the description of philosophical positions, and which, again, is an instance of descriptive foundationalism. And, finally, Derrida's use of the term "logo-centrism" is descriptively foundationalist: he is asserting that this is a basic feature of an enormous range of philosophies (i.e. Western thought from Socrates on), and also that it can be appropriately used to criticise those philosophies.

There is not necessarily anything wrong with descriptive foundational-ism; however, the problem is that, in many cases, it is adopted without argument, simply by the use of a given descriptive vocabulary. Very often, too, it is difficult to see what arguments could lie behind it, and, in particular, behind its *critical* use: what follows, as far as the evaluation of somebody's thought is concerned, from the fact that it can be described as X? To take Heidegger for an example: granted that all of Western thought has been as based on metaphysics as he says it was, what follows from that? Very often these connections are not made explicit, and the argu-ment – such as it is – seems to rely on somewhat imprecise metaphors about infection and contamination (for someone's thought to be – let us say – based on the philosophy of identity, is for it to be *infected* with such a thing, and therefore to be avoided).

There is, again, a problem with descriptive foundationalism when it comes to historical scholarship: it tends to force the adoption of a fixed terminology, which can be tremendously constraining. Thus, if one has an idealist background, and thus tends to describe all thought in terms of "subject" and "object", one faces problems with the history of medieval philosophy, because the medievals also used terms like "subjective" and "objective", but with approximately opposite meanings to the idealist ones (thus, the medieval "subjective" means something like the idealists' "objective", and vice versa). Similarly, the medievals' use of terms like "signification" can lay unexpected traps for historians with an analytic background, since it means something rather different from our concept of signification.

## Argument and Beyond

Even in the most rigorous scientific or technical writing, not every move-ment of thought is brought about by the methods of formal logic. This much is uncontentious. What is contentious, however, is the attitude that one takes to this state of affairs. There is hardly anyone left who believes in the possibility of completely formalising any significant piece of philo-sophical argument; it was, certainly, part of the programme of logical pos-itivism, but nowadays philosophers are generally much too aware of the complexity of most real problems to believe that they could be completely translated into formal terms. There are three main attitudes that one can take to this.

The first one would be to say that, although in fact non-formal elements (metaphor, narrative and so on) necessarily do form part of philosophical writing, they can nevertheless be regarded as promissory notes: we can, if we are lucky, fill out the content of any given metaphor, and transform it into a rigorous piece of argument. There is a fair amount of evidence that supports this view: probably the most significant is the success of twentieth century mathematics in doing just this, that is, in providing rigorous reconstructions of areas of mathematics which, in the past, had been done by non-rigorous means – arguments by analogy, pictures, and so on. A remarkable example of this is algebraic geometry, which was notorious in the nineteenth century for its informality and lack of rigour, but which has been made rigorous in the twentieth century in such a way as to recover almost all of the content of the nineteenth century subject. By analogy, this would lead to a view of philosophy as a subject in which rigorous and non-rigorous methods were used, in such a way as to mutually condition one another: the non-rigorous methods being more tentative and exploratory, while the rigorous methods would support and correct what had been conjectured by the non-rigorous methods. The only obstacle, then, to making everything rigorous would be the complexity of the subject, lack of time, and such like manifestations of human finitude, and there would thus be no difference in principle between what could be done by non-rigorous, and what by rigorous, means.

The second position would maintain that there are things which cannot in principle be established by the methods of formal logic. Hegel's position is typical: according to him, philosophy had a method – called dialectic – which went far beyond what could be achieved by formal logic, which was, despite this, rigorous, and which could be used to develop almost all of the content of Hegelian metaphysics. Thus, if Hegel's claims are right, not only would one not need to establish the results of dialectic by formal means, but it would be impossible: dialectic was a method which was superior to logic, so that one simply could not establish its results by logical arguments. Hegel's dialectic was taken up by Marx, and has had a long career among both Hegelians and Marxists. However, it is extremely contentious: hardly any of the results of dialectic – in either the Hegelian or the Marxist forms – seems to have been definitively established in such as way as to be unchallengeable; much of Hegel's philosophy (including almost all of his philosophy of nature) seems to be quite clearly wrong, and to have been quietly forgotten by even the most doctrinaire Hegelians. Consequently, even Hegel's supporters disagree quite strongly about what the dialectical method is, about what subject matter it is appropriate for, and about its degree of rigour. This is not to deny Hegel's significance, or the value of his philosophy, and it is certainly not to say that it is all wrong; however, his own position on the dialectical method is so strong that not even his supporters can plausibly maintain it.

There are other positions which are analogous to Hegel's, in that they claim to have a specifically philosophical method which is not reducible to formal logic. One of these is Husserl's method, which he called phenomenology; there are many philosophers who are, directly or indirectly, influenced by Husserl, and who consequently use some sort of phenomenological method or other – for example, Heidegger, Sartre, de Beauvoir, and Lyotard all claim to be doing phenomenology. However, this does not mean that they are all doing the same thing: there are disagreements between, for example, Heideggerean phenomenologists and those who remain faithful to Husserl, and even the Husserlians are split between those who follow the early Husserl and those who follow his later writings.

There is also a large group of philosophers who claim that philosophy does have methods distinct from those of formal logic, but that they are not specifically philosophical: they are simply the philological, historical methods of humanist scholarship. This is a position with a long and respectable history – since the Renaissance, there have been philosophers who have advocated it – and it has prominent contemporary representatives, notably Foucault with his method of archaeology and, in the Anglo-Saxon world, what is called "ordinary language philosophy".

The third attitude to our problem would be to agree that there are elements in human thought which cannot be represented using the vocabulary of formal logic, but one would refuse to take any normative attitude towards this: that is, one would not try to make any sort of "method" out of the non-argumentative elements. One would simply admit their presence, and say that part of the task of philosophy is to investigate these elements of human thought – almost in the manner of an anthropologist – without attempting either to purge them from human thought or to make a "method" of them. One *could* turn this into a sort of therapy – one would perhaps try to treat the pathologies to which such thought might give rise – or one's message might simply be that these are elements of the human situation which we ought to acknowledge and come to terms with. In any event, though, this attitude would be less narrowly and technically "philosophical" than the previous two: one would not be claiming that these elements of human thought are to be regarded as rational, or are to be made rational, but simply that they are there, that we cannot do without them, but ought to acknowledge them. Nietzsche is the most prominent representative of this school, but there are many contemporary representatives, particularly among the French – Lyotard's philosophy, with his detailed investigations of narrative, is one of the most important. This attitude also lies behind a good deal of work being done in cognitive psychology and linguistics – George Lakoff's work is a good example of this.

There is, of course, nothing which prevents a philosopher from taking more than one of these attitudes: many philosophers combine them in various ways, particularly the second and third. Thus Lyotard has a phenomenological method (i.e. in this respect he represents the second attitude) and uses this method to investigate the role of narrative in human thought (the third attitude). Combinations of the first two are also not uncommon: for example, there are analytical philosophers who work on Hegel, Marx, or Husserl, and who take the first attitude to them – that is, they view Hegel's, Marx's, or Husserl's thought, as fruitful and stimulating, but not rigorous, and they view their own task as that of giving a rigorous reconstruction of what was established, tentatively and non-rigorously, by their nineteenth century predecessors. Habermas, for example, uses the theory of speech acts stemming from analytic philosophy in order to reinterpret Marx's thought, and in this way he takes up the first attitude.

As should be clear by now, this is a fairly tangled issue, and one that is responsible for a great deal of the friction between analytic and European philosophy. Typically, European philosophers take the second or third attitude, whereas analytic philosophers take the first one. This certainly marks a significant difference in philosophical culture, and makes communication between the two parties very difficult. However, it is very hard to say whether there is anything more to it than simply a *cultural* difference; do the attitudes even contradict one another? Probably not, because a significant number of philosophers hold combinations of them. Again, it may well be that one of the attitudes is more appropriate to certain subject matter, and another to different subject matter – the first attitude to the philosophy of the natural sciences, for example, or the second and third attitudes to the philosophy of the human and social sciences. In such a case, the choice of problems that analytic or European philosophers work on could have a profound effect. Analytic philosophers quite frequently work on problems drawn from the natural sciences, whereas European philosophers concentrate on problems from the human sciences or politics (although this should be regarded as a very rough generalisation). Thus the two groups of philosophers could find themselves choosing different methods because of the influence of their typical problems.

These cultural differences are certainly persistent and influential, but one should not take them for granted. They give sociological explanations of why people behave in the way that they do, but they are hardly laws of thought (in either the descriptive or the normative sense). The dividing line between the natural and human sciences is constantly varying, and cannot be assumed to be immovably fixed; and certainly any naïve equation of analytic philosophy with the natural sciences, and European philosophy with the human sciences, would be unwarranted. Although both types of philosophy may incline more to one side or the other of the dividing line, there is no law that says so – and, in any case, the facts do not bear out any sort of naïve dichotomy. Hegel's favourite subject at high school was physics, Husserl's background was in mathematics, and there is a good deal of both subjects in their respective philosophies. Even Heidegger wrote extremely good summaries of both relativity theory and intuitionistic logic in the initial paragraphs of *Being and Time*.

## Authority

It is quite clear that both types of philosophy acknowledge different sorts of authority. Analytic philosophy inclines towards the natural sciences and logic; European philosophy relies on history and the exegesis of texts. That, at any rate, is the ideology of both sides. However, simply because a group of people profess to treat something as authoritative does not mean that they in fact do so: they might not try, and even if they do try to obey the authority they might not do so successfully. So it is in this case. The average analytic philosopher's grasp of logic corresponds to the state of logic in the 1930s and 1940s; formal logic has changed quite substantially in the mean while, but analytic philosophy, on the whole, shows no sign of wanting to keep up to date. Similarly, European philosophers' dealings with history often amount to no more than vague and unsubstantiated references to the "Western metaphysical tradition". There are exceptions on both sides, but what is striking is the rigidity and conservatism of philosophers' dealings with their professed authorities. This is hardly deliberate, but it seems to be a sad fact that, when one treats something as authoritative, one's attitude to it can be very constrained and, hence, conservative.

This is especially true here, when both authoritative subjects (history and logic) are external to philosophy. They thus both need interpretation: to use them in philosophy, one needs to know the "philosophical meaning" of, say, a logical formula, or a historical event. These "meanings" tend to be very slow to change; they are part of the reason why philosophy's use of its authorities is so conservative. One will find it difficult to assimilate a new logical result, or to incorporate a piece of historical research into one's thinking, until that new element has been provided with a philosophical interpretation.

This state of affairs can have quite paradoxical effects. It turns out that some of the most interesting recent history of philosophy has been done by analytic philosophers – for example, there is the work of Kretzmann and his school on medieval philosophy, or Sorabji's work on the Hellenistic period. Conversely, there are several very creative logicians with "European" philosophical allegiances – Lawvere is a Marxist, for example. One should not deduce from this anything about the superiority of one tradition over another: all it shows is how constraining an authoritative tradition can be.

## Philosophical Engagement

What, then, has European philosophy to contribute that is distinctive? Why ought one to read it? A perfectly good answer to this question would be that many European philosophers are worth reading because they are good philosophers and have said interesting things. Some of the things that they have said – for example, about the relation between philosophy and politics – have been somewhat neglected in Anglo-Saxon thought; other things – such as Heidegger's critique of foundationalism – are concerned with matters that have been extensively discussed in Anglo-Saxon philosophy, but, nonetheless, give an informatively different perspective on those matters. This would certainly be an *adequate* answer, but hardly an exciting one.

There is a rather more exciting answer, however. It is simply that European philosophy has taken seriously – as analytic philosophy, arguably, has not – the notion of philosophy as *engaged*, as involved in a critical dialogue with the intellectual, cultural and political events of the time. And in this respect, the philosophers described in this book provide a series of important models for how such engagement can take place; almost all of them thought of their work as having a dual aspect, discussing purely philosophical questions on the one hand, and, on the other hand, bearing on the political and social conditions of the societies that they lived in. Although individual analytical philosophers may also have been thus oriented – Bertrand Russell springs to mind – it is not something that is *systematically* practised in the analytic community; it is, as it were, a hobby for analytic philosophers, but part of one's professional orientation for the Europeans.

An engaged philosophy is one which becomes involved with extra-philosophical questions. Particularly, it concerns itself with problems from history, politics, literature, and the social sciences. What, then, can we learn about engagement from the European philosophers that we cover in this book? Engagement can be problematic if – as European philosophy is – the philosopher is very conscious of the tradition he or she stands in: one may simply take the traditional account of philosophy's role, and blindly apply it to contemporary problems. The frequent attacks by European philosophers on long dead movements (such as positivism) is a witness to such traditionalism, but there are more serious cases where it could be a danger. One is the problem of social structure: it seems to have been taken for granted, in much post-war European philosophy, that the main problem facing society was too much structure; that society, and individuals, were constrained by social structures that were repressive, or at least overly bureaucratic and conformist. We are now living in a society where, in many parts of the world, the main problem seems to be not an excess of structure, but a lack of it: the former Yugoslavia, of course, comes to mind, but is far from the only example. Thus the equation of structure with repression is very problematic, at least according to the *naive* reading of the European tradition. There are, of course, resources in the European tradition which will allow one to say more constructive things about this problem, but exploiting them will certainly mean reading the sources attentively and sensitively.

## Methodology

This is another problematic area, and one which is fraught with both academic and political dangers. Academically, there seems to be a tendency to absolutise various competing philosophical methodologies (phenomenology, deconstruction, archeology, hermeneutics...) which are learned by imitation, from teacher to student, without ever being described accessibly enough so that one could get a good idea of their limitation, or even whether they really are compatible, or incompatible, with each other. Furthermore, one could well ask whether there is anything about such methodologies which makes them immune from the political critique of dialectic described in the last chapter of this book. The philosophical and the political critiques, of course, reinforce each other: insofar as a "method" can only be learned by imitation, by personal contact from teacher to pupil, it will naturally lead to the formation of an élite.

One ought, then, to be a little sceptical about the question of methodology: specifically, one ought to be doubtful of claims that philosophy is only possible with an appropriate methodology (something which seems to be empirically false, and in any case is very hard to argue for), and one ought also to examine very carefully the connection between philosophers' professed methodologies and the way that they actually reason; there can be quite significant divergences. Ironically, this is yet another issue on which analytical and European philosophy have crossed over; fifty years ago, analytical philosophy made very strong claims about methodology, claiming that philosophy ought to be carried out according to an explicitly formulated method, and it has now given up almost all of these claims.

## The Philosophers

A book such as this, of course, cannot replace reading the philosophers themselves, and cannot replace a serious engagement with their thought. *That* can be difficult, infuriating, mystifying, but also rewarding: difficult, because good philosophy can be difficult; infuriating and mystifying, since one is dealing with writings produced in an intellectual culture that one does not know; but, of course, rewarding, since Europe has produced a great deal of good philosophy in the nineteenth and twentieth centuries. One must also be prepared to disagree: very few of the people discussed in this book would be happy with any sort of slavish intellectual discipleship, and, after all, many of the things that they said are quite controversial. And this is only consistent with the picture of philosophical engagement that we are trying to build; it would be odd if any particular philosopher – or philosophical movement – could give all of the answers to the philosophical, political, or social problems that we face now, or could warrant the sort of discipleship that some philosophers seem to attract. The essays collected in this book are written from a variety of standpoints, but they all share a willingness to disagree with the philosophers that they study; it is hoped that, in this way, this book can be an aid to intelligent debate with the tradition of European philosophy.

## Philosophy in a Particular Situation

This, then, is the position argued for here: it is a plea for a serious engagement, by philosophers, with political and social issues; but it is equally a plea to be aware of the necessarily contextual nature of that engagement. In a given context, certain philosophical issues will turn out to be politically or socially germane, others not. Consequently, one cannot expect there to be any philosophical concepts or methodologies – or any particular philosophers – that are guaranteed to be automatically on the side of the angels. And philosophical arguments which attempt to discover such privileged concepts, or methodologies, must inevitably seem rather suspect; many of them seem to establish conclusions which are implausibly strong (claims, for example, that essentialism is always politically repressive, or that realism is always a product of false consciousness). There surely are links between philosophy and political or social practice, but these links are strongly contextual; and so, if we want ourselves to be, as philosophers, socially or politically engaged, we must be prepared to be involved in a particular situation, to know the relevant areas of philosophy, and to bring the philosophy to bear on the problems of the particular situation. If this is an accurate picture of philosophical engagement, then any attempt to establish – almost *a priori* – some sort of privileged methodology, or to establish a fixed correlation between political and social ideas, can only fail. Grandiose strategies of this sort, although they may be good for philosophers' self-esteem, are hardly constructive; they facilitate neither one's involvement with the world one lives in, nor properly cooperative relations with one's philosophical colleagues, other than the members of a small clique, and are probably best discarded.

# 3  G.W.F. Hegel
## Robert Stern

Writing in 1946, Merleau-Ponty declared that "all the great philosophical ideas of the past century – the philosophies of Marx and Nietzsche, phenomenology, German existentialism, and psychoanalysis – had their beginnings in Hegel." (Merleau-Ponty, "Hegel's Existentialism", p. 63) Although this is in some respects an exaggeration, Merleau-Ponty's assessment is nonetheless broadly speaking correct, and indeed some other schools of thought, such as critical theory, could perhaps be added to the list. Hegel's work provides the background against which the major developments in European ideas since 1831 have emerged, and for many of the philosophers to be discussed in this book, only once they had come to terms with Hegel could their own thinking begin. Furthermore, as Merleau-Ponty observes, "interpreting Hegel means taking a stand on all the philosophical, political, and religious problems of our century", for often the central debates within post-Hegelian continental philosophy have been couched in terms of competing readings of his work. Hegel is therefore a good place to start for two reasons: firstly, because he decisively influenced the thinking of those who came after him, if only negatively, and secondly because so much European philosophy has been written by developing different aspects of his thought, and by providing competing approaches to problems in his terms.

Georg Wilhelm Friedrich Hegel was born in 1770, and was part of an important generation of German thinkers which included the poet Hölderlin and the philosopher Schelling, both of whom Hegel knew from his youth in Tübingen, where they had all attended the Protestant theological college together. Although later on personal and philosophical differences came between them, in the early years they shared a deep concern with the revolution in France, an impatience with the orthodox theology they were taught at Tübingen, a dissatisfaction with Kant's philosophy, and a desire to overcome the fragmentations and divisions they perceived in the social and intellectual outlook of their times. In an early work, published after he was reunited with Schelling in Jena in 1801, Hegel states that "[t]he sole interest of reason" is to "suspend" the antithesis between "spirit and matter, soul and body, faith and intellect, freedom and necessity" (Hegel, *The Difference*, p. 90), arguing that "[d]ichotomy is the source of *the need of philosophy*" (*The Difference*, p. 89). These dichotomies – and there were others, such as that between the individual and society –

were perceived as dividing man from his environment, from his fellow man and from God, and as such it was a primary concern of Hegel and his contemporaries to overcome these oppositions in a more unified world-view.

The poets and philosophers of Hegel's period characteristically identified the Greeks as having possessed such a unity in their social, religious and philosophical outlook, so that the ancient world came to represent for them a lost but exquisite flowering of this desired unity. The emergence of the divided and alienated world-view held by "us moderns" was felt to represent a fall from the innocent harmony of the Greek world, which – as in *Genesis* – could be explained by the awakening in man of the faculty of knowledge, or (more particularly) by the awakening of the sort of reflective self-consciousness which leads to the loss of our original sense of the unity of things. It is important to note, however, that while blaming reflective understanding for this, Hegel nonetheless saw that this mode of thought could not now be given up, and instead believed that the dichotomies it had generated should be resolved in a higher form of knowledge, in which the unified outlook of the Greeks is restored, but at a higher level of understanding and awareness. As we shall see, Hegel shared the confidence expressed here by Hölderlin in the concluding lines of his poetic novel *Hyperion,* that all the contradictions and dichotomies suffered by us moderns could be overcome:

> Like lovers' quarrels are the dissonances of the world. Reconciliation is there, even in the midst of strife, and all things that are parted find one another again. The arteries separate and return to the heart and all is one eternal glowing life. So I thought. More soon. (Hölderlin, *Hyperion*, p. 170)

## The *Phenomenology of Spirit*

Hegel's thought is notorious for its systematic and all-inclusive nature, a feature which characterises his work from around 1801 onwards. In the Jena lectures of 1803-6, which he delivered as a *Privatdozent* or unsalaried lecturer, he put forward the outlines of his early philosophical system. While at Jena he wrote his first major work, the *Phenomenology of Spirit*. ('Spirit' is one possible translation of the German word *Geist,* a term that has no exact equivalent in English, and which can also be rendered as 'mind'.) The publication of the *Phenomenology* was delayed until 1807, as Hegel was forced to leave the city in the wake of the Napoleon's defeat of the Prussians at the battle of Jena, and move to

Bamberg in Bavaria, where he became a newspaper editor. In 1808 Hegel was appointed headmaster of a school at Nuremberg, where he stayed until 1816. From 1816 to 1818 Hegel was professor of philosophy at Heidelberg, and in 1817 he published the *Encyclopaedia of the Philosophical Sciences* in one volume, which is an outline of his system as a whole, consisting of three parts: logic, philosophy of nature and philosophy of mind. This became a three volume work by the time of the third edition of 1830, each volume containing one of the parts of the system. In 1818 Hegel became professor at the University of Berlin, where he published the *Philosophy of Right* in 1821. After his death in 1831, a group of friends compiled an edition of his works in which his lectures on aesthetics, philosophy of religion, philosophy of history and history of philosophy were published, all of which provide further elaboration and discussion of specific parts of his system. This edition also began the practice of adding students' notes and lecture material (*Zusätze*) to the text of the *Encyclopaedia* and the *Philosophy of Right,* as these were used as handbooks for Hegel's teaching courses. In the next two sections, my aim will be to show how the various elements that make up Hegel's *Encyclopaedia of the Philosophical Sciences* relate to one another, in order to provide an overview of his philosophy as a whole.

However, in order to understand Hegel's aim in his developed system, it is necessary to begin with his *Phenomenology of Spirit,* which Hegel himself said should be treated as a "ladder" to the absolute systematic standpoint adopted in the *Encyclopaedia* (*Phenomenology,* p. 14). The *Phenomenology* is a strikingly original work, and its dense and allusive prose and considerable length make it hard to read and follow. Nonetheless, its general aim is clear: it is to trace the development of thought and consciousness through various modes of thought and experience, from the lowest level of human awareness to what Hegel calls "absolute knowledge". The consciousness in question is not just that of a single individual mind taken in isolation, but also that of human culture in general, which is why the *Phenomenology* contains echoes of historical and literary episodes (such as the French revolution, Diderot's *Rameau's Nephew,* Sophocles' *Antigone*) and of diverse philosophical systems. The movement or evolution goes through various necessary stages, which are plotted out in the *Phenomenology.* At each stage, consciousness (or *Geist*) adopts a certain way of viewing the world (including itself), only to find out that this is incoherent, as a result of which a more adequate conception evolves. Hegel compares this movement from partial to absolute knowledge with the Christian account of the movement of spirit through suffering toward redemption and rebirth, when finally "it arrives at knowledge of what it is in itself", and with this finishes its journey along the "pathway of *doubt,* or more precisely the way of despair" (*Phenomenology,* p. 49).

In following spirit's journey towards absolute knowledge, the *Phenomenology* traces the collapse of each inadequate theoretical and practical standpoint adopted by consciousness along the way. The *Phenomenology* is therefore peppered with the "deconstruction" of various inadequate forms of knowledge, such as sense-certainty, perception, empiricism, the scientific understanding of the natural sciences, observing reason, Enlightenment rationalism, and so on. It also follows the collapse of various practical standpoints, such as the master-slave relationship, hedonism, virtue, human and divine law, ethical action, and morality. In revealing these theoretical and practical positions as inadequate and incoherent, the *Phenomenology* aims to show why spirit must move beyond them and arrive at a form of consciousness (absolute knowing) in which their incoherence is resolved.

Now, Hegel's explanation for the development of consciousness through these various standpoints is not based on some idea of historical necessity or goal-directed evolution, as is sometimes alleged. Rather, consciousness develops in its conception of itself and the world because this conception is causing it to see things in the wrong way, so that it is continually being led into contradictions and one-sided modes of thought. It is the failure of consciousness to use the right concepts and categories that forces it to move from one standpoint to another, as each inadequate conception breaks down. The journey of consciousness through the *Phenomenology* only ends when consciousness has arrived at those categories which enable it to avoid a felt contradiction in its experience, and thereby attain absolute knowledge.

In particular, Hegel suggests, consciousness develops in its conception of itself and the world when a certain outlook involves a tension between the categories of *universal* and *particular*, which it tries to resolve. This tension is generated because consciousness often turns out to be using these two principal categories in an inadequate way, leading it to treat the universal on the one side as distinct from the particular on the other. It is only when the opposition between these two categories is overcome that this tension in our conceptual scheme can be resolved, and a unified world-picture emerge.

Hegel focuses on these two categories because he holds that they are central to our way of thinking. At the metaphysical level, we oppose the universality of the ideal to the particularity of the real; the universality of essence to the particularity of existents; universal properties to particular entities; the universality of form to the particularity of matter; and the universality of God to the individuality of man. At the epistemological level, we contrast the universality of thought with the particularity of feeling, and the universal concept with the particular intuition. And at the moral and political level, we distinguish the universality of the genus from the particularity of the individual; the community as universal from the citizen as individual; the universality of the general will from the particularity of the individual will; and the universality of laws from the freedom of the individual. Associated with the categories of universal and individual, therefore, there are crucial issues of metaphysics, epistemology, ethics, political and religious philosophy, and the *Phenomenology* traces the movement of consciousness through all these dimensions. Hegel tries to show that no coherent metaphysical, epistemological or ethical outlook can be attained until these various oppositions are transcended, which can only be achieved when the correct conception of universal and particular has emerged, and we abandon a one-sided understanding of these categories. Thus, when Hegel talks of the failure of consciousness to overcome the dichotomy between universal and particular, he is using this to account for a whole series of divisions in our view of the world, between abstract and concrete, ideal and real, one and many, necessity and freedom, state and citizen, moral law and self-determination, general and particular will. Hegel believed that the dichotomy between universal and particular lies behind all these dichotomies, and in demonstrating how these categories interrelate, he sought to demonstrate how all these other dichotomies could also be overcome.

So, for example, in the discussion of sense-certainty and perception at the beginning of the *Phenomenology,* Hegel tries to show how consciousness gets into difficulties in its conception of objects by treating particular entities as being distinct from their universal properties; for then we are forced to view particulars as indeterminate "Thises" or bare particulars. This Hegel thought was absurd, on the grounds that such pure particulars could not be identified or discriminated from one another. And, at the social level, in the well-known section on the master-slave dialectic, self-consciousness is shown to fall into contradiction in that it opposes itself, as particular, to all other particulars, and thus because it cannot recognise that it shares a universal essence with others, that they are all selves. Hegel comments in the passage from the *Encyclopaedia* that incorporates this section of the *Phenomenology:*

In this determination lies the tremendous contradiction that, on the one hand, the 'I' is wholly universal, absolutely pervasive, and interrupted by no limit, is the universal essence common to all men, the two mutually related selves therefore constituting one identity, constituting, so to speak, one light; and yet, on the other hand, they are also two selves rigidly and unyieldingly confronting each other, each existing as a reflection-into-self, as absolutely distinct from and impenetrable by the other. (*Philosophy of Mind*, §430Z pp. 170f.)

The aim of the master-slave dialectic is thus to show that we cannot view ourselves as pure, unique particulars, and to show that we must come to an awareness of others as selves in their own right, by recognising that we all share a common universal essence. And, as a final example, at the ethical level, Hegel shows that a one-sided emphasis on the individuality of conscience, as one's own inner moral voice, will lead us into conflict with the universal interest of the community, and individuality must be reconciled with the general will if this tension is to be resolved. (*Phenomenology*, pp. 400f.) Using the categories of universal and particular as a focus, therefore, Hegel is able to diagnose and represent most of the crises and contradictions that he and his contemporaries believed beset modern consciousness.

As it is presented in the *Phenomenology,* however, consciousness is not *itself* aware that its difficulties are generated by its inadequate conception of the categories of universal and particular. Rather, only we, as philosophical observers of its journey, have seen that the true cause of consciousness's problems has been its failure to reach a coherent worldview, owing to its one-sided understanding of these categories. In short, while consciousness has been implicitly operating with these categories throughout the *Phenomenology,* it has not yet subjected these categories themselves to an explicit examination, for it has merely been using them in an unreflective way. Once consciousness has reached the end of the *Phenomenology,* however, it is able to give these categories *explicit* treatment, and it is this that we find in Hegel's *Science of Logic:*

In life, the categories are used; from the honour of being contemplated for their own sakes they are degraded to the position where they serve in the creation and exchange of ideas involved in intellectual exercise on a living content.... As impulses the categories are only instinctively active. At first they enter consciousness separately and so are variable and mutually confusing; consequently they afford to mind only a fragmentary and uncertain actuality; the loftier business of logic therefore is to clarify these categories and in them to raise mind to freedom and truth. (*Science of Logic,* pp. 34, 37)

# The *Encyclopaedia*: Logic

Hegel's account of logic exists in two versions: the *Science of Logic* (sometimes known as the "Greater Logic"), published between 1812 and 1816, and written as an independent work, and the so-called "Lesser Logic", which is a condensed version of the *Science of Logic*, and was published as the first part of Hegel's *Encyclopaedia of the Philosophical Sciences*. Each work contains substantially the same material and has largely the same structure, although the *Science of Logic* is more detailed and elaborated. Both can therefore be read together, as forming the first part of Hegel's developed system, to which the *Phenomenology* constitutes the "ladder".

As we have seen, in his *Logic* Hegel sets out to offer an explicit treatment of the categories of thought that were only unreflectively used in the *Phenomenology*. Hegel's suggestion is that in all our thinking we use fundamental concepts or categories (such as being, cause and effect, force) and that these categories carry with them important metaphysical, epistemological and practical implications, and it is Hegel's aim to make us examine such categories more closely:

> ... everyone possesses and uses the wholly abstract category of being. The sun *is* in the sky; these grapes *are* ripe, and so on *ad infinitum*. Or, in a higher sphere of education, we proceed to the relation of cause and effect, force and its manifestation, etc. All our knowledge and ideas are entwined with metaphysics like this and governed by it; it is the net which holds together all the concrete material which occupies us in our action and endeavour. But this net and its knots are sunk in our ordinary consciousness beneath numerous layers of stuff. This stuff comprises our known interests and the objects that are before our minds, while the universal threads of the net remain out of sight and are not explicitly made the subject of our reflection. (*Introduction to the History of Philosophy*, pp. 27–8.)

In a crucial passage of his *Philosophy of Nature,* Hegel makes clear that once the *Logic* has completed its task of investigating and criticising our categories, our ways of thought will be forced to undergo a conceptual revolution, from which a vast cultural, historical, and scientific change will follow:

> ... metaphysics is nothing but the range of universal thought-determinations, and is as it were the diamond-net into which we bring everything in order to make it intelligible. Every cultured consciousness has its metaphysics, its instinctive way of thinking. This is the absolute power within us, and we shall only master it if we make it the object of our knowledge. Philosophy in gener-

al, as philosophy, has different categories from those of ordinary consciousness. All cultural change reduces itself to a difference of categories. All revolu-
tions, whether in the sciences or world history, occur merely because spirit has
changed its categories in order to understand and examine what belongs to it,
in order to possess and grasp itself in a truer, deeper, more intimate and unified
manner. (*Philosophy of Nature*, §246Z I p. 202.)

Hegel therefore hopes that by clarifying our categories in the *Logic,* we
will be led to abandon some of our old and incoherent ways of thinking,
and develop a new set of concepts which will enable us to see things in a
new and better way.

As we have seen, Hegel and his contemporaries were unhappy with our
current way of thinking about the world because it involves deep and
unresolved tensions between (for example) freedom and necessity, faith
and reason, mind and body, finite and infinite and so on. Likewise, in the
*Phenomenology,* we saw that consciousness was led into crisis because it
could not resolve the felt contradictions in its experience. Now, in the
*Logic,* Hegel explicitly deals with the metaphysical categories that lie
*behind* these contradictions and dichotomies, and tries to develop a set of
categories that do not lead to this inadequate world-view. The method he
uses is one of immanent critique: that is, rather than beginning directly
from his own preferred set of categories, he begins instead with the categories of ordinary thought, but shows that on their own they are incoherent, and must be taken up into higher categories. In this way, the *Logic*
aims to arrive at a set of categories that will not involve disunity and fragmentation, but instead will enable us to overcome the false dichotomies
we are faced with in our previous ways of thinking, so that a more unified
world-picture can emerge.

As we have also seen, Hegel suggests that the categories of universal
and particular are particularly central to how we conceive of the world,
and these categories are fully analysed and discusses in the final subdivi-
sion of the *Logic*. Prior to his account of universal and particular, Hegel
examines other important categories, such as being and nothing, quality
and quantity, finite and infinite, identity and difference, whole and part,
one and many, essence and appearance, substance and attribute. Hegel's
analysis of these and other categories is designed to show how none of
these terms is fully intelligible on their own, and only when we see how
each one is related to the other can we use these concepts properly, and
arrive at a rational conception of things. Now, reason (*die Vernunft*) has a
very definite meaning for Hegel, which must be explained if the purpose
of the *Logic* is to be made comprehensible.

Hegel's account of reason both stems from and is a critique of Kant's conception, as developed by the latter in his *Critique of Pure Reason*. Like Kant, Hegel draws a definite contrast between reason and the understanding (*der Verstand*), and Hegel himself acknowledges his debt to Kant in drawing this distinction (*Logic*, §45Z p 73). However, while Kant had a dim view of reason as leading into metaphysical error, and put forward the understanding as yielding the only possible form of (albeit limited) knowledge, in Hegel the order of priority is reversed: Hegel argues (against Kant) that reason *can* attain knowledge of ultimate reality, and that as a consequence reason stands above the understanding, which has only a limited range.

Furthermore, Hegel's account of *why* the understanding is limited also differs from Kant's. For the latter, the understanding was limited because it must work within the bounds of possible experience; certain infinite objects (such as God, the extent of the world, the soul) lie outside possible experience, however, and so cannot be known through the understanding. For Hegel, by contrast, the understanding is more crucially limited than that: the understanding is limited because the categories with which it conceives the world are finite, and cannot be used to think about infinite objects such as God or the world as a whole. In more general terms, Hegel's point is as follows: the understanding is limited because the categories it uses in its conception of the world are one-sided and opposed to their "opposite", while an infinite object (such as God or the soul) is apparently contradictory for the understanding because it is *not* one-sided in this way, but seems to encompass opposites, by being both finite and infinite, one and many, limited and unlimited, and so on. This criticism of the understanding, for operating with one-sided and limited categories, comes out clearly in the following passage:

> The metaphysics of the understanding is dogmatic, because it maintains half-truths in their isolation: whereas the idealism of speculative philosophy carries out the principle of totality and shows that it can reach beyond the inadequate formularies of abstract thought. Thus idealism would say: the soul is neither finite only, nor infinite only; it is really the one just as much as the other, and in that way neither the one nor the other... We show more obstinacy in dealing with the categories of the understanding. These are terms which we believe to be somewhat firmer – or even absolutely firm and fast. We look upon them as separated from each other by an infinite chasm, so that opposite categories can never get at each other. The battle of reason is their struggle to break up the rigidity to which understanding has reduced everything. (*Encyclopaedia Logic* §32Z, pp. 52–3)

As this last sentence indicates, whereas understanding operates with a firm distinction between its categories, reason for Hegel reveals that these distinctions are not tenable, and so forces thought to move beyond the opposed categories of the understanding, to a higher category in which such oppositions are resolved. Thus, while the understanding insists on using categories that divide the world up into mutually exclusive aspects, reason is able to see how these aspects cannot be divided and separated from each other, but must be brought together and viewed as interdependent. This, in essence, is what is meant by calling Hegel a dialectical thinker: his aim was to show that by treating certain categories as simply opposed to one another, we will be led into contradictions in our world-view (as was shown in the Phenomenology), and that unless we find a way of rethinking these categories in which this opposition is resolved, we cannot hope to arrive at a coherent picture of reality, and so claim to have absolute knowledge. Contrary to what is sometimes suggested, this does not show that Hegel somehow wanted to do away with the law of non-contradiction: indeed, it is precisely because certain ways of conceiving of these categories do lead us into contradiction that Hegel seeks to establish these conceptions as inadequate, as arising from the understanding and not from reason.

This account of understanding and reason comes out clearly in Chapter VI of the *Encyclopaedia Logic,* entitled "Logic Further Defined and Divided". In this short chapter, Hegel distinguishes three stages in the development of thought, which he identifies as

> (a) the Abstract side, or that of understanding; (b) the Dialectical, or that of negative reason; (c) the Speculative, or that of positive reason. (*Logic*, §79 p. 113)

The first stage, or understanding, is characterised as that faculty of thought which treats categories not as unified and mutually inclusive, but rather as apparently discrete and finite; it thereby

> sticks to fixed determinations and the distinctness of one determination from another: every such limited abstract it treats as having a subsistence and being of its own. (*Logic*, §80 p. 112)

Hegel insists, however, that the categories or concepts cannot be kept apart in this way, but are essentially connected to one another. The leads to the second or dialectical stage, which is the inherent self-sublation of these finite determinations and their transition into their opposites. (*Logic* §81 p. 115)

As a result of this dialectic, therefore, the understanding's attempts to treat its categories as mutually exclusive is undermined, as such categories are shown to pass over into their opposite, thereby making a nonsense of understanding's efforts to keep them apart. These then leads on to the third and final stage, that of of *reason*, which

apprehends the unity of the determinations in their opposition – the affirmation, which is embodied in their disintegration and their transition (*Logic* §82 p. 119)

Thus, after the dialectical stage, in which each finite category passes over into its opposite, they are then taken up by reason, and brought together in a unity. We can therefore summarise Hegel's position by saying that for him, to think rationally is to set aside the distinctions imposed on things by the understanding, and to see the various determinations of reality as dialectically interrelated.

An example may help here: according to Hegel, it is characteristic of the understanding to treat the categories of freedom and necessity as utterly distinct, so that something is either free, or it is necessarily determined. Now this, of course, leads directly to the traditional free-will problem. But, Hegel argues, the understanding can be shown to be mistaken in thinking that freedom and necessity can be separated so easily: in fact, unless we mean by freedom something fairly minimal and unsatisfactory, like chance, it is clear that freedom must involve necessity at some level. This, however, the understanding finds very hard to accept, because it feels the categories should be distinct. Nonetheless, through reason we are able to arrive at a conception of freedom on the one hand and necessity on the other than shows them to be compatible, so that while the understanding's view of these categories is contradictory, reason's is not (see *Logic* §§155–159, pp.218–222).

Now, Hegel argues that the categories of thought which are most closely interrelated in this way are the categories of universal, particular, and individual, which must be brought together if consciousness it to avoid the problems it faced in the *Phenomenology*, and if we are to resolve the antinomies of traditional metaphysics. The mistake we make, according to Hegel, is to think that the universal and the particular are distinct from one another, because we think of universals as self-sufficient, ontologically independent Platonic entities on the one hand, and particulars as concrete, material particulars on the other; whereas, Hegel argues, every uni-

versal must be exemplified in an particular, while particulars are constituted as what they are by a universal essence. It therefore follows from this
that only if we are working with what Hegel argues are inadequate and
false conceptions of the universal and particular will we separate the ideal
and the real, or will we see any ultimate division between these two categories. Likewise, Hegel argues, many of the other dichotomies that have
plagued "us moderns" will be resolved once we see the unity of universal
and particular in this way, and a more unified conception of things has
emerged:

> The Idea itself is the dialectic which for ever divides and distinguishes the self-
> identical from the differentiated, the subjective from the objective, the finite
> from the infinite, soul from body. Only on these terms is it an eternal creation,
> eternal vitality, and eternal spirit. But while it thus passes or rather translates
> itself into the abstract understanding, it for ever remains reason. The Idea is the
> dialectic which again makes this mass of understanding and diversity under-
> stand its finite nature and the pseudo-independence of its productions, and
> which brings the diversity back to unity. (*Logic* §214 pp. 277–8)

## The *Encyclopaedia*: Nature and Mind

Having analysed our categories of thought in the *Logic*, and having shown
how this analysis leads towards a unified world-picture, Hegel moves on
the *Philosophy of Nature*, which is the second book of his *Encyclopaedia*.
In it, he examines the categories as we use them in thinking about the natural world, and suggests how this thinking might be altered once his categorial revolution is accepted. He criticises some of the ways in which
inadequate categories are used in science, particularly when they lead us
to view nature in an atomistic way, arguing that the Newtonians are especially guilty in this regard (e.g. *Philosophy of Nature* §276II, pp. 17–18).
At the same time, Hegel allows that, although the *Logic* implies that the
highest form of knowledge is one that treats the world in a unified, rational manner, not *all* entities in nature are unified and rational in this sense.
That is why Hegel says that nature constitutes "the Idea in its otherness".
(*Logic* §18, p. 23) Nonetheless, although Hegel accepts that limited, one-
sided categories might do quite well in the understanding of some natural
phenomena, a conceptual revolution *is* required to comprehend the higher
realms of nature, for example the animal organism; for the animal organism displays the kind of holistic structure that can only be grasped using
dialectically interrelated categories (as developed in the *Logic*), and otherwise will remain incomprehensible to the scientific understanding.

In the third part of the *Encyclopaedia*, Hegel turns from the natural world to mind (*Geist*), and makes the same point regarding our understanding of the mental:

> When in the two modes of treatment already described, empirical psychology takes the individual on the one hand, and the universal on the other, each as a fixed, independent category, it also holds the particular forms into which it analyses mind to be fixed in their limitation; so that mind is converted into a mere aggregate of independent forces, each of which stands only in reciprocal relation with the others, hence is only externally connected with them. For though this psychology also demands that the various spiritual forces shall be harmoniously integrated... this gives expression to a unity of mind which only ought to be, not to the original unity, and still less does it recognise as necessary and rational the particularisation to which the Notion of mind, its intrinsic unity, progresses. This harmonious integration remains, therefore, a vacuous idea which expresses itself in high sounding but empty phrases but remains ineffective in the face of the spiritual forces presupposed as independent. (*Philosophy of Mind* §378, p. 4)

Thus, in the first section of the *Philosophy of Mind*, Hegel is concerned to show how his conceptual revolution will also change the way we view the world. He then goes on, in the second section, to consider what he calls "objective mind", by which he means ethical, social, and political life. Given its importance, this aspect of Hegel's thought will be discussed separately in the next section.

# The *Philosophy of Right*

While an outline of Hegel's political philosophy is given in the *Philosophy of Mind*, in his account of the ethical and social development of *Geist*, an extended and more developed account is given in his *Philosophy of Right*, which was published as a separate volume in 1821. Aside from the *Phenomenology*, this is perhaps Hegel's best-known work, and is a central text in modern political thought. However, it is a work that, like many of Hegel's other writings, is open to divergent interpretations, and the meaning and significance of Hegel's political philosophy has remained the focus of agitated and heated debate. Immediately after Hegel's death in 1831 there emerged two schools, known as the Young (or Left) Hegelians and the Old (or Right) Hegelians, who offered radically different readings of the *Philosophy of Right* and of Hegel's thought as a whole. The Left Hegelians (like Marx, Feuerbach and Engels) saw in Hegel a utopian view of freedom, community and the triumph of the human spirit, a vision that they tried in their own work to complete; while the Right Hegelians saw in Hegel a theocratic defence of the Prussian state and support for the *status quo* of absolute monarchy. Since then, almost every shade of political opinion has had protagonists offering what they consider to be a legitimate interpretation or extension of Hegelianism. Even today, Hegel's influence on both left and right wing thinkers continues, while both left and right have denounced him as the enemy. If one looks carefully at this bewildering list of followers, interpreters and critics, however, one central feature of Hegel's political philosophy emerges as the focus of interest for both the left and the right: namely, Hegel's searching critique of what he calls "civil society", and by which he means something like the liberal commercial society that constitutes the basis of the modern state. It is this critique that has led some (like Karl Popper) to accuse him of totalitarianism and authoritarianism, while his supporters on both the left and the right have used Hegelian ideas to challenge the fundamental presuppositions of liberalism and modern capitalist societies.

In trying to understand Hegel's political philosophy and his critique of civil society, it is important to remember that it is part of his philosophical project as a whole, which (as we have seen) aimed to develop a more unified world-view by revolutionising our fundamental concepts and ways of thought. The understanding, which employs one-sided and limited categories, is inclined to view the world, including the social world, in a fragmented and atomistic way, whereas after his categorial revolution, Hegel hoped our conception of things would be more unified, including our conception of the social realm. Only when this re-thinking of our social categories has been achieved, Hegel suggests, will a better integrated and less atomistic community be realised. Moreover, he argues that the dialectic of universal and particular is unresolved within civil society, and that the synthesis of these aspects can only be achieved in a higher form of community, which Hegel calls the state. Let me begin, then, by explaining what Hegel means by civil society, and his criticisms of it.

For Hegel, civil society is in many respects the greatest achievement of the modern age, and its emergence marks a crucial break between ourselves and the ancients. He argues that it has developed as a creation of individualism, as a direct result of the discovery of individual freedoms and rights. The modern age was brought about by the Protestant reformation, the French revolution, the new science, the industrial revolution, Cartesian and Kantian philosophy, and the achievements of the Enlightenment, which all served to liberate the individual from previous restrictions. This new freedom is given political expression in civil society.

Civil society is based on an economic system in which individuals work and trade to satisfy their needs, together with the civil institutions needed to manage such a system: markets, courts and an administration of justice, public works, minimal welfare and antimonopoly systems. It is a society composed of free, rational maximisers, who are economically interdependent, who recognise each other as sovereign agents within the bounds of the law, and who accept merely formal structures of recognition. Civil society is a form of association that has evolved to accommodate the kind of disinterested, autonomous, asocial agent that has emerged in modernity, and that was not recognised by the ancients. In earlier societies, there was no separation between a person's identity as a person and his or her definite social role. As is well known, Aristotle argued that "man is a political animal', who can no more exist outside society than an isolated draughts piece can exist as such off the draughts board. There was consequently no form of recognition set up for "human beings as such", and no developed concept of purely human rights. In civil society, by contrast, we recognise each other as pure, abstract *persons*, free to move throughout the social structure, and independent of any social role. We only interact in so far as we require economic cooperation to fulfil certain needs, and we treat each other as autonomous individuals, protected as such by the law. In this way, Hegel pictures the minimal liberal state as a distinctive achievement of modernity.

However, Hegel's attitude to civil society is somewhat complex. While, as we shall see, he offers certain fundamental and important criticisms of it, he recognises that it nonetheless represents an important advance on the social structures of the ancients, in so far as it incorporates the modern notion of individuality; but while he never claimed that modern society should abandon its discovery of human rights and liberties, or reject the market mechanisms of modern institutions, he argued that this could not be the whole story, the form of community with which history might end. Thus, while Hegel, like the thinkers of the Enlightenment, celebrated the achievements of modern individuality at one level, he tempered this enthusiasm with some critical observations on the limitations of civil society. These may be summarised as follows: freedom, individuality and community as recognised within civil society are one-sided and abstract. Let us look at each of these in turn.

As Hegel pictures it, civil society clearly corresponds to the "night-watchman" state as envisaged in classical liberal theory, with its conception of freedom as the absence of restrictions. According to this conception, I am free if others do not interfere with me and do not force me to do what I do not wish to do. For Hegel, however, this notion of freedom is inadequate and one-sided: being able to do what one wants does not constitute real freedom, as what one wants may be irrationally determined. (*Philosophy of Right* §15, p. 27) In fact, Hegel argues (following Kant) that it is on our ability to pull back from our desires and rationally reflect on them that our genuine freedom is realised. To be truly free, therefore, I should be able to rise above the arbitrariness and subjectivity of my individual desires and inclinations, and instead act as a rational agent, who acts in accordance with more concrete, objective, moral ends. (*Philosophy of Right* §152, p. 230) In civil society, however, Hegel argues that the emphasis is one-sidedly on freedom as mere individual choice, and the satisfaction of individual need, and not on rational self-determination. In this respect, Hegel implies, we find in civil society not true freedom, but the slavery of individuals to their subjective, and ever increasing, desires. (*Philosophy of Right* §185, p. 123) Hegel therefore criticises civil society for embodying only a limited, one-sided conception of freedom, a freedom to do as one wants as a pure individual, without providing the moral, educational and social context whereby one can transcend this pure particularity and recognise that one's freedom is always circumscribed by the universal, by the moral law and by the general good. In order for this to be achieved, we must institute the less minimal social structures of the State, which, as we shall see, Hegel sets above civil society. Before outlining Hegel's conception of the State, however, let me continue with the other criticisms he offers of civil society.

Hegel's second claim is that individuality as recognised in civil society is one-sided and abstract. The point here is that in civil society each individual is only recognised in the most abstract, legalistic way: they are treated merely as *persons*, protected from others by legal rights, who are also treated in an equally formal way. Moreover, in so far as civil society is founded on and constituted by a market economy, in which we all cooperate for our own self-interest, we all begin to become subordinated to the dehumanising mechanism of the market. The economic system of civil society threatens to trivialise life and convert all human relations into commodity relations. We come to see that we are all mutually dependent on the market for our livelihoods, and so come to treat each other as partners within a scheme of economic cooperation: but the basis for our interaction and recognition is merely that of self-interested need. (*Philosophy of Right* §183, p. 123)

As a result, and this is Hegel's third claim, civil society is one-sided and abstract. Hegel argues that modern society, based on market mechanisms and abstract rights, uproots individuals from their communities, depriving their lives of the weight given them by traditional roles and values. Human relations, as we have seen, become matters of contract, and there is nothing to be respected for itself. We treat our fellow citizens as abstract persons, but do not have any deeper feeling for them: we respect their freedoms, but do not feel any underlying identity with them. This erosion of the community in modern times means that traditional values and meanings have been lost, and with them the sense of belonging to any particular group. Instead, we feel contingently aligned with particular class interests within the market, but have lost the more concrete unity to be found in more traditional societies. We treat each other as means to our ends, but do not feel that we are related by anything other than an external conjunction of interests: we have lost the sense of community. (*Philosophy of Right* §182Z, pp. 266–7)

Despite his recognition of his achievements, therefore, Hegel stands as a formidable critic of modern liberal society, and it is this that has endeared him to both the left and the right: thinkers on the left have endorsed his criticism of the market as dehumanising and exploitative, and of the hollowness of liberal freedoms, while thinkers on the right have echoed his worries about the erosion of community and public sentiment in modern society. Given these limitations of civil society, therefore, Hegel argues that there must be a form of association over and above that of the market place, and this is Hegel's State.

It is not possible to produce a full analysis of the details of Hegel's picture of the State (which is in many respects rather unconvincing). All I can bring out here is how the State was supposed to act as a form of association beyond that of civil society, in which the purely abstract freedom, individualism and community of the latter would be transcended. Three features of the State in particular were meant to bring this about.

First of all, in the State the abstract freedom of civil society is transcended because in the State one does not act as a purely self-interested individual driven by egoistic desires and needs, but rather as a citizen, who recognises that one has certain duties and social responsibilities. Hegel argues that this is only superficially a limitation of one's abstract freedom, and only appears as such due to a one-sided emphasis on individuality: in fact, the truly rational agent, who adopts a more universal outlook, comes to see that his or her duties are the expression of the rational will, and so are rather expressions of a higher freedom. In the State, Hegel argues, one does not feel a tension between one's individual will and the universal laws: rather, they coincide. (*Philosophy of Right* §261, p. 161)

Secondly, in the State the abstract individuality of civil society is transcended, in so far as the individual is not acknowledged to be more than a mere person by society, and is treated as a concrete individual, someone with a determinate place within the social whole. This comes about because as political, not merely economic, agents within the State individuals no longer view themselves as atomistic units, but see themselves as engaged in a wider project, as parts of an overarching social whole.

Thus, thirdly, the State embodies a more concrete notion of community than that found in civil society. Hegel argues that the self-interested motivations of the market place give way to the general interests of the State, as individuals come to feel themselves to constitute one society, with a shared culture and ethical life at stake.

In Hegel's political philosophy, we have an expression of hope: a hope that out of the self-interested, atomistic, narrow individualism of civil society, which is based on the marked and individual rights, a more concrete community will emerge, a community in which we acknowledge our civic duties, our responsibilities for others, our shared culture and our social unity. Hegel did not wish to impose these duties or this community upon us, and in this sense he cannot be called authoritarian: rather, he believed that we would come to feel the emptiness, inadequacy and absurdity of life merely within civil society, and ourselves construct a higher form of community within the State, and bring about the unity of individuality and universality within the social sphere.

However, it is I think fair to say that Hegel underestimated the difficulties of bringing about this reconciliation. In particular (as critics on the left have observed) it is not clear that the State can arise by incorporating the market and market rationality, but may have to abolish it. Nor is it clear (as thinkers on the right have observed) that the State will be viable without recourse to anti-democratic political structures: Hegel himself argued for a constitutional monarchy. Hegel is a significant political thinker, then, not because he provided answers, but because he raised important questions, questions that plague liberal orthodoxy even now: namely, notwithstanding the evident achievements of modern, liberal, capitalist States, are they the final word? Must we be content with the alienation, *anomie*, exploitation, mechanisation, abstract freedom and collapse of community that accompanies modern civil society? Or can we hope that history and the development of human culture will evolve one further, final social norm, in which the benefits of liberalism can be retained without these drawbacks? Hegel, and those whom he has influenced on both the left and right, argue that we can, while the defenders of modern liberalism hold that this hope is misguided, and that in seeking to go beyond the freedoms of civil society, and passing into the State, we may gain in some respects, but we risk losing what Hegel admitted was the greatest achievement of modernity so far: individual freedom itself.

In the political realm, therefore, Hegel's attempt to reconcile individuality and universality, freedom and community, has fallen short, and the tension between these social categories remains. Indeed, the same might be said of Hegel's philosophical project as a whole: to his critical successors (such as Marx, Feuerbach, Kierkegaard and Adorno), the dichotomies Hegel spoke of, and which he tried so hard to transcend, were not successfully resolved in his system, and fundamental antitheses remained.As Adorno puts it,

> Dialectics serves the end of reconcilement... but none of the reconcilements claimed by [Hegel's] absolute idealism – and no other kind remained consistent – has stood up, whether in logic or in politics and history. (Adorno, *Negative Dialectics*, pp. 6–7)

The dissolution of the Hegelian synthesis, and the failure of his project of reconcilement, is the background against which subsequent European thought developed, and it is this failure which forced continental philosophy to face once again the very contradictions and crises that Hegel had tried so hard to overcome.

# Further Reading

Hegel's works are fairly challenging; however, some of the lecture notes – for example the *Lectures on the History of Philosophy* – have a considerably more accessible style than his more technical writings. The *Phenomenology of Spirit*, although difficult, has been extremely influential in the later history of philosophy. There is a good collection of selections from Hegel, edited by M. J. Inwood. Among the secondary literature, *Hegel and Modern Society*, by C. Taylor, is a helpful introduction, as is *Freedom, Truth and History*, by S. Houlgate, and *The Cambridge Companion to Hegel*, edited by F. C. Beiser, is a useful reference.

# Bibliography

Theodor W. Adorno, *Negative Dialectics*, tr. E.B. Ashton, London: Routledge 1973.
Frederick C. Beiser (ed.), *The Cambridge Companion to Hegel*, Cambridge: Cambridge University Press 1993.

G.W.F. Hegel, *The Difference between Fichte's and Schelling's System of Philosophy*, tr. Walter Cerf and H.S. Harris, Albany NY: State University of New York Press, 1977)

——*Introduction to the Lectures on the History of Philosophy*, tr. T.M. Knox and A.V. Miller, Oxford: Oxford University Press 1985.

——*Logic*, tr. William Wallace, third edition, Oxford: Oxford University Press 1971.

——*Philosophy of Mind*, tr. William Wallace and A.V. Miller, Oxford: Oxford University Press 1971.

——*Philosophy of Nature*, tr. M.J. Petry, London: Allen and Unwin 1970.

——*Philosophy of Right*, tr. T.M. Knox, Oxford: Oxford University Press 1952.

——*Phenomenology of Spirit*, tr. A.V. Miller, London: Allen and Unwin 1977.

——*Science of Logic*, tr. A.V. Miller, London: Allen and Unwin 1969.

——*Selections*, ed. M.J. Inwood, London: Macmillan 1989.

Friedrich Hölderlin, *Hyperion*, tr. Willard R. Trask, New York: The New American Library 1965.

Stephen Houlgate, *Freedom, Truth and History: An Introduction to Hegel's Philosophy*, London: Routledge 1991.

Maurice Merleau-Ponty, "Hegel's Existentialism", in *Sense and Non-Sense*, tr. Hubert L. Dreyfus and Patricia Allen Dreyfus, Northwestern University Press 1964, pp. 63-70.

Charles Taylor, *Hegel and Modern Society*, Cambridge: Cambridge University Press 1979.

# 4 Arthur Schopenhauer
## Jenny Teichman

Arthur Schopenhauer, who is generally known as "the philosopher of pessimism", was born in Danzig in 1788 and died in Frankfurt in 1860. He was the son of a rich merchant, a fact which enabled him to devote his life to writing and private study.

To say that Schopenhauer despised the mainstream Hegelian philosophy of his time would be something of an understatement. Schopenhauer described Hegel as "ponderous and witless" and "a lasting monument to German stupidity"; when outlining the history of philosophy as it developed after Kant he wrote "... the greatest effrontery in serving up sheer nonsense, in scrabbling together senseless and maddening webs of words, such as had previously been heard only in madhouses, finally appeared in Hegel." As to the works of Hegelian university professors, these, he said, were "false and bad", "monstrous abortions", "absurd and senseless". According to him, Hegelian professors misunderstood Kant, ignored contemporary non-Hegelian philosophy, and praised one anothers' books "with corybantic shouting". They were "bombastic sophists", grovellers who followed the rule "I sing the song of him whose bread I eat".

Schopenhauer, a wealthy man, never held a university professorship, but he did once try to give some lectures. This was in 1820, in Berlin, and he deliberately chose a time of day when Hegel was also lecturing, seeking no doubt to draw the crowds away from the object of his hatred. But, as one of his biographers, Frederick Copleston, writes, "[t]he enterprise was a complete failure and Schopenhauer gave up... after one semester".

Schopenhauer complained that his contemporaries ignored his books, but that was not entirely true. He was admired by the poet Goethe and by one or two philosophers in Germany, and he won a Norwegian prize for an essay on freedom. On the other hand he was not really well known until the last years of his life. He remained confident, however, that his work was of the kind to be remembered and read by future generations. It should also be noted that in spite of what he himself believed his philosophy has points of similarity with the work of the Hegelian school. Like Hegel and others, Schopenhauer surmised that the world contains some feature or entity which could explain *everything*; thus the role of the Will in his philosophy is somewhat similar to the role of Reason or Spirit in Hegel's.

Schopenhauer owes a large debt to Kant, which he acknowledges in full. He also has a high regard for Berkeley, whom he describes as the bearer of an immortal reputation. The first sentence of his best known book runs "The world is my representation", and echoes Berkeley's well-known dictum "To be is to be perceived".

The most notable feature of Schopenhauer's philosophy is his metaphysical pessimism. Another characteristic is a cosmopolitan interest in foreign writers and foreign systems of thought. He quotes many authors and scholars and and makes several references to the ancient literature of both East and West. He ingeniously combines ideas from very different sources, arguing, for example, that the philosophical ideas of Kant and Berkeley had already been recognised by the Greeks and, earlier still, by the Indian sages of the long distant past. Schopenhauer interpreted Kantian philosophy in his own rather special way and then associated that interpretation with the Indian doctrine of Maya. Since 'Maya' means illusion, Schopenhauer is able to identify it with the Kantian notion of phenomenon. Another feature of his thinking, and a rather unfortunate one, is his extreme contempt for women. Since no-one has psychoanalysed him, even *in absentia*, there is no way of knowing how and why this intelligent son of a cultivated father and an intellectual mother became a misogynist.

The title of Schopenhauer's *magnum opus* is variously translated as *The World as Will and Idea* or *The World as Will and Representation*. The title has to do with reality and illusion. The world as representation is constituted by all those things and events which are explained by science. These things and events are not the ultimate reality but merely a collection of appearances. Science and common sense have to do only with the way things seem to be, not with the way they really are. Behind appearances lies reality, and according to Schopenhauer reality is a blind force or urge which he calls the Will. The real world of the Will is objectified, or pictured, or represented, by the phenomena which we wrongly take to be real in themselves. The nature of the metaphysical Will, that is to say, of ultimate reality, is fundamentally cruel and evil.

# The World as Representation

Our human apprehension of the world is not direct but indirect in that nothing can be apprehended at all until it has been filtered, as it were, through the five senses and through the human intellect. Consequently the world as an object of apprehension, of knowledge, of science, is nothing but ideas or representations. Schopenhauer remarks that the deep gulf between phenomena and reality is like the motion of the earth; we cannot feel it, we cannot be directly aware of it, but once philosophers realise that there is such a gulf "[they] can have no rest." In the end though it turns out that true philosophy will tell us about the reality that lies behind our ideas.

Schopenhauer says that Kant's most important contribution to philosophy was the way in which he drew the distinction between the world of phenomena, on the one hand, and the world as it really is, on the other. Locke and Berkeley had already argued that what is known of the material world, if there *is* a material world, consists merely of the data provided by the five senses. Since our knowledge of the empirical world is determined by the senses, Berkeley formulated the drastic theory that the world consists entirely of spiritual beings and their ideas or perceptions. Others have argued that there is a real material world, adding, however, that it lies behind "the veil of perception" and cannot be known by us.

Kant added a second veil to the veil of perception. He reasoned that phenomena do not exist for us in higgledy-piggledy fashion – if they did they would be unintelligible. We perceive things in a frame, as it were, of certain conditions. First, we have to perceive what we take to be material objects as existing in space and time, and mental events as existing in time. Second, when we apprehend events we have to apprehend them as governed by causality. Yet we cannot perceive causality with the senses. Time, space and causality are necessary for thought and perception, and Kant attributes the necessity to the nature of the human mind. Time, space and causality are not independent realities; but are superimposed on the world by the mind, so that the nature of what we think we know is determined, not only by perception, but also by intellect. We see the world through a veil of intellect as well as through a veil of the senses. Schopenhauer accepts this thesis of Kantian philosophy as true beyond all question. For him, space, time and causality are "in the head".

Now Kant held that beyond the veils of sense and intellect there exists a real world, the world of things-in-themselves, or, as he called it, the world of *noumena*. Schopenhauer accepts this too as true beyond all question, but unlike Kant he does not hold that the transition from knowledge of representations (*phenomena*) to knowledge of reality (*noumena*) is impossible. On the contrary, he argues that philosophy can tell us something about the true nature of ultimate reality. Moreover he gives the notion of an ultimate underlying reality his own special twist.

# The World as Will

Schopenhauer's gloomy philosophy of metaphysical pessimism is founded on his concept of the metaphysical Will. Scientifically minded materialist philosophers believe that the ultimate underlying realities are matter and energy; idealist thinkers, and notably Berkeley, argue that the underlying reality of the world is mind or spirit, plus ideas. Schopenhauer rejects both materialism and idealism, because for him ultimate reality consists of a blind universal eternal force, or urge, or striving. All the different things and events that common sense and science, and materialist or idealist philosophy, take to be real, are merely manifestations of this blind striving, the metaphysical Will. And to understand this is to understand that there is a way of knowing about the real, noumenal world. The ultimate reality which Kant thought was unknowable can be known after all.

The way in which Schopenhauer reaches his conclusion about the possibility of knowledge is rather complex. To start with, it has to be agreed provisionally that the only world that I can know about is the world of my own perception and intellect. Things exist, *for me*, only as I perceive them and understand them. Furthermore, if the world of visible tangible things is for me made up of my perceptions, then my own body must also be a perception, since my body is a visible tangible thing. However, this does not mean that my desk, for instance, or my body for that matter just *is* my understanding and perception of it; it means that that is all it can be for me. And as to my body, it is clear that it is not *me myself*. I am more than my body because I am an entity who perceives it (and other things). Call this perceiving entity the subject of perception. Then the objects of perception are simply the things I, the subject, perceive. The things in the material world exist (for me) as perceived objects. Schopenhauer reasons from this that the perceiving subject and the perceived object cannot be separated. He writes "matter and intelligence are inseparable correlates, existing only for one another, and therefore existing only relatively". Because matter and intelligence are, as we might say, stuck together by their need for one another, it follows, according to him, that intelligence as well as matter is merely part of the world as representation. Intelligence too is illusion or Maya.

This is the first step in Schopenhauer's chain of thought, and we can pause here to consider it, and maybe even to question it. Suppose we agree for the sake of argument that intelligence *qua* intuition and perception is nothing but representation, still, isn't there another kind of intelligence, namely, the capacity for abstract reasoning, for philosophical thinking? Knowledge of concepts is different from perception and intuition. Why then assume that we cannot reach reality through the exercise of the power of abstract reasoning? Schopenhauer's answer (which I find unsatisfactory) runs somewhat as follows. All reason is useful, insofar as it is an instrument for satisfying human desires. Even abstract reason has a biological function: it too is a servant of the body. Schopenhauer thinks we are forced to conclude that abstract reason belongs to the world of representation and cannot be the ultimate reality. Descartes' dictum "I think therefore I exist" must be discarded.

This move is perhaps not very convincing, but as it happens it is only a side issue. In the second part of his search for knowledge Schopenhauer argues that human reason can after all find a way, though only one way into reality. He calls this way "the single narrow door". To locate the single narrow door we have to engage in introspection. (Is introspection perhaps a form of reasoning?) Introspection, or "inner consciousness", will reveal to each individual his or her own acts of will, which means that individual acts of will are known directly. Moreover inner consciousness informs us that an act of will, and the bodily action which follows it, seem to be one and the same thing. Will and action are not cause and effect, rather the bodily action is, as it were, a picture of the will, its representation. The body itself, Schopenhauer infers, is therefore nothing more or less than a representation of the will. We have stumbled on a representation (the human body and its actions) which represents a directly known thing-in-itself (the will).

There are two conclusions. First, for every individual there is one reality – the will – which can be known directly and infallibly. Second, the relation between that reality and the world of human bodily phenomena – i.e. the relation between will and action – is known directly and infallibly. The relation is known directly and infallibly because actions are representations, as it were pictures, of the will.

Perhaps the chief defect of this line of argument is that it seems to overlook the fact that individual acts of will, like all mental phenomena, are apprehended in time, and since time is part of the "veil of the intellect" there seems no reason to regard "the single narrow door" as a door leading anywhere that other introspectively discovered doors might not also lead.

# Unity and Individuality

Schopenhauer concludes that the whole of reality consists of the Will as such. The Will as such, or metaphysical Will, is one will, it is unitary and undivided. It has no ends or purposes, and no knowledge, and it is completely blind and non-rational. It is just *there*.

Reality is unitary; plurality and multiplicity are aspects of the merely phenomenal world. But of course the existence of the pluralistic world, the existence of everything, depends on the ultimate reality. The unitary metaphysical Will has plural manifestations: it manifests itself as a multiplicity of individual willings and other phenomena. When the Will objectifies itself as phenomena, it displays individuality and sometimes has specific ends and purposes. For example, when the Will objectifies itself as the actions and strivings of this or that individual living animal body it strives for life. But because the metaphysical Will is the ultimate reality, it follows that all nature, inorganic as well as organic, consists of its manifestations. All natural events are aspects of the Will, the behaviour of vegetables, of iron and of planets and magnets just as much as the behaviour of human and other animals.

The plurality of phenomena, as described by Schopenhauer, makes up a hierarchy of an almost Aristotelean kind. At the bottom are the forces of inorganic nature, then a little higher up come vegetables, then the non-human animals, then mankind. The Will, considered purely in itself, is devoid of knowledge: in itself it is blind. We perceive this urge, and its blindness, in the motions of inorganic and vegetable nature, and in their laws. The blindness as well as the urge can also be detected in our own human life. Human impulses, such as love and altruism, live in disguises; their true nature is cruel and selfish. Like Freud after him, Schopenhauer believes that the real origins of human actions are unconscious.

By extending the concept of Will to everything whatsoever, Schopenhauer returns the natural world to the realm of the real. Inorganic things act on us and on each other, and because of this we are forced to concede them a being-in-itself, a reality, of some kind. Thus lifeless bodies do not exist solely and simply as representations. Moreover, inorganic matter has "unfathomable properties", properties which science cannot explain. Science can quantify gravitational attraction, for example, but it cannot say what gravity is, or where it comes from. In claiming that all the forces and motions of animate and inanimate nature are manifestations of a metaphysical Will, Schopenhauer presents a theory which seems to answer questions which science cannot. The natural world, he says, is not as science and materialistic philosophy present it: it is not a mechanically organised conglomerate of matter and energy; on the contrary, it is governed by that which governs human existence. The desires and longings and struggles and evils which we think of as specifically human are in fact universal, because the striving of the Will is everywhere.

What the Will wills is always life, so that Schopenhauer writes "It is immaterial if instead of saying 'the will' we say 'the will to live'".

Schopenhauer produces many examples of the manifestations of the metaphysical Will in the world of representation. In every species of animal we see the instinctual urges to self-preservation, reproduction, and protection of the young, strivings which, he believes, are clearly instances of Will. Human strivings, whether they be instinctual, or intellectual, or technological, or political, or economic, are also nothing but representations of the same underlying reality.

It may be asked why Schopenhauer gives the title *Will* to blind incessant urge and strife. If it is blind why not call it energy or force? One reason might be that energy and force are terms belonging to a science which takes matter to be real without giving any reason for that assumption. Another reason is epistemological, having to do with the fact that *knowledge* of reality comes to the philosopher through "the single narrow door" revealed by introspection.

## The Torture and Slavery of the Will to Live

Ultimate reality is gloomy and unpleasant. From the point of view of the individual every unsuccessful act of willing is a painful frustration, while every successful one necessarily results in disappointment. Sexual life, for example, results in two possible states of affairs: on the one hand frustrated longings, on the other hand an expense of spirit in a waste of shame. Matters are just as bad if we try to take a wider view. The metaphysical Will manifests itself in the animal kingdom as a host of warring species, each one of which tries to survive at the expense of the others. Strife is especially obvious in the case of human beings, for they are in perpetual conflict, not only with inanimate forces and other animals, but with each other. Worse still their struggles are fundamentally cruel and irrational, and opposed to everything that is noble and good:

> ... this world of humanity is the kingdom of chance and error... and along with them folly and wickedness also wield the scourge. Hence arises the fact that everything better struggles through only with difficulty; what is noble and wise

very rarely makes its appearance, becomes effective, or meets with a hearing, but the absurd and perverse in the realm of thought, the dull and tasteless in the sphere of art and the wicked and fraudulent in the sphere of action, assert a supremacy that is disturbed only by brief interruptions... the chief source of the most serious evils which afflict man is man himself: *homo homini lupus* [man is a wolf to man]. Whoever keeps this last fact clearly in view sees the world as a hell which surpasses that of Dante through the fact that one man must be the devil of another.

As evidence for the hellish nature of human life Schopenhauer describes in some detail many different manifestations of the hard-hearted and devilish character of mankind: war, greed, torture, slavery, and every kind of injustice. He insists, of course, that there is no point in blaming anyone for the damage and suffering inflicted by human beings on the rest of creation and on humanity itself. If the blame is to fall anywhere it must fall on ultimate reality. All the evils in the world are the fault (as one might say) of the thing-in-itself.

## Aesthetics and Asceticism

Schopenhauer thinks it is difficult but not impossible to escape from the horrors and sadness of the world of representation. There are two ways to escape: one is through art, and the other is through asceticism. The preliminary answer to the question: How shall I live? is: Create art or contemplate it, and the final answer is: Will nothing and do nothing.

The contemplation of works of art is an essentially disinterested activity, which therefore does not induce anxiety. Contemplation of works of art should be contrasted with the desire to possess things; clearly if one's contemplation induces a desire to possess the art work it will no longer escape from anxiety. Insofar as one has no desire to possess, then one has escaped from the slavery of the will, at least for a short time. Schopenhauer, like Nietzsche after him, and like the whole German Romantic movement, exalts artistic genius, concluding that even the capacity to appreciate the genius of others has a sort of grandeur. Aesthetic contemplation, like aesthetic creation, enables us to transcend the subjection to desire.

Schopenhauer draws up a hierarchical classification of the arts which throws some extra light on his notion of the relation between phenomena and the metaphysical Will. Landscape gardening and architecture come at the bottom of the scale because they deal with dead matter. On the next level up there is historical painting and sculpture, which both deal with mankind. Higher again is poetry, because it concerns itself with concepts. Above poetry is tragedy; and above tragedy, music. Tragedy is high in the hierarchy because it depicts the true character of human life: its injustice, its evil, its unending pain. Music is highest of all because it represents nothing; it is pure form. Music is not representation, therefore it has a kind of reality, it reveals the nature of the ultimate. Listening to music is the highest type of aesthetic contemplation.

The second way to escape from the horrors of the world is through renunciation of the will to live. Since the individual will to live is a source of evil, it follows that to avoid evil one must deny the will and attempt, too, to deny the individuality of the self. We see here the influence of Indian thought. The wise man of India is represented as wishing to escape from anxiety and illusion and as pursuing his aim by reducing the needs of the body.

It might be thought that self-denial expresses itself most thoroughly in suicide. However, Schopenhauer rejects the option of suicide, on the grounds that self-destruction is an expression of the individual will. The desire for death is a desire like any other, and so it too must be denied.

How then is one to deny the self? What form can self-denial take? Schopenhauer explains the problem in terms of Maya, or illusion. One's own individuality is itself an illusion, the most pernicious illusion of all. Insofar as there are many different individuals, individuality as such implies plurality. But true reality cannot be plural, true reality is a unity. The correct and proper purpose of self-denial is to try to achieve a full realisation of the fact that the self is not a separate entity but is part of a unified wholeness. A person who has understood this fundamental truth will adopt a life of poverty, celibacy, and self-mortification. He will feel towards other human being, not love exactly (for ordinary human love is mere selfishness), but rather sympathy.

## Some Objections to Metaphysical Pessimism

One obvious objection concerns Schopenhauer's advice on how to live. His advice seems to be contradictory: he says that suicide is ruled out, because it involves the will, but might not self-mortification also involve acts of will? Well, perhaps Buddhism has an answer here. According to Buddhism it is possible to allow the will to "fade away". However, that idea is less helpful than it might appear, insofar as it presupposes that the nature of the will is such as to allow it to fade away of itself if given the chance. Whether or not that is true, it is clear that a will which tends to fade away of itself would be nothing like Schopenhauer's blind and all-devouring urge. The Buddhist answer also assumes that negative acts (for instance, allowing something to happen) do not require acts of will. But this is by no means certain. In sum: on the one hand it is perhaps not possible to will not to will; on the other hand, if human willing really is the objectification of a blind and violent metaphysical Will, it seems unlikely to fade away of itself.

Another possible objection to metaphysical pessimism is that it presupposes that overall comparisons can be made between existence and non-existence. I think it is very doubtful whether such comparisons can be made. Do we really understand the proposition that it would have been better if the world had never existed? It is easy, of course, to imagine smaller possibilities, to imagine, for instance, a world in which some particular person or state of affairs did not exist. It is not difficult, indeed, to imagine a state of affairs in which one does not exist oneself; for example when you imagine the Battle of Hastings in 1066, or the future world of Space Oddysey 3000, you imagine states of affairs from which you yourself were or will be absent. It is possible, too, to *compare* the actual world with an imaginary world; for instance, one might draw a comparison between the real world of today with a Utopian future in which war and illness and famine are unknown, and one could (and doubtless would) decide that the actual world is less good than the ideal one. But none of this amounts to making comparisons between the existence and non-existence of a huge totality, of the universe. For one thing comparisons of this kind, if conceivable at all, would have to be abstracted from all possible points of view, make them inherently reasonless.

## The Metaphysical Will as Hypothesis

Schopenhauer believed that he had succeeded in rigorously deducing the nature of ultimate reality from Kantian premises. Since the deduction is not rigorous, and so fails, some commentators have suggested that we ignore it. Instead, they argue, we should think of the metaphysical will as an *hypothesis*. Its value lies in the fact that it is a *completely new* hypothesis, having little to do with Kant or any previous philosopher. Schopenhauer was convinced that this world is a horrible place, and he speculated about how best to explain all the sadness and pain. The hypothesis that the world is built on conflict, the idea of the ultimate reality as a blind and pointless striving, appeared to him to explain all human misery. Perhaps it was only after he had arrived at his hypothesis that he attempted to deduce it from the philosophy of his great predecessor Immanuel Kant.

# Further Reading

Schopenhauer's main work, *The World as Will and Representation*, appeared in several editions; Volume Two of the third edition (that of 1859) is much easier than the rest of the book, because it contains many quite everyday examples. The aphorisms – the *Parerga and Paralipomena* – which will be irritating to at least some readers, are also extremely accessible. Copleston's *Arthur Schopenhauer* is an excellent commentary.

# Bibliography

F.C. Copleston, *Arthur Schopenhauer: Philosopher of Pessimism*, London: Burns, Oates & Washbourne 1946.
Arthur Schopenhauer, *The Fourfold Root of the Principle of Sufficient Reason*, tr. E.F.J. Payne, La Salle, Ill.: Open Court: 1974.
——*On the Freedom of the Will*, tr. R.J. Kolenda, New York: Bobbs-Merill 1960.
——*Essays and Aphorisms,* tr. R. Hollingdale, Harmondsworth: Penguin 1983.
——*The World as Will and Representation* (2 volumes), tr. E.F.J. Payne, New York: Dover 1969.

# 5   Søren Kierkegaard
## Robert Stern

Kierkegaard is often described as the first existentialist, one of the nine-teenth century precursors of a philosophical movement which, according to Sartre, "puts every man in possession of himself as he is and places the entire responsibility for his existence squarely upon his own shoulders." (Sartre, *Existentialism and Humanism,* p. 29) Certainly there is much in Kierkegaard's work to justify such an attribution: he shares with his twen-tieth century successors, such as Sartre, an emphasis on choice, subjectivi-ty, despair, irony, anxiety, isolation, and a distrust of abstract philosophis-ing, together with a literary and personal style of writing that is recognisably modern. And yet these themes are all worked out within the context of a theism which was not shared by later existentialists, but which has made him a central figure for subsequent Christian thought. Kierkegaard himself most often likened his position to that of a Christian Socrates, an heroically individual thinker faced with the struggle of faith.

It is not only his work that has led later commentators to call Kierkegaard an existentialist, but also the manner of his life. Søren Aabye Kierkegaard was born in Copenhagen, Denmark in 1813, the youngest of a family of seven children born to Michael Pedersen Kierkegaard and his second wife Anna. He describes his father as being afflicted by a "fright-ful depression", which formed part of the "dark background of my life from its earliest beginning." (*Journals* VI p. 72) He asks

> Why did I not thrive as other children do, why was I not wrapped around in joy, why did I come to look into that region of sighs sĭo early, why was I born with a congenital anxiety which constantly made me look into it, why were nine months in my mother's womb enough to make me so old that I was not born like other children but was born old. (*Journals* V pp. 232-3.)

In 1830, at the age of seventeen, Kierkegaard entered the University of Copenhagen, where after a period of study for which at times he lacked any real enthusiasm, he completed a degree in theology in 1840. Two other events were more significant during this period: the unexpected death of his father in 1838, and his meeting with Regina Olsen a year pre-viously. Shortly before his death, his father had told him how, as a young boy tending sheep on the Jutland heath, he had cursed God for the misery of his life, and that he regarded his subsequent worldly success as a preparation for divine punishment, interpreting the death of his wife, two sons and a daughter in this light. Kierkegaard assumed that this punishment was to be visited also on himself, but when his father died instead, he viewed this as some sort of "sacrifice" made on his behalf, in order that he might fulfil a religious task. He therefore began to take his theological studies seriously at last, and completed them within a year. Then, in September 1840, after announcing his engagement to Regina Olsen, the daughter of a highly-placed civil servant, Kierkegaard prepared for a professional life in the Church and life as a family man. However, a year later he returned the ring, an act that caused him enormous emotional suffering, but to which he felt compelled. The separation from Regina Olsen was a crucial turning point in his life, leading him to abandon the safety and comforts of society, family and Church, and embark on a future of agonised isolation and devotion to his purely personal vocation.

In 1841 Kierkegaard travelled to Berlin, in order to hear Schelling's lectures on the philosophy of revelation, which involved a highly charged attack on Hegel from a Christian perspective. Kierkegaard had already formed an unfavourable impression on Hegel's philosophy before he went to Berlin, and was critical of the growing influence of the Hegelian system on thinkers within the Danish Lutheran Church at this time. He therefore welcomed Schelling's attack, but was unimpressed by the latter's own attempts at positive speculation. On February 6th 1842 Kierkegaard remarked in a letter to his brother, "Schelling talks endless nonsense... I am leaving Berlin and hasting to Copenhagen... not, you understand, to be bound by a new tie... [but] to complete *Either/Or*." (*Journals* V, p. 201.)

Published in 1843, *Either/Or* was the first of a series of "pseudonymous" works by Kierkegaard that appeared in the next few years. These works were published under a series of transparently fictitious names with the aim of exhibiting, for each of a number of invented *personae*, the connection between life and authorship. Also published pseudonymously were *Repetition* (1843), *Fear and Trembling* (1843), *Philosophical Fragments* (1844), *The Concept of Dread* (1844), *Stages on Life's Way* (1845) and the *Concluding Unscientific Postscript* (1846). It is on these works, particularly the latter, that Kierkegaard's reputation is based. In addition, during this period Kierkegaard also published twenty-one "edifying" discourses on religious themes under his own name.

Then, in December 1845, another event occurred that marked Kierkegaard's life. In that month, a collection of literary essays was published which included an attack on *Stages on Life's Way* by one P.L. Møller. Greatly annoyed by Møller's article, Kierkegaard responded by publishing a reply in which he revealed Møller's connection with a disreputable satirical weekly called *The Corsair*. As a result, in the following weeks *The Corsair* turned its attentions to Kierkegaard himself, making him an object of public ridicule. This only served to increase his isolation from society, begun by the scandal of his broken engagement with Regina and reinforced by the odd nature of his books. It also confirmed in him his sense of the cowardliness and moral depravity of those in civic life, and strengthened his vocation as outsider and scourge of the establishment.

His subsequent publications include *The Sickness Unto Death* (1849) and *The Training in Christianity* (1850), two of the most important of his works as a Christian writer. Then, after a few years in which he produced little, he began a vitriolic and impassioned campaign against the State Church ("Christendom"), provoked by comments made by Hans Martensen, a theologian, in the funeral oration for Bishop Mynster, the Danish primate. This attack was principally carried on through Kierkegaard's own broadsheet *The Instant*, which went through nine issues until he fell ill and died in 1855.

Filled as it was with self-destructive pride and perversity, high courage, absurd melodrama, deep melancholy and self-inflicted suffering, Kierkegaard's life is a model for that of the existential hero, as by his sacrifice of any conventional solace he struggled to develop the distinctive viewpoint and "voice" that one finds within his work.

## Kierkegaard against Hegel.

As with many nineteenth century thinkers, Kierkegaard's philosophy is marked by his encounter with Hegel, and his dissatisfaction with the Hegelian system. However, while the "left" Hegelians like Marx, Engels and Feuerbach attacked Hegel from a humanistic and materialistic perspective, Kierkegaard's attack was from a religious standpoint. As Kierkegaard declared in a posthumously published work, "the unifying thought of the whole authorship is: becoming a Christian" (*The Point of View*, p. 75); and his basic objection to Hegel's philosophy was that it makes becoming a Christian impossible. In order to understand this claim, it is first necessary to say something about the equivocal relationship between Hegel's thought and the religious outlook, so that we can see why Kierkegaard feared that, with the ascendency of the former, the latter would be undermined.

Hegel typically declares that "religion can exist very well without philosophy, but philosophy cannot exist without religion, which it rather encompasses in itself". This contains a twofold claim: firstly, that religious thought is independent of philosophy, and the latter is dependent on the former, but secondly that philosophy "encompasses" or "includes" religion, meaning that religion, like everything else, is incorporated within the Hegelian system. Now, to a thinker like Kierkegaard, the apparent assurance of sovereignty for religion contained in the first claim is undermined by the threat posed to religion in the second, for in "encompassing" it, philosophy can leave no room for religious faith. Kierkegaard therefore has deep misgivings regarding the Hegelian project, of overcoming religion positively, by appropriating it within philosophy.

In fact, Hegel's appropriation of Christianity is two-fold, taking place at both the metaphysical and ethical levels. At the metaphysical level, Hegel argues that philosophy presents the content of religion in the form of thought, by transforming religious images and representations into metaphysical categories, and "cashing out" the metaphors of religion into the hard currency of philosophical thought. Thus, Hegel argues that we find in the Christian doctrine of the incarnation a pre-reflective expression of the unity of universal and individual, finite and infinite, as the figure of Christ represents this unity in concrete form, which consciousness later comes to understand philosophically. Moreover, once it has divested revealed religion of its picture thinking, and conceptualised it philosophically, consciousness no longer views the incarnation as incomprehensible, but now sees in it the expression of a deep philosophical truth. Thus, at the metaphysical level, Hegel appropriates religion by transforming the realities of faith into mere representations for higher conceptual thought, arguing that the mysteries of Christianity can be philosophically "taken up" once his dialectical re-interpretation of the categories of universal and individual, infinite and finite, has been achieved.

Hegel also sets out to appropriate religion ethically and politically, by trying to use Christianity in such a way that its potentiality as a folk religion could be realised for socio-political purposes. Using the Greek city state as an example, Hegel argues that religion can play an important role in underpinning the civic life of a community, unifying its members around a shared set of beliefs, and acting as a vehicle for ethical instruction. However, following Rousseau, Hegel claims that historically Christianity has not operated in this way, and has acted more as a socially divisive force, based on individual conscience, introspection and the worship of a transcendent God, with the result that it has encouraged the neglect of social and political obligations, and has undermined civic and communal ties. Nonetheless, Hegel believes that potentially Christianity could serve as a folk religion if its outlook could be transformed in certain ways, and in particular if Jesus could be seen as a prophet of ethical life. Thus, Hegel places considerable emphasis on the development of the Christian community, and its ethical function within the state:

> In the Protestant state, the constitution and the code, as well as their special applications, embody the principle and the development of the moral life, which proceeds and can only proceed from the truth of religion, when reinstated in its original principle and in that way as such first becomes actual. The moral life of the state and the religious spirituality of the state are thus reciprocal guarantees of strength. (Hegel, *Philosophy of Mind* §552, p. 291)

Both at the metaphysical and ethical levels, therefore, Hegel hoped to "encompass" religion by giving it a role within his system. For Kierkegaard, however, to accept this two-fold appropriation of Christianity by philosophy would be to trivialise the special significance of the former, and he set out to show that religious belief could not be seen in this light. In his attack on Hegel's treatment of religion, and in developing his own, anti-Hegelian picture of the meaning of religion for human life, Kierkegaard sets out to undermine the former's rationalistic and ethical appropriation of Christianity, and with this initiates his distinctive critique of the whole project of traditional philosophy.

# The Paradoxes of Faith

In order to overturn Hegel's attempt to "encompass" religion at the metaphysical level, Kierkegaard emphasised that two paradoxes lie at the heart of Christianity which cannot be incorporated within philosophy: firstly, the *object* of faith is paradoxical, and secondly the *act* of faith is paradoxical. Kierkegaard therefore argues that the Hegelian attempt to include religion within philosophy must fail, since religion involves an aspect of deep irrationality that no amount of philosophical thinking can resolve.

Kierkegaard claims that the object of Christian faith is paradoxical because we are asked to believe in the incarnation, and accept that the "absolute" difference between God and man was nonetheless bridged: "That God has existed in human form, has been born, grown up, and so forth, is surely the paradox *sensu strictissimo*, the absolute paradox." (*Concluding Unscientific Postscript*, p. 187) The claim that the deity has lived in human form implies, in philosophical terms, that "the eternal truth has come into being in time: this is the paradox". (*Concluding Unscientific Postscript*, p. 187) The two terms 'temporal' and 'eternal' are for Kierkegaard mutually exclusive or at least qualitatively different, making it impossible for us to understand how God can exist in time, and become a particular man:

> Christ's appearance is and still remains a paradox. To his contemporaries the paradox lay in the fact that this particular individual human being, who looked like other human beings, talked like them and followed the customs, was the son of God. For all subsequent ages the paradox is different, for since he is not seen with the physical eye it is easier to represent him as the son of God, but the shocking thing now is that he spoke within the thought world of a particular age. (*Journals* III, p. 400)

Kierkegaard therefore sees in the incarnation an insuperable obstacle to the philosophical consciousness, as it involves an "absolute paradox" which cannot be comprehended.

Now, Hegel himself had suggested that the unity of God and man as represented in the incarnation should be understood as follows:

> In the Church Christ has been called the God-Man. This is the extraordinary combination which directly contradicts the Understanding; but the unity of the divine and human natures has here been brought into human consciousness and has become a certainty for it, implying that the otherness, or, as it is also expressed, the finitude, the weakness, the frailty of human nature is not incompatible with this unity, just as in the eternal idea otherness in no way detracts from the unity which God is. This is the extraordinary combination the necessity of which we have seen. It involves the truth that the divine and human natures are not implicitly different. (Hegel, *Philosophy of Religion* III, pp. 76–77)

According to Hegel, therefore, although the incarnation is puzzling if one assumes an absolute difference between the divine and the human, once one sees that there is in fact no fundamental dichotomy, that each incorporates the other in dialectical unity, then the paradox of the God-Man dissolves. Hegel bases his position here on the claim, common to many thinkers in the rationalist tradition, that "the divine and human natures are not implicitly different", in so far as all human beings can become infinite and divine in thought, *qua* thinking beings. This is an idea that has its roots in the Greek conception of *nous* as a divine element in man, as what enables human beings to see the world from the perspective of God. Hegel identifies God with the thinking element in man, arguing that "[r]eason is the divine element in man" (Hegel, *Introduction to the History of Philosophy*, p. 91), and that "[p]hilosophy is knowledge, and it is through knowledge that man first realises his original vocation, to be the image of God". (Hegel, *Logic* §24Z) For Hegel, therefore, the historical event of the incarnation is by no means incomprehensible, as it is merely the figurative representation of the philosophical claim that by becoming fully rational the human mind can approximate to the divine.

For Kierkegaard, however, there is something absurd in the rationalist claim that as human beings we can come close to the standpoint of God. He argues that we are finite, temporal creatures, whose understanding of things is invariably limited by this existential predicament, and who cannot approximate to the view of reality afforded to an infinite and atemporal being like God:

> An existential system cannot be formulated. Does this mean that no such system exists? By no means; nor is this implied in our assertion. Reality itself is a system – for God; but it cannot be a system for any existing spirit. System and finality correspond to one another, but existence is precisely the opposite of finality... Anyone who is himself an existing individual cannot gain this finality outside existence which corresponds to the eternity into which the past has entered... But who is this systematic thinker? Aye, it is he who is outside of existence and yet in existence, who is in his eternity forever complete, and yet includes all existence within himself – it is God... Such a thinker would either have to be God, or a fantastic *quod libet*. (*Concluding Unscientific Postscript*, pp. 107–8)

For Kierkegaard, the "absolute difference that distinguishes man from God" is not that "between more or less of intellectual talent", as the rationalist suggests, but rather

> that man is a particular existing being... whose essential task cannot be to think *sub specie aeterni*, since as long as he exists he is, though eternal, essentially an existing individual, whose essential task is to concentrate upon inwardness in existing; while God is infinite and eternal. (*Concluding Unscientific Postscript*, p. 195)

The rationalist philosopher – Hegel, for example – affords the comic spectacle of trying to resolve the existential predicament of being human by abstracting from finitude and individuality through adopting the standpoint of pure thought; but he cannot manage to do so, and must remain an existing individual, trapped within a merely human perspective.

Kierkegaard is therefore important, and deserves to be known as the first existentialist, because he inaugurated the critique of rationalism from the standpoint of individualism. For rationalism, the aim was to achieve an objective perspective on the world, an understanding free of the limitations imposed by the merely human, or subjective, viewpoint, and thereby

to approximate to the divine. This, Kierkegaard argues, is a doomed project, in so far as we cannot transcend our own, individual perspective on
the world without transcending what it is to be human, and what it is to be
ourselves, which is absurd. As particular individuals, we can only know
and experience reality from within a limited standpoint, and we must
abandon the rationalist attempt to adopt a view from nowhere.

Kierkegaard thus goes on to question the traditional emphasis on the
connection between objectivity and truth, arguing against the rationalist
like Hegel that something can be true for me without being true for all.
The rationalist tries to loosen our commitment to those things we merely
believe as individuals, and tries to get us to accept only those propositions
we can get others to share with us; but Kierkegaard allows that there can
be beliefs that we take to be true, but which are truths for us alone, which
no one else has reason to accept. Central among those subjective truths
are our religious beliefs, for which the believer recognises and demands
no objective, rationally defensible warrant:

> When subjectivity, inwardness, is the truth, the truth becomes objectively a
> paradox; and the fact that truth is objectively a paradox shows in turn that sub-
> jectivity is the truth... The paradoxical character of the truth is its objective
> uncertainty; this uncertainty is an expression for the passionate inwardness,
> and the passion is precisely the truth. (*Concluding Unscientific Postscript*,
> p. 183)

Kierkegaard therefore moves from his insistence that the *object* of faith
– that is, the God-Man – is paradoxical, to an insistence that the *act* of
faith is paradoxical: that is, that faith rests not on objective truth, but on
an objective uncertainty, making it irredeemably subjective. This contrast
of inner certainty and objective uncertainty he calls the passion of faith.
Faith is paradoxical for reason because as a psychological state it cannot
be brought about rationally (by a demonstration of the existence of God,
for example) but only through an ungrounded decision, or leap. Indeed it
is precisely the absence of rational justification (not to say the irrational
and contradictory nature of the claim that the infinite can be incorporated
in the finite) which provides the occasion for such an act, or leap, of faith.
Thus whereas for Hegel the content of religion could be made rational, so
that no act of faith would be required, for Kierkegaard the truth of
Christianity remains paradoxical, and its only warrant is subjective certainty based on inner conviction and a leap. This leap is only made when
one feels the contradictions which Hegel had tried so hard to dispel. It
rests on our need to overcome the separation of finite and infinite, of death
and eternal life, and on our inability to do so rationally. Only after this
absolute contradiction is affirmed can the leap be taken, only after it has

been accepted that our existential predicament cannot be transformed through reason, but through faith alone.

# The Suspension of The Ethical.

While in his masterwork, the *Concluding Unscientific Postscript,* Kierkegaard is primarily concerned with undermining Hegel's appropriation of Christianity at the metaphysical level, his rejection of Hegel's ethical incorporation of Christianity is a theme of many of his most important works. He sets out to show that a morality based on the will of God is inimical to the Hegelian morality of civic life, and that the one cannot be successfully incorporated within the other. The underlying tension between the ethical conceived in the Hegelian way, and the ethical grounded on the will of God, is clearly brought out in *Either/Or* and in *Fear and Trembling.*

*Either/Or* represents a clash between what Kierkegaard calls the aesthetic and the ethical standpoints. Pseudonymously written under the name of Victor Eremita, the book presents two sets of papers, "A's Papers" offering the reader a picture of various aspects of the aesthetic attitude to life, and "B's Papers" offering a picture of the ethical attitude. A's papers are an eclectic mix of material, containing (*inter alia*) scattered aphorisms, discussions of tragedy (*Antigone*), opera and the erotic (Mozart's *Don Giovanni*), and concluding with a detailed account of an elaborately planned seduction. B's papers, by contrast, are written in a sober and deliberate manner, by a respectable married man, Judge William. They are apparently written to the A of the first part, to try and convince him of the need to maintain "the equilibrium of the aesthetical and the ethical in the composition of the personality" (*Either/Or* II, p. 159), and to extol the benefits of marriage over merely romantic love (a topic of deep interest to Kierkegaard after his broken engagement to Regina Olsen).

In his portrayal of Judge William, Kierkegaard produces something of a caricature of the Hegelian position, while at the same time pointing beyond it. (It should not be forgotten, perhaps, that William was Hegel's middle name.) Judge William's intention is to convince A that the aesthetic attitude towards life, the immediate, romantic infatuation with the instant, must be replaced by the enduring love of marriage, and its ethical and social obligations. Judge William speaks of the way in which the universal and the individual can be united within the family, in a manner that clearly echoes Hegel's claim that the family constitutes the "ethical root of the state". (Hegel, *Philosophy of Religion* §255, p. 154) The Judge claims that one must strive to realise "a social, a civic self", not an abstract one that "fits everywhere and hence nowhere" (*Either/Or* II, p. 267), and argues that marriage, having a useful job or occupation, undertaking civil and institutional responsibilities, are all necessary from this point of view. Like Hegel, he suggests that to the ethical individual the duties of the community are not an external limitation, for "he who lives ethically expresses the universal in his life, he makes himself the universal man, not by divesting himself of his concretion, for then he becomes nothing, but by clothing himself with it and permeating it with the universal". (*Either/Or* II, p. 260) As a spokesman for civic morality, therefore, Judge William represents the standpoint of a true Hegelian.

However, looked at more closely, it is possible to detect non-Hegelian elements in the Judge's portrayal of the ethical. There are several passages where he seems to acknowledge the pull of subjectivity and conscience, as he emphasises the place of individual choice within moral life, the importance of which Hegel had tried to undermine:

> The act of choosing is essentially a proper and stringent expression of the ethical. Whenever in a strict sense there is a question of an either/or, one can always be sure that the ethical is involved. The only absolute either/or is the choice between good and evil, but that is also absolutely ethical... If you will understand me aright, I should like to say that in making a choice it is not so much a question of choosing the right as of the energy, the earnestness, the pathos with which one chooses. Thereby the personality announces its inner infinity, and thereby, in turn, the personality is consolidated. (*Either/Or* II, pp. 170–1)

Here, it seems, Judge William is suggesting that the ethical must remain at the level of individual choice, and cannot be made objective and universal, something merely to be found in the moral law of the community. As it turns out, the reason for this is that good and evil originate from within a *religious* context, in the will of God, which lies outside the civic life of the community, and has priority over it. As Hegel himself had been aware, and had analysed in his critique of Christianity as a private source of morality, the good that we choose in the religious context may force us to decide against the good of the merely civic life, and the ethical can thereby be suspended by faith.

This phenomenon is vividly illustrated and dramatically represented by Kierkegaard in *Fear and Trembling*, another work he wrote pseudonymously under the name of Johannes *de silentio*. Here faith is represented as lying beyond the province of Hegelian civic morality, as represented by Judge William. The centrepiece of the work is a discussion of the biblical account of Abraham (the "father of faith"), who was called upon by God to kill his son, Isaac, by offering him as a sacrifice. Abraham set out to follow his instructions, until at the last moment God withdrew his command, and he sacrificed a lamb instead. To the religious believer, Abraham is seen as having acted as a worthy servant of God, as a "knight of faith".

> In order to perceive the prodigious paradox of faith [writes Johannes *de silentio*], a paradox that makes a murder into a holy and God-pleasing act, a paradox that gives Isaac back to Abraham again, which no thought can grasp, because faith begins precisely where thought stops – in order to perceive this, it is now my intention to draw out in the form of *problemata* the dialectical aspects implicit in the story of Abraham. (*Fear and Trembling*, p. 53)

On this basis, Kierkegaard takes up the problem: "Is there a teleological suspension of the ethical?" Following Kant and Hegel, he understands the ethical as essentially universalisable, as defined by the categorical imperative that one "ought never to act except in such a way *that I can also will that my maxim should become a universal law*." (Kant, *Groundwork of the Metaphysics of Morals*, p. 67) Thus, for an ethical individual, the aim or *telos* is to reconcile themselves to the universal, which can be used to justify their actions to others, and which they must recognise as the arbiter of right or wrong: "As soon as the single individual asserts himself in his singularity before the universal, he sins, and only by acknowledging this can he be reconciled again with the universal." (*Fear and Trembling*, p. 54)

Kierkegaard argues, using the story of Abraham, that this ethical outlook is suspended within the religious context. Abraham stands isolated and alone, not claiming to be able to justify his action to others, which at the level of rational thought and conduct can be seen as outrageous, even mad: for he contemplates the murder of his son solely on the grounds of hearing a voice telling him to do so. If his action is justifiable, it can only be by reference to a divine command that is addressed to him alone and whose content is such that it cannot be made acceptable by purely human standards, according to which he is contemplating an immoral act. He has accepted as a binding duty an action that cannot be seen as part of the moral law, or based on civic morality, but is grounded simply in the will of God, so that the ethical is annulled by Abraham's act of faith:

> By his act he transgresses the ethical altogether and had a higher *telos* outside it, in relation to which he suspended it. For I certainly would like to know how Abraham's act can be related to the universal, whether any point of contact between what Abraham did and the universal can be found other than that

Abraham transgressed it... Abraham's act is totally unrelated to the universal, is a purely private endeavour. (*Fear and Trembling*, p. 59)

Kierkegaard therefore uses the story of Abraham to show two things: that there is an essential difference between the religious and ethical outlooks, and that the ethical *can* be suspended in favour of the religious, although this suspension can only be achieved through an act of faith, not on objectively rational grounds. Whereas from an Hegelian perspective what Abraham was prepared to do was ethically wrong, and was based merely on conscience and religious feeling, from a religious point of view, as Kierkegaard points out, Abraham is a "knight of faith", a servant of God, and as such has a pull on us as a religious hero. Moreover, even outside the religious context, we can see in Abraham something to admire, while viewing his proposed action with horror; and this is because we acknowledge the significance and grandeur of Abraham's choice, as a pure individual: "The story of Abraham contains, then, a teleological suspension of the ethical. As the single individual he became higher than the universal. This is the paradox, which cannot be mediated." (*Fear and Trembling*, p. 66)

Ultimately, therefore, Kierkegaard's case against Hegel, and against philosophy itself, is that it is superficial: it claims to have solved problems, to have overcome difficulties, to have resolved dichotomies, and to have set individual and social life on a reasonable footing, but in fact it has merely glossed over them. In man's relationship to God, in the juxtaposition of the finite and the eternal, however, all these questions re-emerge, as we fight to come to terms with out limitedness, our doubts, and our isolated individuality, and are thereby forced to base our existence on an ungrounded choice, an act of faith, a leap. Philosophy glosses over the rich texture of human life, the tragic uncertainties of human existence, and it is in Kierkegaard's efforts to cast light on these neglected issues that the originality of his perspective lies:

It is supposed to be difficult to understand Hegel, but to understand Abraham is a small matter. To go beyond Hegel is a miraculous achievement, but to go beyond Abraham is the easiest thing of all. I for my part have applied considerable time to understanding Hegelian philosophy and believe that I have understood it fairly well; I am sufficiently brash to think that when I cannot understand particular passages despite my pains, he himself may not have been entirely clear. All this I do easily, naturally, without any mental strain. Thinking about Abraham is another matter, however: then I am shattered. I am constantly aware of the prodigious paradox that is the content of Abraham's life, and, despite all my passion, my thought cannot penetrate it, cannot get ahead by a hairsbreadth. I stretch every muscle to get a perspective, and at the same instant I become paralysed. (*Fear and Trembling*, p. 33)

# Further Reading

Of Kierkegaard's own works, both *Fear and Trembling* and *Repetition* are very accessible, and *Repetition* is not nearly as gloomy as the usual stereotype of Kierkegaard would suggest. Among the secondary literature, Gardiner's *Kierkegaard* is a good introduction to Kierkegaard himself, and Weston's *Kierkegaard and Modern Continental Philosophy* describes the recent influence of Kierkegaard.

# Bibliography

Edward Craig, *The Mind of God and the Works of Man*, Oxford: Oxford University Press 1987.

G.W.F. Hegel, *Logic* tr. William Wallace, 3rd. ed., Oxford: Oxford University Press 1987.

——*Philosophy of Mind* tr. William Wallace and A.V. Miller, Oxford University Press: Oxford 1971.

——*Philosophy of Right*, tr. T.M. Knox, Oxford: Oxford University Press 1952.

——*Lectures on the Philosophy of Religion* tr. E.B. Spiers and J.B. Sanderson, new ed., 3 volumes, London: Humanities Press 1962.

Immanuel Kant, *The Groundwork of the Metaphysic of Morals*, tr. H.J. Paton as *The Moral Law*, London: Hutchinson 1948.

Søren Aabye Kierkegaard, *Concluding Unscientific Postscript*, tr. David P. Swenson and Walter Lowrie, Princeton: Princeton University Press 1944.

——*Either-Or*, tr. David F. Swenson and Lillian Marvin Swenson, with revisions by Howard A. Johnson, Princeton: Princeton University Press 1959.

——*Fear and Trembling* and *Repetition*, ed. and tr. Howard V. Hong and Edna H. Hong, Princeton: Princeton University Press 1983.

——*Soren Kierkegaard's Journals and Papers*, ed. and tr. Howard V. Hong and Edna H. Hong (7 vols), Bloomington: Indiana University Press 1978.

Søren Aabye Kierkegaard, *The Point of View of My Work as an Author*, tr. W. Lowrie, New York: Harper and Row 1962.

Jean-Paul Sartre, *Existentialism and Humanism*, London: Eyre Methuen 1948.

# 6 Karl Marx
## Gill Howie

Karl Marx (1818–1883) studied law at Bonn and Berlin, but soon became more interested in philosophy and history. In his early life he was influenced by the philosophy of Hegel, the ideas of Feuerbach, and the works of the economist David Ricardo, but later developed his own powerful and very influential theory, a theory intended to explain historical processes, economic facts, and political and social forces and norms.

At the time Marx was writing, European societies had already been undergoing massive social upheavals for some time. Conventional explanations of these changes focus on the Enlightenment, the French Revolution and the Industrial Revolution. The Enlightenment is seen as the first indication of the secularisation of society, replacing religious orthodoxy with faith in science and reason and freeing people from false mystical beliefs and from the authority claimed by religious and aristocratic hierarchies. The French revolution is thought to have established the principles of universal suffrage, freedom, and equality before the law, principles which form the basis of liberal democracy. The Industrial Revolution established new social relations which allowed "man" to control nature, to increase production and to satisfy "his" needs.

This explanatory model, however, does not account for the unevenness of European transitions from feudalism to capitalism, or for the early English Revolution which significantly liberalised pre-Enlightenment mercantile capitalism in that country, or for the unpopularity of orthodox religious institutions in France and elsewhere.

Marx held that crises are a necessary consequence of liberal capitalism. Conflicts are an endemic part of a social organisation founded on a systematic exclusion of most people from natural resources. According to Marx, liberal capitalism contains the seeds of its own dissolution: the subjection of people to industrial productive relations increases even as formal conditions for democracy emerge. This contradiction between freedom and subjection leads to crises. Because expectations raised and encouraged by liberalism cannot be met within liberal capitalism, conflict can only be resolved by the dawning of a new age. Only a class aware of the reasons for the crises and conscious of its collective power would be able to alter the relations producing conflict.

Nietzsche, too, forsaw a tendency towards crises in liberalism. However, he explained these in terms of general problems with epistemology, and his continental followers likewise explain the crises of liberalism in epistemological terms. It is my intention to challenge this understanding of our contemporary situation by showing that challenges to legitimacy cannot be reduced to problems of epistemology; the crisis has a different cause, which it is the function of scientific Marxism to elucidate.

## Legitimacy and Crisis

Liberalism takes power to be legitimate when the rules which govern it are neutral as to moral ends, impartially negotiate conflicting interests, and deliver and distribute benefits while protecting basic rights. If there is evidence of consent then all the better. The individual, who is free by nature, forms a contract with the state by which freedom is exchanged for civil liberties and the subject undertakes obligations to obey the laws of the state. The contract can hold explicitly through the act of voting or tacitly with the receipt of benefits. If there is little civil disobedience then legitimacy is manifested in the harmony between the state's activities and the beliefs held by all law-abiding rational citizens.

A crisis of legitimation can thus arise in one of two ways. A government might transgress the conditions which determine legitimacy. This would not be a crisis over legitimacy but with the legitimacy of a particular government. A more fundamental crisis would follow if the actual conditions defining legitimacy were to be rejected.

Marx claims that all liberal governments are, on their own terms, necessarily illegitimate, because they cannot abide by their own criterion of state neutrality; they must uphold the right to private ownership. The legitimacy of liberal capitalism also requires smooth economic production in order to supply the promised benefits. In theory, the state is supposed to govern social relations but not the economic relations of production, but the relation of government to the economy is in fact articulated as management rather than as participation. During economic recessions this curious role tends to come under scrutiny. Dissatisfaction is expressed as demands for social justice.

## Marx's Ontology

Scientific Marxism proceeds from the assumption that there is a world independent of the senses. The natural world exists independently of the mind and so too do certain social forms or structures. However Marx is not a reductive empiricist. First, he holds that nature alters through our practical engagement with it, an engagement which transforms us in turn. He also argues that objective social forms and structures are the result of intentional human agency within historically transmitted limits. Lastly, he emphasises that it is through our labour, our productive activity, that we create and understand the natural-social world.

The human being is a natural entity with instincts, needs and dispositions.

> Man as an objective, sensuous being is a suffering being – and because he feels that he suffers, a passionate being. Passion is the essential power of man energetically bent on its object (Marx, *Economic and Philosophical Manuscripts*.).

It should also be noted that Marx's account of human beings is relational. As social beings we are constituted in and through our active engagement with the world and with other people. Historically these relations take different forms. A social relation can be objective in the sense that it is established as the usual form of engagement. Social relations are taken to be essential. This does not mean that the human being can be "explained away" as a product of those relations; it only means that a human being comes alive in its contact with nature and with other people.

The claim that consciousness and self-consciousness are social does not mean that we cannot distinguish between true and false beliefs. There is, however, a degree of ambivalence in Marx's theory of knowledge. The world exists independently of human senses, yet human senses are part of the world. Our perception and understanding of the world have natural limits and empirical investigation will be informed by these limits. Investigation is a social practice, and because it is a social practice it is constrained by its own history; its autonomy is relative. As a social practice science has its own dynamic and inherits beliefs and ideas from previous scientific paradigms. As well as this, scientific practitioners are social creatures and cannot cannot leave all their other non-scientific beliefs at the door of the laboratory. Contemporary feminist scientists suggest that scientific theories suffer because scientists are socially located. Ideas common in society exert their influence, even in perception and observation, and are more likely to bias the interpretation of empirical 'data'.

## The Labour Theory of Value

In order to understand the current legitimation crisis, we need to understand the basic processes of capitalist society, or, as Marx called then, the relations of production of capital. Marx's method, historical materialism, is a study of changing and dynamic social (productive) relations. His examination of capitalism traces the historical stages of development of productive systems from ancient times through feudalism to capitalism and socialism.

Marxist economics focuses on the social relations involved in the production of commodities. Goods satisfy needs; they have use-values. Commodities are goods which stand in relation to other goods; they have exchange-values. This relation is a measurement: if, for example, two chairs can be exchanged for one table, a table has twice the value of a chair. Since we are able to measure the relation between different commodities they must all share something. As they have different and incommensurable uses, what they share must be the fact that they are products of labour. Their values depend on the amount of labour needed to produce them. The measurement is in all cases the same – it is based on labour – but measures different amounts of labour; we can reformulate this by saying that what is measured is qualitatively the same but differs quantitatively. This is not a measurement of particular labour but is an abstract measurement. It is the socially necessary labour time taken to produce use-values under conditions of production normal for a given society. The abstraction assumes an average degree of intensity of labour and an average degree of skill. Once abstracted from particular productive endeavours we are left with the average amount of labour measured in time units. So measurement of value in terms of abstract labour regulates the process of trade: trade is the circulation of commodities, and thus the circulation of value.

The capitalist invests a sum of money in the means of production (tools, machinery, raw materials) and labour (skills, knowledge, techniques). During the process of production the raw materials are transformed into new use-values. The capitalist releases these use-values on the market. The use-values also have exchange-values. The money received by the capitalist for these commodities is larger than the money originally invested. The exchange-value of the commodity is larger than the exchange-value of the machinery and of the present labour. The value of any commodity is the sum of the past labour measured in units of time (exchange-value of the machinery, raw materials) and the present labour socially necessary to the production of the object. For the value of the commodities to be greater than the value of the original investment value must be created in the system of production. Because the value of past labour (machinery, materials) is simply transferred to the new commodity, it must be the present labour which adds value. This account of value explains how it is possible for the capitalist to accumulate value. It is present labour which produces value additional to the value of "dead" labour in the system of production. For there to be profit available, the value of labour must differ in magnitude from the exchange-value of the commodity produced by the labourer. The value of labour must be less than the value produced by the labourer in a working day. This difference in magnitude is surplus-value, for which the capitalist claims the profit.

In this process, the worker sells a commodity, i.e. labour power, for its exchange value; according to the labour theory of value, this must be the amount of socially necessary labour taken to produce and reproduce it, measured in terms of time. This will amount to the labour value of the bundle of commodities consumed by the worker and family in the production process. In this sense, the worker can be paid a fair wage under capitalism, defined in terms of the exchange value of labour power. and the difference between the value of labour and the value produced by labour is surplus value,

However, this commodification of labour depends on treating the labour process – a transformative and creative activity – as a measurable quantity. This transformative and creative activity is what gives labour its *use* value, rather than its exchange value. The capitalist appropriates this human capacity under the guise of a fair wage contract.

There are thus two aspects to exploitation under capitalism. Quantitatively, private ownership of the means of production entitles the capitalist to appropriate the surplus value produced by the worker, and this can happen even if the worker is paid a fair wage; this is the particular manner in which exploitation takes place within capitalism, hidden and obscured by the wage-form. Qualitatively, exploitation occurs simply because a transformative and creative activity is measured in terms of time units.

The labour theory of value is concerned with ratios between values, where value is understood as socially necessary labour time. Obviously commodities are not exchanged in this simple fashion. There is one commodity which mediates between exchanges. This for Marx is gold, or its monetary equivalent.

# Essence, Appearance and Ideology

Marx criticises those political economists who have simple demand-supply economic models for siding with appearance. This is not to say that the concept of demand is irrelevant to the Marxist account since demand for use-values effects the concentration of capital in certain industries, and explains the movement of capital between productive sectors. Yet focussing on demand would be to conceal the essential social relations governing production. The demand-supply model hides the fact that value is not a natural measurement but an abstract one. The social counterpart of this abstract measurement is the mobile pool of exploited labour. So in conventional political economy things are not understood as they really are. Market economics makes it appear that the objects have a power to command prices. But to understand fluctuations of prices, or the difference between price and value, one needs first to grasp the substance of value, which is constituted by the social relations of capital. This requires empirical studies of the relations of production and the extraction of surplus value. Because these relations are social relations, capitalism is only one, alterable, way of organising production. But market economics reifies these relations by presenting them as natural and immutable.

Ideology is the one-sided presentation of social relations in the realm of appearance. For example, market economics presents goods as commanding prices whereas the commodity actually commands a price because it has a value and it has a value determined by labour power. Ideological thought attempts to abstract from social relations in favour of what it takes to be essential, as though the relations were irrelevant to a proper understanding. But what appears to be a relation between absolute goods is in fact a product of a relation between people; and in dialectical materialism, empirical investigation and critical procedures combine to uncover the concealed essential pattern of social relations, and in so doing decipher why certain beliefs are false. In capitalism ideological beliefs are usually those which function to hide or distort the relations of production. Described as part of the intellectual and cultural superstructure of society, ideological thought justifies the base – private ownership and the appropriation of surplus-value.

"The ideas of the ruling class are in every epoch the ruling ideas, i.e. the class which is the ruling material force of society is at the same time its ruling intellectual force". (Marx, *The German Ideology*) The ideas of the bourgeois ruling class tend to be ideological. Its beliefs and ideas appear to present a coherent picture of the world but it is coherent in a problematic way. Bourgeois ideology presents people with private utopias, in the form of religion, popular literature, and commodity fetishism, which function to release the stress of conflict. But because the conflicts arise from the way that social relations are organised in capitalism the release is only temporary. The search for utopias itself provides an expanding market, which advertisers manipulate to aid the redistribution of surplus value.

Even though a liberal government might appear to satisfy its own conditions of legitimacy, it must still operate within the limits of capitalism. By ensuring stability it encourages a climate of affluent production, which in effect means the ongoing extraction of surplus-value and the accumulation of profit. But the production of surplus-value, privately accumulated by the capitalist, is not in everyone's interest. A liberal government securing stability sides with the interests of capitalists. The neutral negotiation of conflicting interests which is supposed to take place actually operates operates only at the level of appearance. "Interests" are considered in abstraction from the social relations which produce them and so the fact that conflicts of interests primarily arise not between individuals but between classes is hidden.

## Civil Society and the State

The edifice of liberalism is upheld by an historical demarcation of economic activity from state government. Economic activity is a private contractual matter between individuals. The principal political relation is between individual members of civil society and the state. The system of government mapped by this vertical political relation (individual-representative government) excludes the economy from the political relation except in the form of taxation. The right to property is usually presented in liberal democratic theory as a natural right, discovered by reason in accordance with natural law. This right embodies in law the outcome of various historical struggles between social groups over access to material resources. Obviously the bourgeoisie did not create the concept of property, but with technological innovations access to the means of production became a critical issue. With capitalism, the right to property came to mean the right to own surplus value. Thus, according to Marxism, the description of the right to property as natural is false. The description of the economy as a private matter between individuals is false. The idea of a free contract at the origins of human society is a fiction. However these ideas continue to legitimise the merely formal democratic structures of representative government.

The rights to liberty and equality are similarly illusory. The concept of civil liberty, integral to any liberal contract theory, draws on a hidden and contestable ontological assumption. Likewise, in liberal theory, equality means equality under the eyes of the law, to which has been added one person one vote, and equal opportunity. In effect, the numerical equality of the vote means little given the merely structural function of the liberal

capitalist state. How the right to this kind of equality can effect the distri-
bution of goods is not at all clear. According to Marx in liberalism the
right to equality is the subjection of the majority of people to a single
standard of measurement, it is the 'right to be the same' in the exchange
of labour at value:

> [i]t is a right of inequality, in its content, like every other right. Right by its
> nature can consist only in application of an equal standard; but unequal indi-
> viduals (and they would not be different individuals if they were not unequal)
> are measurable only be an equal standard in so far as they are brought under an
> equal point of view, are considered in one particular aspect only, for instance,
> as in the present case, are regarded only as workers and nothing more is seen
> in them, everything else being ignored. (Marx, *Critique of the Gotha
> Programme*)

These abstract rights constitute the ideology of civil society. They
establish as legitimate certain social and economic relations; this ideology, however, is false. Even when the state, by upholding these rights,
appears to be pursuing a policy of non-intervention in civil society, it
secures the basic exploitation inherent in the capitalist process itself. This
is not to claim an easy relationship between the state and the "private"
economy of civil society; there state may indeed have a certain relative
autonomy vis-a-vis the operation of capital. However, liberal civil society
and the state basically constitute each other, and this combination of relative autonomy and fundamental interdependence leads to a succession of
crises, including crises of "legitimate" state activity.

# The Legitimation Crisis Reconsidered.

Capitalism is structurally riddled with contradiction. Crises inevitably
occur due to the relation between concrete useful value of labour and the
socially abstract aspect of labour, between the use value of a commodity
and its exchange-value. Capitalism is defined by its manner of extracting
and accumulating surplus. The production is social but the accumulation
is private. This tension is expressed as a conflict between wage labour and
capital. In addition, unless there is a market for the goods produced by the
worker, who is only paid subsistence, then there will be a gap between
production and consumption. Although capital has various ways of
accommodating this, crises in production are likely.

In searching for profit capitalists introduce innovative technology in
the production process. This has the effect of reducing the value of the
commodity. For Marx this is entirely consistent with the increase in sur-

plus-value generated by mechanisation. As outlined above, the reduction in value is not immediately apparent because the value of a commodity is an average for that industry. Competition for the profit encourages other capitalists to introduce similar technology. The overriding tendency is for the value of the commodity to fall across the industry. As what is called the organic composition of capital increases – that is, as the amount of mechanisation increases – the amount of dead labour to be transferred in the cost of production likewise increases. Given the fall in the amount of socially necessary labour time taken to produce the commodity, the capitalist has restricted options. S/he might extract greater labour from the worker. By increasing the rate of exploitation, increasing the working day, increasing the intensity of work or decreasing the value of labour power, the capitalist might maintain her or his level of profit. However, as Marx points out, there is a natural limit to the working day and to the value of labour power. There are countervailing tendencies, too. The value of labour power might fall because the cost of subsistence falls, but this is relevant only if wages decrease to reflect the real value. The value of a given amount of capital might fall in a similar fashion. The capitalist might continue to over-produce and find markets to consume this surplus, for example through wars. It is also possible that the machines may embody less dead labour and therefore have a lower value.

There are thus economic realities which have corresponding social effects, and these social effects may include problems over the legitimation of state activity, because state activity is defined in terms of the provision of benefits, of a stable culture for affluent production, and in terms of consent. During a recession, it becomes more difficult for the state to provide benefits or a stable culture, and consent is likely to be withdrawn. In such a situation, the activity of the state can well become more overtly repressive, although this can usually be disguised with language like "the enemy within".

# Epilogue: Marx in the Twentieth Century

There have been significant challenges to Marxism on three counts. One is the idea that Marxism cannot account for the power bases of international capitalism; multinational corporations can thus exercise a monopolistic control over the market, and therefore increase profit by controlling prices. Another is the so-called "post-Fordist" challenge, namely that the nature of industrial production has changed so much that Marx's theories are no longer applicable. The third and related type of challenge comes from such diverse sources as cultural studies, feminist theory, literary theory, continental philosophy and psychoanalysis. In effect Marxism is rejected for trying to explain all phenomena and events as products of a class struggle.

## International Monopoly Capital

The first challenge based on the phenomenon of international monopoly capital, ignores several phenomena. The first is that capitalism is growth-oriented. Globally competitive industries, driven by the logic of accumulation, plunder and appropriate natural resources, and environmental crisis is not far away. Because the post-colonial age is an age of industrial and cultural imperialism crises can be envisaged between nation-states and within "underdeveloped" countries. Without an economic theory of combined and uneven development it is difficult to see how multi-national interventions in "underdeveloped" economies can be analysed or politically instabilities accounted for.

The second feature is that, if the labour theory of value holds, then the global market still functions by the extraction of surplus value. Full automation would not produce any value, partial automation reduces the value of goods. Profit is made by the capitalist because the value is set by less machine intensive industries and cheap international labour raises the average rate of surplus value. This results in the concentration of capital in other counties effecting crises in European domestic markets. Domestic crises precipitate a high borrowing requirement. A higher borrowing requirement affects not only the internal operation of the market but also places the nation-state in a precarious position of dependency. Because capitalism has a tendency towards globalisation, the structural booms and slumps of capitalism provoke crises in national economies irresolvable at national level. This explains the emergence of supra-national structures. The third feature to be highlighted is that capitalism is necessarily and organisationally dynamic. Forms of social intercourse will adjust to variations in the relations of capitalism. Technological innovations transform our relation to the cultural environment, to knowledge and to our work practices. But this is not a transformation in the relations of production when defined in terms of ownership and control. In fact shifting technological relations (the internet, the hyperreal, cyberspace) aggravate the atomism characteristic of alienated civil society. Combined with an emergence of a drug culture this is likely to entrap further working people and the unemployed in relations of exploitation and alienation. The concept of the nomadic worker promoted by certain postmodernists is the ideal theoretical expression of these changing technological relations. Their arguments tend to mystify the reasons why the increasingly global workforce, and the unemployed pool of labour, is subjected to greater regulative surveillance. It could be argued that the radical pluralism and cultural heterogeneity endorsed by some postmodernists is consistent with a stage in communism removing the final fetters of production.

## Post-Fordism and Nietzscheanism

The second challenge is the post-Fordist description of economic relations of production; there are three main claims here. Firstly, that there is a move to smaller firm sizes with less bureaucratic structures, and a greater degree of interaction between firms. Secondly, capital can now be much more fluid due to strategies of manufacturing production where supplies are kept low and are acquired exactly when needed, which is now possible because of better inventory control as a result of computerization (this is the so-called Just In Time strategy). The previous relations of production, understood by means of a binary worker/capitalist model, have definitely shifted and a new nomadic workforce appeared virtually ready to work for virtual companies. These three points can be summed up in the belief that there is no obvious concentration of power: power is dispersed. Given this, then the Marxist theory of crisis and contradiction is outdated; there is, however, still a legitimation crisis, since the nation state cannot cope with these virtual relations of production.

The third challenge develops and departs from the above. Marxism is rejected for being a story which attempts to be the one story, for being a Grand Narrative. If God has died, then there can be no one story, no one truth and certainly no scientific Marxism. If there is no objective or absolute truth then no theory, state or government can appeal to objective principles, or to appropriate states of affairs, or to consent, in order to legitimise itself; it is all a question of epistemology, and it is for this epistemological reason that there is a legitimation crisis.

And this, say the Nietzscheans, is not capitalism's only flaw. Because it reduces social relations to those between worker and capitalist, it simplifies power relations and forms of social interaction: all differences – those of gender, culture, sex, and colour – are considered to be irrelevant. This neglect of difference is taken to be thoroughly modernist; and the Nietzscheans attempt to move beyond this modernism by asking "how is identity constructed?" They hope thereby to able show up techniques of organisation, surveillance and regulation, and thus to demonstrate mechanisms of power operating "behind the scenes". This critique relies on a

Nietzchean perspectivism, which gained favour in France during the debates of the 1960's about structure and agency. However, there is a hidden ontology behind this perspectivism; an ontology of physical flux, which leads to a scepticism about the stability of knowledge.

Marxism can meet these challenges in two ways. One is through the notion of praxis; this is a term used by Marx to suggest a philosophy of action that neither relegates nor reduces the import of sensuous, conscious and social experience to action. Because the human being is a natural being and a species being s/he has dispositions, needs, desires, passions, beliefs and an ability to reason. The second way is by using the resources of Marx's materialism, which identifies factors of the world which can be known, even though such knowledge is historical. And against the Nietzscheans, one must stress that – even though These theorists do illuminate complicated phenomena on the boundaries between sociology, psychology and history, but one must stress that it is capitalism, and not epistemology, which is the totalising system. The legitimation crisis, if indeed there is one, is not an epistemic one; cultures and differences vanish because everyone is subjected to the global ratio of measurement, in relations of production that appropriates exploited labour. If we were to accept Nietzschean perspectivism, then we would lose any critical distance between essence and appearance, and thus we would mistake social conflicts as conflicts between stories – stories which would then be resolved ideologically in some overarching story about competing drives, preferences and desires.

To sum up: governments face legitimation problems because the criteria of legitimacy are not fully compatible with the social relations of capitalism. This point is made apparent during inevitable economic crises. Nation-state governments intervene during economic crises by shouldering a portion of production costs, by protectionist policies, by direct legislation (trade union laws) and by redistributing collective goods (welfare provision, housing). This intervention transgresses the original liberal definition of legitimate state activity, which presupposed both the provision of benefits and also that economic activity is a private concern of individuals. A rising gap in income differentials, high unemployment, the concentration of capital in other countries are consequences of partial automation, cheap labour and the irrationality inherent in the search for profit. Specific to this trade cycle are at least three interrelated, factors. The first is that the consequences of shifting technological relations are increased wage differentials and high domestic unemployment. The second is the redundancy of the nation-state. With technological innovation the nation-state is unable to perform its function of surveillance and regulation in relation to capital and aspects of domestic policing. In addition, the global market places an impossible strain on the state. It is at once expected to control the devastating effects of the flight of capital and due to the flight unable to pay for the welfare provisions necessary to ease crises. With de-industrialisation combined with a greater proportion of the work force heading for retirement, states are forced to cut back pension provision. Because state employee pensions count for a large section of pension output states must "roll back their frontiers". This is, of course, an unpopular move. The final factor is the role of highly technical and rapid international exchange markets in equalising values across national boundaries. The exchange market sets the ratios against which currencies will be exchanged. A series of judgments concerning what constitutes a healthy economy forces currencies to exchange above, on or below their value. The money form as a commodity intersects with the money form as universal equivalent of exchange. Nation-state economies are constrained by this speculation and nation-state governments become further redundant.

Whether this crisis of legitimacy becomes a crisis over legitimacy is a different matter. It is true that logically the first indicates the second. With domestic employment in Metropolitan countries restructured towards luxury and leisure goods the effects of de-industrialisation are omnipresent. One question, a question only answerable empirically, is whether governments can contain the impact of real and relative poverty. A crisis over legitimation implies a subjective aspect previously unconsidered and would require a recognition and rejection of liberalism as liberal capitalism by those whose surplus labour is appropriated by the capitalist. Only then would the liberal right to liberty be properly realised as emancipation from wage slavery and the formal structures of representative democracy given substance.

# Further Reading

A familiar and comparatively easy work by Marx and Engels is *The Communist Manifesto*. Their major work is clearly *Capital*, which is long and full of economic detail. However, there are many shorter and more ostensibly philosophical works by Marx, particularly among the early writings; the collection edited by McLellan has many of these.

The debate over international monopoly capital can be found in the works by Sweezy and Cataphores; more on the debate between Nietzscheans and Marxists can be found in Harvey's book. MacKinnon's article is a good introduction to the extensive and rich Marxist feminist literature. Bhaskar's work represents a fundamental contribution to the elucidation of Marx's concept of dialectical materialism; Collier's recent book is a good introduction to Bhaskar's philosophy.

# Bibliography

R. Bhaskar, *Scientific Realism and Human Emancipation*, London: Verso 1986.

T. Bottomore (ed.), *A Dictionary of Marxist Thought*, Oxford: Blackwell 1983.

G. Cataphores, *An Introduction to Marxist Economics*, London: Macmillan 1989.

A. Collier, *Critical Realism: An Introduction to Roy Bhaskar's Philosophy*, London: Verso 1994.

G. Cohen, *Karl Marx's Theory of History: A Defence*, Oxford: Clarendon 1979.

W. Connolly (ed.), *Legitimacy and the State*, Oxford: Blackwell 1984.

D. Harvey, *The Condition of Post-Modernity*, Oxford: Blackwell 1989.

N. Keohane et al. (eds.), *Feminist Theory: A Critique of Ideology*, Sussex: Harvester 1982.

E. Mandel, *Late Capitalism*, London: New Left Books 1975.

C.A. MacKinnon, "Feminism, Marxism, Method, and the State: An Agenda for Theory", in Keohane et al., *Feminist Theory*.

K. Marx, *Selected Writings*, ed. D. McLellan, Oxford: Oxford University Press 1990.

K. Marx and F. Engels, *The Communist Manifesto*, tr. S. Moore, ed. D. McLellan, Oxford: Oxford University Press 1992.

——*Capital*, tr. B. Fowles and D. Fernbach, Harmondsworth: Penguin 1978–1992.

C. Offe, *Disorganised Capital*, ed. J. Keane, Cambridge: Polity 1985.

J. Plamenatz, *Ideology*, London: Macmillan 1970.

P. Sweezy, *Modern Capitalism*, New York: Modern Reader Paperbacks 1972.

# 7    Friedrich Nietzsche
## Jenny Teichman

Friedrich Nietzsche was born in 1844 and died in 1900. He was a brilliant scholar who became Professor of Classical Philology in the University of Basel at the age of 25. He volunteered for army service during the Franco-Prussian war and served in the medical corps before being invalided out.

Nietzsche's first book, *The Birth of Tragedy* (1872), was written under the influence of Wagner, who he had met in 1868. Nietzsche thought Wagner was about to create a new culture for Germany, a culture akin to, but different from, that of ancient Greece. His feelings about Wagner changed dramatically after the first Bayreuth Festival, held in 1876. In 1878 he resigned from his professorship with a sickness pension, and from then on he lived a somewhat nomadic life, moving about between Italy and Switzerland. In 1888 Nietzsche went mad, and many believe that his insanity was the result of syphilis. At first, the illness manifested itself in bouts of terrifying euphoria, and on January 3 1889 he collapsed in the street in Turin. His sister Elisabeth took charge of him, dressing him up in a white robe and inviting visitors to meet "the Sage".

Nietzsche's writings are often very destructive; at the same time, there is a feeling of disappointed nostalgia for the things being destroyed, and a longing to find something to put in their place. He was fond of making prophecies, and two of these are of special interest since they turned out to be true. He predicted that the twentieth century would be a time of terrible wars, and he predicted that his own name would come to be associated with evil and catastrophe. Since his sister Elisabeth became a supporter of Nazism and insisted that Nietzsche would have been a Nazi too, had he lived, his name is indeed associated with evil and catastrophe.

The American scholar Walter Kaufman, in *Philosopher, Psychologist, and Anti-Christ*, tries to defend Nietzsche against the charge of proto-Nazism. Kaufman is an example of what some call "the gentle Nietzscheans". The latter say (for example) that Nietzsche's attacks on Judaism don't prove that he was anti-Semitic. As we will see in a later section, Nietzsche saw Christianity and Judaism as religions of the mob, suitable only for the slavish herd; thus he attacks both Christians and Jews, and is anti-Christian and anti-Semitic at the same time. His well-known anti-anti-Semitic remark, which occurs in one of his letters ("anti-

Semitism is vulgar") probably means that *Christian* anti-Semitism (like everything else about Christianity according to him) is vulgar.

An astonishing megalomania appears in his later works, yet at the same time it is possible to read even the most megalomaniacal passages as a kind of black joke against pomposity and academic seriousness. It is hard to decide whether these passages should be seen as signs of his oncoming madness, or, alternatively, as nothing more than extreme examples of an inveterate tendency to irony.

# Culture Criticism

Nietzsche is a *culture critic*. Note that not all such criticism is philosophical; Utopian novels are a form of culture criticism, and so are novels of pessimism such as Orwell's *1984* and Huxley's *Ape and Essence*. Culture criticism as philosophy attacks (or, less commonly, defends) the ideologies of one or more human communities, usually the philosopher's own. It explains or debunks the society's moral teachings, or political structures, or art and aesthetics, or all of these. Nietzsche's own writings are a prime example of culture criticism as philosophy; so too are Marx's attacks on capitalism and the bourgeoisie, and Foucault's accounts of the history and significance of social customs such as gaoling people, placing people in asylums for the insane, admiring and respecting professors, and forbidding homosexual acts. Academic feminism quite naturally takes the form of culture criticism, a good example being Simone de Beauvoir's book *The Second Sex*, and further instances can be found in the works of those contemporary French philosophical feminists who argue that language itself is infected by a false ideology of male supremacy.

Nietzsche's critique is carried out from a number of different angles. He considers the mores of 19th century European societies, culture as a historical phenomenon, and culture in general. His investigation relies heavily on what he calls *genealogy*. Now genealogy in the ordinary sense of the word means the study of the ancestry of particular families, but in the Nietzschean sense it refers to an enquiry into the historical, etymological and psychological "ancestors" of ideology, that is to say, into the ancestors or origins of morals, religion, political theory, aesthetic theory. It is obvious from his writings that he found the culture of his own time and country completely suffocating.

Nietzsche's first interest lay in the field of aesthetics. A little later he turned to ethics and to general questions about value, questions, for example, about mediocrity and its opposite, about what is necessary for human society, and about what threatens human survival. He also wrote about the place of science in nineteenth century life, and about war, and race, and evolution, and (briefly) about the relations between the sexes.

Perhaps Nietzsche's most significant contributions to philosophy are, first, the twin theses comprising the idea that all our most central conceptions are errors, and the idea that these errors are necessary for life; second, his speculations about the will to power and the coming of a new kind of being, the Superman; and third, the metaphysical supposition that everything that happens occurs over and over again – the idea of eternal recurrence. Another notable feature is his great dislike of the philosophy and personality of Socrates.

# Necessary Fictions: The Fiction of Absolute Truth

Nietzsche claims that our most fundamental ideas are fictions. Such fictions, however, are necessary for human life, hence they are to be found in every age and every nation. Absolute truth is itself a fiction, an ultimate illusion which underlies all the others: these include religion, morality, and the fictions of logic and epistemology. Associated with the attack on the concept of truth is the thought that the search for truth needs a critique. Man must take responsibility for his science, for the knowledge he seeks, for the questions he asks, and for the consequences of the answers he discovers: otherwise science and knowledge and love of truth will turn out to be terribly dangerous.

Before considering this it will be useful to look briefly at what Nietzsche says about untruth. He discusses many types of untruth, or falsehood, but does not distinguish between them. For him all untruths are *lies*. Lies include fiction in general (i.e. the genre), self-deception, errors in philosophy and religion (theoretical untruths), ordinary lies, ordinary mistakes, the falsification of what is natural, and false gods.

Behind knowledge is the will to know, which is part of the will to power. Nietzsche argues that the search for truth must be seen as an exercise of power, not as something holy, an idea taken up by Foucault, as we will see in a later chapter. Scientists are proud to "seek the truth whatever the consequences", hence it is not surprising that their discoveries are so often used for destructive purposes. The assumption that the search for truth is a good thing in itself leads to perdition. The search is rendered even more suspect by the fact that secular crusaders for truth and justice fight for world domination, seeking a substitute for the non-existent heavens of religion. In his notebook for 1878, Nietzsche wrote

The unselective drive to knowledge resembles the indiscriminate sex drive – they are both signs of vulgarity.

He also wrote

Science depends on philosophical opinions for all its goals and methods. Philosophy, not science itself, has to consider the level to which science should be permitted to develop – philosophy has to determine the value of science.

And

Science barbarises, it serves only practical interests. Artistic powers are needed to break the unlimited drive to knowledge.

And

Science is like laissez-faire economics, it has faith in absolutely beneficial results [i.e. of its own activities].

# Necessary Fictions: Religion

## *Religion and the Greeks*

Nietzsche was perhaps an artist *manqué*, but he certainly does not think that culture is the same thing as art (still less does he regard it as entertainment). The culture of an age is its whole way of thinking: its morality, its religion, its science, its aesthetics. It can be argued, however, that Nietzsche saw art as the most important ingredient in this amalgam.

The main source for Nietzsche's philosophy of art is his first book *The Birth of Tragedy from the Spirit of Music;* in this book we find, too, some of his most important ideas about religion – albeit in a somewhat undeveloped form.

Nietzsche had no training in logic, nor indeed in philosophy, and *The Birth of Tragedy* contains a lot of slapdash argumentation. There are two large flaws which are specially likely to confuse a reader. The first is a failure to distinguish between tragedy as an aspect of reality and tragedy as a literary genre. This creates a fundamental muddle at the heart of the book. It is indeed true that, in later works, Nietzsche was inclined to proclaim that one must live life as if it were a work of art, a recommendation which assumes that there is in fact a difference between life and art; nevertheless, the difference is not made at all clear in *The Birth of Tragedy*. The second flaw consists in a confusing oscillation among three kinds of viewpoint: Nietzsche sometimes writes from a universal point of view, sometimes from a genuinely historical point of view, and sometimes from the point of view of pseudo-history, the 'history' of myths or his own imagination.

Like much of his other work *The Birth of Tragedy* is melodramatic in tone and somewhat self-glorifying. Nietzsche can be a wonderful stylist, but this, his first philosophical publication, is the least well written of all his books.

He asks three "genealogical" questions. The first is: What were the origins of tragedy, and what made it possible? The second question is: How did tragedy come to die? The third is: Can tragedy be reborn?

The origins of the genre of Greek tragedy, that is to say, the cultural phenomena which made it possible, are explained in terms of an opposition or duality linking Apollo, the sun god, and Dionysos. Apollo represents light, reason and order; he is also the god of possibilities, the things we create or control. Dionysos is the god of wine and frenzy; he is the god of necessities, the things we cannot control. Tragedy, the genre, is a type of art in which something essentially terrifying, namely the Dionysian aspect of the world, is controlled and made bearable by the addition of Apollonian reason, light and order.

Tragedy – and here Nietzsche means both the genre and also a certain way of looking at the world – is necessary because human life itself is terrible, awful, appaling. The idea that human life is awful came to Nietzsche from Schopenhauer, whose works he greatly admired, at least for a time. Although he eventually came to develop Schopenhauer's ideas in new ways, he never abandoned the vision of life as tragic.

Those who refuse to face the fact that human life is awful cannot produce tragic works of art, nor can they have anything but a shallow culture. The Greeks were able to "look into the abyss", and hence able to create great art and a truly significant culture. On the other hand, the culture of nineteenth century Germany was, according to Nietzsche, shallow, boring, middlebrow and trivial.

Can tragedy be reborn? Nietzsche seem to have seriously believed that Richard Wagner's new artistic genre, the music drama, was destined to be the foundation of a new tragic outlook. He saw Wagner's role in modern Europe as akin to the role of Aeschylus or Sophocles in ancient Greece, failing to notice some very obvious differences between the Greeks and Wagner. For instance, Aeschylus and Sophocles use real myths but Wagner invents bogus ones (rather like Tolkien). Nietzsche was later to pour scorn on Wagner's "kitchen" Valhalla.

Here perhaps is the place to mention the case of Socrates. Nietzsche argues that, when Socrates arrived on the scene, tragedy, and the tragic outlook, were both doomed. Socrates, he says brought triviality to the culture of the Greeks. It is perhaps not too difficult to see why Nietzsche loathes Socrates. First, Socrates, in spite of his apparent personal modesty, clearly hoped that human reason, and his own reasonings, are in principle capable of answering ultimate questions about virtue, about God, and about the soul and the afterlife. Although he sometimes displayed doubts about human wisdom, these doubts always occurred in the context of an unquestioning faith in the existence of ultimate truth. Socrates was deeply interested in questions about virtue and justice, abstract entities which he took to be true realities. Plato himself extended the original Socratic range of philosophical questioning to logic, politics, the theory of knowledge, and the nature of the universe, showing that he too had the same confidence in human reason as his master. Secondly, in Plato's *Republic* Socrates is represented as recommending that poetry, drama, and art in general should form no part of education. According to this Platonic Socrates, the arts are dangerous guides for the young, who should be kept away from literature and music and taught mathematics and philosophy and military skills instead. This wholesale rejection of art and the aesthetic must have been anathema to Nietzsche. Thirdly, Socrates, as depicted by Plato, was a great optimist. He was optimistic about the possibility of acquiring wisdom and knowledge, and about the possibility that the soul is immortal: in short, he did not have a tragic outlook. Finally, Socrates, though brave in battle, was no Superman. If the descriptions of him by Plato and Xenophon are any guide, he was squat and ugly and entirely unaristocratic in appearance.

The overall message of *The Birth of Tragedy* is this. In Greece, religion and art between them created a system of value. But religion now is dying and tragedy is dead; as a result, the modern age has no deeply rooted understanding of life. Art must take on a new and double role, a role in part akin to that manifested in Athenian tragedy, and in part a sort of replacement for religion. It is up to the artists, the poets, painters, and musicians, to create a new system of values, a new unity, a new culture.

## Religion and Metaphysics

In *The Gay Science* (1882) there is a section called "The Story of a Madman" in which a tale is told about the death of God. The people have killed God, but do not realise that he is dead. Only the madman understands, and only he can see that there is a catastrophe ahead: "there will be wars such as have never been before."

Two of the main fictions of metaphysics are the belief in God and the belief in an immortal soul. In "The Story of a Madman", loss of belief in these necessary fictions is described as a cultural event, that is to say, an event which has a profound importance for human culture and for humanity itself.

Marx argued that capitalism contained the seeds of its own destruction. Nietzsche claims, in a somewhat similar way, that Christianity cannot help destroying itself. Both these ideas doubtless owe something to Hegel.

Christianity encourages a desire for truth and spiritual certainty, and also a hatred of earthly things. This combination leads inexorably to loss of faith in God. Science then takes over, teaching or preaching the dogmas of materialism and determinism. These dogmas lead in turn to a denial of mind, and then to a denial of responsibility. The Christian search for the truth causes, first, death of belief in God, then death of belief in mind, and finally death of belief in responsibility. Nietzsche regarded this as a situation fraught with danger for the whole human race. Various solutions, possible ways of overcoming the danger, suggested themselves to him at different times. The first of these, as we have seen, was the notion that art has the power to create new myths and a deeper culture. Later solutions can be found in the concept of the superman and the idea that values must be "transvalued".

In ancient Greece, religion and tragedy were vital expressions of a deep understanding of the nature of life. The fiction of the gods was necessary for the Greeks and is, or was, just as necessary for us, since religion has, or had, a profoundly important function: without religion, or something similar, man is nothing but a mischievous animal whose survival cannot be guaranteed. Unfortunately a lost fiction cannot be artificially reinstated; a new culture, a new cultural bedrock, is needed to take its place.

## Judaism and Christianity

When Nietzsche discusses non-Greek religions, that is, Judaism and Christianity, he gives a different and more cynical account of necessity. He interprets the necessity of Judaism and Christianity as nothing more than a love of power, the will to power of weak people.

Now according to his overall account, necessity is always relative. Every community has its own fictions, and the stability of each society depends on its own particular ideology. Yet Nietzsche also seems to say that fictions which are associated with weak human types are less deeply necessary than those discovered in, say, Greek religion, or in metaphysics. The clash between these two opinions about necessity is never made explicit, but it shows itself in the different ways in which Nietzsche treats different religions. Greek religion is regarded favourably, as a fount of art and of understanding, but Judaism and Christianity are always castigated, as if they are in some sense fraudulent. It is very significant that Nietzsche shows little interest in the aesthetic productions of Christian culture, and none at all in those of Judaism. He attributes the success of these religions not to cultural factors, not to Jewish or Christian music, drama, painting, poetry or philosophy, but rather to the will to power of human types whom he despises and dislikes. He speaks of Christians and Jews as obedient, ant-like, slavish masses, governed by a slightly stronger type: the priests.

## Religion and the Soul

In *The Genealogy of Morals* (1887) it is argued that belief in the existence of the soul was a necessary stage in the development of the human race. arising originally out of unscientific reflections on the nature of the living body. At the same time belief in the soul was a social necessity; it made men reliable and calculable. It was part of the institution of punishment, in that the soul was supposed to be an eternal immaterial entity destined eventually for Hell or Heaven. The utility of a common belief in the soul's immortality is not permanent, and to cling to it after it becomes redundant is dangerous; yet its loss too is dangerous.

# Necessary Fictions: Morality

## Morality as Created

Schopenhauer claims that morality is not discovered but created, and Nietzsche follows him in this; yet, as we have already seen, he also insists that ethical concepts are absolutely necessary for human life.

The philosopher has to recognise that the necessity of morality masks two fictions. One fiction consists in the assumption that any one system of morality is permanent, the other in the belief that all members of a community are bound by the same moral code. There are different kinds of society and so there will always be a diversity of codes; more importantly, there are different kinds of human beings – masters and slaves. and as a result there must be two codes. Codes which are suitable for slaves are by no means suitable for masters.

Now, in drawing this distinction between human types, Nietzsche implies that there are *real truths* about human beings; an implication which is inconsistent, of course, with his thesis that knowledge and truth are mere fictions. It seems he is less critical of Darwinism than he is of other kinds of science. He classifies human races and human types into the superior and the inferior, along lines later adopted by eugenicists and so-called social Darwinists. Nietzschean and "Darwinian" theories about race were not uncommon in Western Europe and the United States of America up until around 1945.

A somewhat similar quasi-scientific theory appears in *Human, All too Human* (1878-9), a work which explains the origins of human codes and customs along the following lines: when animals evolve into men, they cease to live for the moment and become capable of looking to the future, they stop being motivated by short term satisfactions and come to adopt usefulness as a standard of behaviour. The community itself then begins to compel conformity to standards of behaviour which tend to promote its survival. Eventually this compulsion by and on behalf of the community undergoes a transformation, and becomes the conscience of the individual – a notion soon to be taken up by Freud. Nietzsche concludes that morality is nothing but usefulness..

## Morality and the Superman

Behind Nietzsche's account of ordinary ethics we catch a glimpse of something different, a morality which is not merely useful but also more objective, more real, than any other. This is the code of the strong, of masters, of ruthless men. The matter is discussed at some length in *Beyond Good and Evil* (1886). The title of this work, incidentally, is a typically Nietzschean melodramatic misnomer – it would be better titled *Beyond Conventional Good and Evil*, or *Beyond the Good and Evil of the Nineteenth Century German Herd*.

The new morality turns out to be a code whose utility lies in the fact that it promotes the evolution of the Superman, he who has not yet been born but who will evolve from man as man has evolved from the ape. Ordinary nineteenth century morality is, or was, utility for the herd, and it goes into abeyance when the welfare of the herd is no longer a prime consideration. Nietzsche believed that this point had actually been reached in his own time. The stifling quality of middle class German culture was partly due, he thought, to the fact that it had outlived its usefulness, it had become redundant. The herd had wrongly assumed that its own rules apply to everyone everywhere for all time. But the mores of the herd, and the herd's devotion to equality, hamper the possibility of evolution, and retard the coming of the Superman.

# Necessary Fictions: Epistemology

In his overall approach to epistemology, the theory of knowledge, Nietzsche adapted the philosophy of Kant. As we saw in the chapter on Schopenhauer, Kant argued that human beings are not in a position to understand the world as it really is (that is, the world of things in themselves). Everything we think we know is the result of interpretation; everything we think we know is mediated by our own perspectives. But Kant at least believed that there is only one possible perspective for human beings, a perspective which does indeed cut us off from reality, but which is nevertheless universal as far as the human species is concerned. Nietzsche is a relativist. He holds that our current perspective is only one of an indefinitely large number of historically and biologically permissible perspectives, none of which, therefore, can be regarded as constituting genuine knowledge.

This idea has been enormously influential in twentieth century French and German philosophy, yet it is possible to argue against it. We might, for example, argue that truth is the sum of all possible perspectives, or, alternatively, that there are as many truths as there are perspectives.

# The Fictions of Logic and the "Truth" of Perspectivism

By logic Nietzsche does not mean the domain of formal systems such as the syllogism, predicate calculus, modal logic, and so on. Rather he means certain basic principles, for instance, the principle of non-contradiction (*a proposition cannot be both true and not true*) and the principle of identity (*a thing is itself and not another thing*). These principles permeate all rational and analytic thinking, yet Nietzsche rejects them as fiction. Why? Let us consider the principle of identity. It seems to be necessarily universally true and so we apply it to the shifting world of empirical reality. According to Nietzsche this is a mistake because (like Schopenhauer) he believes that empirical reality is a ceaseless flux; and the principle of identity cannot be applied to a flux. We do indeed speak of "the same river", we do indeed appeal to the idea of sameness, yet in fact the water of the river is never the same. Or consider generalisation. Generalisation about empirical matters cannot be completely exact, but we happily begin our reasoning with statements like 'all swans are white' and 'all ravens are black'. Otherwise we would hardly be able to reason at all. Moreover generalisation, and the other principles and practices of reasoning, must at one time have helped us along the evolutionary road.

Generalisation may be inexact, but at certain times an inexact general assumption may be safer than an exact particular one. If someone is all alone in a forest, the proposition that large animals are without exception always dangerous will be more useful to him or her than precise lists of mild and savage animals. Nietzsche concludes that the human tendency to behave as if the principles of logic are true is, or has been, a competitive advantage in the struggle for existence, but might not always be so useful in the future.

Nietzche's perspectivism is simultaneously a theory of knowledge and a theory of truth. We have seen how he proclaims that there are a number of essential illusions which vary according to the needs, and the points of view, both of individuals and of societies. We may call these illusions 'perspectival falsifications'. For Nietzche the idea of truth itself is just such a falsification. Truth is not absolute, it is not ultimate.

Now it would appear that those who say that truth is an illusion, that there is really no such thing as truth, can easily be hoist with their own petards. For we need only ask them: Is your view, the view that there is no such thing as truth, itself true? Or is it false? If it is true, then there is such a thing as truth after all; if it is false, then once more it follows there is such a thing as truth after all. Again, if there is no truth, how can there be fictions and illusions? Are not fictions and illusions simply negations of truth? And how can one negate the non-existent?

It looks as if Nietzsche cannot, without contradiction, say that his perspectivist theory of truth is *true* – but would he want to say that in the first place?

We cannot know how Nietzsche might have answered this objection, but possibly he would have done so by referring to "the necessary fictions of logic". In this way, perhaps, he could attempt to evade the charge of self-contradiction and paradox. For if logic itself is a fiction, then contradiction and paradox are fictions also; and if there is *no such thing* as a contradiction, *no such thing* as a paradox, then neither Nietzsche nor anyone else can generate a contradiction or perpetrate a paradox.

As we have seen, there are several ways of interpreting Nietzsche's perspectivism. This is because Nietzsche himself sometimes says one thing and sometimes says another. He is not a consistent thinker and it is not much use trying to turn him into one.

One way of interpreting perspectivism would involve looking at it from new perspectives. For example, we could decide to ask about the plausibility of different yet similar theories; or about the plausibility of conclusions drawn from the theory itself, either by Nietzsche or by his followers. We could ask, as he does about other matters, whether perspectivism gives us an evolutionary advantage, or whether, on the contrary, it might be "digging the grave of the human race".

## The Superman and the Eternal Return

The idea of the Superman appears first in *Thus Spake Zarathustra*, (1884/5). In this work Nietzsche expresses his thoughts by devising an imaginary history of the Persian sage Zoroaster (Zarathustra).

Who is the Superman? Nietzsche gives some rather startling descriptions of this being and its relationship to mankind. He says that man is a rope stretched between Superman and the animals, "a rope over an abyss"; man is a bridge and not a goal; man is something which must be surpassed. But the Superman "is the meaning of the earth".

Is the Superman human or is he a new kind of being altogether? Does he evolve biologically from humanity, or is he a production of the human mind? Is he supposed to be a future reality or simply an ideal? An individual, or a species? If a reality, is he a new kind of philosopher? Is he a Free Spirit? Or is he a descendent of the pre-Christian Norsemen, the blond beasts of the past, and, like the Norsemen, a strong, fearless "Aryan" killer? This last interpretation is the Nazi version of Nietzsche's idea.

Many, perhaps most, commentators take the superman to be a myth, a spur and a goal for the higher type of man. However, even a mythical creature can be described, and Nietzsche's hinted characterisation is that of a being which greatly excels mankind, both intellectually and physically, and whose excellence lies in a superior will to power and a final rejection of Judaic and Christian values.

The myth is also an expression of Nietzsche's re-interpretation of Schopenhauerian pessimism. Nietzsche sees life as fundamentally tragic, but insists that, in spite of that, we must say Yes to life, in opposition to Schopenhauer, who he describes as a "Nay-sayer".

In pursuing the idea that we must say Yes to life, Nietzsche invents another myth, that of the eternal return. On a naive interpretation, the idea of the eternal return is a metaphysical theory about the nature of time, according to which every event recurs again and again through all eternity. But, for contextual reasons, it seems better to see it as a proposed test of courage. The myth tests us by asking: could you accept life even if your own life, with all its pains and failures, were to recur again and again, forever and forever? Nietzsche obviously thinks that those who answer Yes are better and more courageous than those who answer No.

It is surely right to credit Nietzsche himself with being a Yea-Sayer, to credit him with saying Yes to life in spite of the pains and failures of loneliness, illness, disappointing friendships, and his own misanthropy.

# The Will to Power

Schopenhauer believed that the Will to Live is an overarching explanation of the way the universe works, a force which can be seen even in inorganic matter. Nietzsche wanted to find a similar large scale explanation, and did so by positing a universal Will to Power. His reasonings here, as elsewhere, are suggestive rather than notably coherent. He begins with an assumption which he takes to be almost self-evident, namely that human action is not free. Nothing we do is a result of choice or purpose, for these very concepts are mere myths. Physical causation is also a myth, it is not a genuine force but only an idea which we have invented in order to "explain" the brute fact that empirical events occur in seemingly regular, seemingly non-random sequences.

Human action is not the result of free choice, nor is it governed by mechanical forces, yet it is predictable. How can this be? Nietzsche's answer is that all our actions are determined by the Will to Power. The Will to Power manifests itself in the conscious and unconscious desires of individuals and races to dominate, crush and enslave other individuals and other races. Nietzsche admires the Will to Power when it appears in strong, straightforward men and races, and despises it when it takes devious or unsuccessful forms. Hence his contempt for Christianity, and Judaism, and democracy, all of which he saw as devious and perhaps, too, as likely to be ultimately unsuccessful.

The Will to Power replaces all other explanations of rational and irrational human behaviour. One of Nietzsche's most telling examples has to do with wealthy people. He notes that the world of big business is regularly rocked by scandals, the reason being that rich men, men who already have far more than they need, are unable to resist the temptation to acquire extra wealth by criminal means. This seemingly inexplicable behaviour is caused by a desire to trick other people, to overcome them and destroy them, in short to exercise hostile power *for its own sake*.

Although, according to the theory, the Will to Power has always existed, some of Nietzsche's followers, notably the Nazis, associated it primarily with the "Aryan" race, which in turn they identified with the

Superman. Unfortunately for Nietzsche's posthumous reputation, there is little doubt that his ideas about power did become part of the ideology used to justify the insanities of National Socialism.

Intuitively one feels that, while the Will to Live must be common to all animal species, the Will to Power is found only in some individuals and in some races. It seems unlikely that the Will to Live is culturally determined, but the Will to Power might well be. Men, women and children all want to live: do they all without exception show a desire for power *for its own sake?* Some manifestations of the so-called Will to Power seem to be defensive actions prompted by fear, mere special cases of the Will to Live. Indeed, *all* of its supposed manifestations could be interpreted, without much difficulty, as manifestations of Schopenhauer's Will to Live.

The Will to Power is supposed to explain everything, but in reality it is not so much an explanation as a way of looking at the world. In our century this way of looking at the world led to behaviour of unexampled vileness. Nietzsche's admirers say he would have abhorred the Nazi ethos, but because of his misanthropy their conclusion remains slightly doubtful.

## Further Reading

Almost everything Nietzsche wrote, with the possible exception of *The Birth of Tragedy*, is very easy to read. His writings became more polemical towards the end of his life; characteristic examples are *The Antichrist*, *The Twilight of the Idols*, and *The Case of Wagner*. More serious works are *Untimely Meditations* and *Beyond Good and Evil*. Among the secondary literature, F.A. Lea's *The Tragic Philosopher* and Kaufmann's *Nietzche* can be recommended.

## Bibliography

W.A. Kaufmann, *Nietzche: Philosopher, Psychologist, Antichrist*, Princeton: Princeton University Press 1950.

F.A. Lea, *The Tragic Philosopher: A Study of Friedrich Nietzsche*, New York: The Philosophical Library 1957.

F.W. Nietzsche, *Beyond Good and Evil: Prelude to a Philosophy of the Future*, tr. R.J. Hollingdale, Harmondsworth: Penguin 1982.

——*The Birth of Tragedy from the Spirit of Music* and *The Case of Wagner*, tr. W.A. Kaufmann, New York: Vintage 1967.

F.W. Nietzsche, *Daybreak: Thoughts on the Prejudices of Morality*, tr. R.J. Hollingdale, Cambridge: Cambridge University Press 1982.

—— *The Gay Science: With a Prelude in Rhymes and an Appendix of Songs*, tr. W. Kaufmann, New York: Vintage 1974.

—— *The Genealogy of Morals*, tr. W. Kaufmann and R.J. Hollingdale, New York: Vintage 1969.

—— *Human, All too Human: A Book for Free Spirits*, Cambridge: Cambridge University Press 1986.

—— *Thus Spake Zarathustra: A Book for Everyone and No One*, tr. R.J. Hollingdale, Harmondsworth: Penguin 1961.

—— *The Twilight of the Idols* and *The Antichrist*, tr. R.J. Hollingdale, Harmondsworth: Penguin 1990.

—— *Untimely Meditations*, tr. R.J. Hollingdale, Cambridge: Cambridge University Press 1983.

# 8 Edmund Husserl
## Graham White

Husserl was born in 1859. He was trained as a mathematician, and studied at Leipzig, Berlin, and Vienna; he received his doctorate, at the latter university, in 1882. In 1883 he took up a post in Berlin, but in that year he was, as it were, "converted" to philosophy; he returned to Vienna to study philosophy with Franz Brentano, and stayed there from 1884 to 1886. Although Brentano was then quite junior, he was to become a very significant figure in the philosophy of the late nineteenth century; his influence on Husserl and others was quite decisive. Husserl then embarked on his own career as a philosopher; he had teaching appointments at Halle, from 1887 to 1901, then Göttingen, from 1901 to 1916, and finally at Freiburg from 1916 to 1929. He died in 1938, his final years having been spent in an atmosphere of increasing rancour and difficulty: he was Jewish and the Nazis had come to power.

He wrote ceaselessly (he is said to have written over 45,000 manuscript pages, in shorthand), but published relatively little. Several of his works stand out; they are significant in themselves, and also delineate the periods of his work. His *Habilitationsschrift* (the formal qualification to teach at a German university) was called *Philosophy of Arithmetic,* and published in 1891; it was severely criticised by Frege, and Husserl substantially changed his views thereafter (although independently of Frege's criticism). The first of his mature works, the *Logical Investigations,* was published (in two volumes) in 1900 and 1901; the next major publication – in 1913 – was the first volume of a projected trilogy called *Ideas.* (The two other volumes were never published by Husserl, but have been published posthumously.) He gave lectures on Descartes in 1929, and these lectures were published in 1950, after his death, as *Cartesian Meditations.* A final significant work is *The Crisis of European Sciences and Transcendental Philosophy,* again a posthumous publication. In what follows, I shall be concentrating on the doctrines of Husserl's middle period, that of *Ideas*, since the thought of *this* period is probably the best approach to Husserl's thought as a whole, and it would be impossible to cover all of Husserl's vast output in an introduction like this. However, there are also important things to be found in his earlier and later work, and the later work in particular has strongly influenced philosophers such as Heidegger.

# The Climate of the Late Nineteenth Century.

The late nineteenth century is in many ways an unfamiliar period – we are quite often blind to the special characteristics of periods immediately preceding our own – but some knowledge of its peculiarities is essential for the proper understanding of someone like Husserl.

## *The Question of Science.*

Science was very much a theme in this period: the natural and biological sciences had made great progress, closely followed by the incipient social sciences. But this progress was certainly not unproblematic; there were notable disputes about the foundations of physics (e.g. between Duhem and the English), the foundations of mathematics were under intense scrutiny (figures like Poincaré were very important), and, especially, there was vigorous dispute over the methods and concepts of logic. The period may seem, in retrospect, to be a golden age of critical enquiry – Poincaré, for example, is one of the great philosophers of mathematics – and certainly Heidegger, a generation later, was to claim that only disciplines which have attained a certain maturity could even be *capable* of a foundational crisis. However, it did not seem that way at the time; many people (including Husserl) thought of the situation as a sort of breakdown, which could only be rectified by the production of new foundations, foundations which could, unlike the old ones, better stand up to critical enquiry. Thus, one of Husserl's later works is called *The Crisis of European Sciences and Transcendental Philosophy;* it is utterly characteristic of Husserl that, firstly, he thought that there *was* a crisis, and, secondly, that he thought that philosophy was what was required to solve it.

We should describe this "crisis" a little more exactly. It revolved around two poles; psychology (taken in the broad sense) and logic (again, taken in an extremely broad sense). The unparalleled success of the natural and biological sciences included the foundation, and expansion, of a genuinely empirical psychology; Wundt, and others, obtained quite significant experimental results. This led, of course, to a great optimism about the scope of the discipline: in particular, many psychologists (particularly Sigwart and John Stuart Mill) attempted to apply these psychological methods to the study of logic, which is, after all, an exercise of human mental capacities. This empiricist atmosphere pervades most of the logical writing of the period; even someone like George Boole – whom we remember now for his results in formal, algebraic logic – published his work under the title *Laws of Thought*, with all the ambiguities that implies. But there are, of course, great dangers: a purely "experimental" study of logic runs the risk of turning logical principles into mere empirical generalisations, which are only true for the most part or under certain assumptions, and might thus deprive logic of its certainty or of its *a priori* character. And this has repercussions beyond logic, since what was supposed to be characteristic of the sciences was their logical procedure; indeed, it was this procedure which was thought to give the sciences their unique value.

Thus, the psychological study of logic was very ambivalent. On the one hand, it promises a new freedom, a liberation from a tradition that had become extremely conservative. There is no doubt that many logicians in fact gained from this freedom – for example, Schröder and Boole both did extremely innovative logical research, and even Frege, bitterly opposed to psychologism though he was, probably benefited from the atmosphere of innovation and critical enquiry. However, psychological enquiry also had a dark side; the risk, namely, of undermining the "foundations" of logic, and with them the foundations of science itself. This can be regarded as a dispute over doctrines ("Are the principles of logic universally valid, or not?"), but it could also be regarded as a dispute over demarcation: what rights do logicians have *vis-à-vis* psychologists, and *vice versa*? And, most crucially, which discipline has the right to lay down methods and norms for the other sciences? This boundary dispute was exacerbated by the fact that psychology was still not an institutionally fixed discipline; most of the people whom we now think of as psychologists – people such as Wundt – in fact occupied chairs of philosophy. It is no surprise, then, that problems of demarcation between subjects are very important for Husserl.

## *Aristotle.*

As we have mentioned, Husserl studied with Brentano, and Brentano had an extremely high regard for Aristotle; in fact, he was a student of the philosopher Trendelenburg, who initiated something of an Aristotle revival in the late nineteenth century. This interest is not merely historical, but had a very deep resonance with the problems of Brentano's and Husserl's periods; Aristotle was important both as a logician and as a psychologist, and, furthermore, he had a picture of the relation between psychology and logic which might, perhaps, extract philosophy from its foundational difficulties. Thus, although Aristotle discussed such things as knowledge in terms of his psychology, this did not lead to the tensions of empirical psychologism; the categories of his logic dovetailed harmoniously with his psychology, and his system can thus be seen as a way of giving each subject its due.

So, although neither Brentano nor Husserl are strictly speaking Aristotelians, they are each strikingly influenced by Aristotle. Some of the most significant influences on Husserl are the following. Firstly, there was – as we have mentioned – Aristotle's reconciliation of psychology with logic and metaphysics. Aristotle can accomplish this because his epistemology is one in which the *forms* of things play a decisive role. Thus, if we know an object, what we know of it is its form; in fact, the form of an object plays a decisive role both on the side of the object and in our mind. On the side of the object, it is responsible for its physical behaviour; in our mind, it is what we know about it and what controls our reasoning about it.

Now Husserl did not exactly have an Aristotelian ontology, or physics, of matter and form, but nevertheless his philosophy has certain decisively Aristotelean characteristics. One important characteristic of Aristotle is that the ideas of part and whole are very important for him. Matter and form are two parts of one whole, and he explains change by saying that the matter has lost one form and acquired another one. Related ideas – substance and accident, for example – play a similarly prominent role in Aristotle. Furthermore, questions of part and whole mark out significant ontological divides: the human intellectual soul is indivisible, for example, whereas the sensory soul is spatially extended and thus has parts (indeed, it is only in this way that it can have sensory experiences, which likewise have parts). For Husserl, as we shall see, analysis into part and whole was likewise very important; indeed, it was his main analytical tool.

Another, and extremely significant, characteristic of Aristotle's thought is his view of science. For him, there was a sharp distinction between everyday knowledge (*doxa*) and scientific knowledge (*episteme*). The latter, unlike the former, was certain; and it was certain because it is knowledge of the right sort of objects, knowledge formulated in appropriate terms, and it is knowledge which is solidly based on sure principles. Furthermore, science is divided into an ordered hierarchy of particular sciences, a hierarchy which comes about because each science deals with its own particular sort of object (thus, biology deals with living beings, botany with plants, zoology with animals, and so on). All of these features are also characteristic of Husserl's view of science, all of them quite deeply modified, but still present.

# Phenomenology

However, apart from all this background, Husserl's philosophy had a quite distinctive shape of its own. His most characteristic doctrine is his reliance on what he called phenomenology; neither the word, nor the concept, started with him, but he was the first to make it central in a philosophical programme. Phenomenology means the study of phenomena, the study of what appears to us. There are two components to Husserl's programme: firstly, the study of phenomena, and, consequently, the reliance of philosophy on what he called intuition; secondly, the use of free imaginative variation in connection with intuition. The first means that philosophy should rely constantly on what is immediately given; that is, that it should neither speculate nor should it rely on premises that are merely *assumed* to be true, but it should depend at every stage on direct insight into the things that it is talking about. This is not, of course, a demand that only Husserl makes – many philosophers, from Socrates onwards, have claimed something like this. Similarly, many philosophers have talked about intuition, meaning thereby some facility whereby things, or experiences, were directly given to us. However, these thinkers all meant different things by intuition, depending on precisely what their views on experience were; and so Husserl's demand for direct, intuitive insight remains an empty slogan until we know what he himself meant by words like "intuition" and "immediately given"; it is here (rather than in the mere idea of a phenomenological method) that Husserl's distinctive contributions lie.

## Intuition and Imaginative Variation.

Suppose that we see something – for example, a blue patch. We can imagine it to be different: it could be red, it could be a different shade of blue, it could have a different shape, or a different texture, it could be transparent or opalescent or specular, and so on. We have, then, an ability to imagine how things could be, other than the way that they are. Husserl not only used this imaginative capacity, but he also thought that it was part of the *intuition* that we have of a thing; thus, not only does intuition tell us how a thing is, it also tells us how it might otherwise be. It is this grasp of how a thing might be – a grasp of what Husserl called a thing's essence – on which Husserl bases his phenomenology. It is this, indeed, which makes it a very distinctive philosophical method, because it postulates that things have essences, and, indeed, very rich and complexly structured essences. The phenomenological method is designed to give us direct access to those essences and thereby to open up a new realm for philosophy.

It goes without saying that this doctrine of intuition goes far beyond what most philosophers (especially those in the empiricist tradition) have thought of as intuition; it gives us far more than simply sense data. Thus, the empiricists would hold that experience only gives us a grasp of how things actually are, and that possibilities are things that we construct. Thus it is that, although Husserl's *programme*, of relying purely on intuition, is quite a common philosophical programme, the results that he gets from it are far from ordinary; it is his very unusual doctrine of intuition – and, in particular, the role that he gives to imaginative variation, and the emphasis on possibility, rather than just actuality – that gives his system its distinctive character. So where did he get this group of doctrines from? There are two possible sources: mathematics and Aristotle.

## *Mathematics*.

Let us deal with mathematics first. Husserl's doctoral thesis was in a part of mathematics called the calculus of variations, and the calculus of variations is the following procedure: one studies a situation – the movement of some mechanism, for example – by looking at all of the ways in which it could have been different (each individual piece of the mechanism could have moved faster or slower, they could have had different sizes or shapes, and so on). One thinks, then, of the *actual* behaviour of the mechanism in connection with a collection of imaginative variations of that behaviour; and a proper understanding of these variations will tell you, not just what the motion actually is, but also why it is *that* motion rather than any of the other possible motions that it could have been. The phenomenological procedure, then, can be regarded as a sort of philosophical calculus of variations. The philosophical and mathematical procedures have, to be sure, rather different goals (the philosophical version does not generally show why *this* object is actual, rather than one of its variations), but they have in common the principle that one should consider not only the isolated, actual situation, but the entire system of possible variations of it.

We should also note, in connection with the doctrine of intuition, that the philosophy of mathematics of Husserl's time put a heavy emphasis on that concept. In particular, Poincaré had a Kantian philosophy of mathematics according to which mathematics was distinct from logic; the latter subject was purely formal, and independent of experience, whereas mathematics depended on experience for its basic insights into arithmetic and geometry. This basic insight – mathematical intuition – comes from our experience of everyday objects (and is impossible without it), but is an insight into their *structure*, and is thus more abstract than sensory knowledge. The same sort of things seem to be true of Husserl's concept of intuition: it, too, is impossible without experience of everyday objects, but it, too, yields insights into structure, rather than simple knowledge of what is actually the case.

## Aristotle

Aristotle is another source for this group of doctrines. He has a doctrine of intuition which is quite similar to Husserl's: he claims that we can have direct intellectual intuition of a thing's essence. (Although one should note that free imaginative variation does not play any role in Aristotle's account of science.) Furthermore, the distinction between potentiality and actuality recurs throughout Aristotle's thought, and is his basic way of analysing change. Any change – for example, a physical object becoming hot – is the result of that object becoming actually hot where it was previously potentially hot. Another feature of Aristotle's account is worth noticing: he tends to analyse such changes in terms of the composition of things out of matter and form. Thus, if an object becomes hot, it will have acquired a certain entity (a form of heat) which it did not have previously. And a physical object is supposed to be a complex whole, made up of a series of parts: its matter, the substantial form (which makes it whatever sort of object it is), and various accidental forms which are responsible for various characteristics that it can gain or lose (being hot or cold, being a certain colour, and so on). There is room for a great deal of argument about how literal this language of whole and parts is, because some of these "parts" seem to behave in rather an odd way – for example, matter (although a part of a matter-form composite) cannot exist without any form at all, although a particular piece of matter is not tied to a particular form; this behaviour is rather different from that of the literal parts of a physical whole, which can be separated from it. But the important thing is that Aristotle did use this language of whole and parts as part of his basic analysis of change; it is also part of Husserl's technical vocabulary, and is something that we need to discuss in its own right.

# Mereology

When philosophers discuss technical matters, they generally need some sort of analytical language – a set of technical terms and conceptual distinctions – to do it in. This is a truism. What is perhaps not so obvious is that, historically, these things have varied a good deal: in fact, such variations tend to be part of the large cultural differences which demarcate the major schools of philosophy, differences which tend to make these philosophical schools incomprehensible to each other. Thus, the main analytical language of contemporary Anglo-Saxon philosophy is the language of logic and set theory; by contrast, philosophers in the Kantian tradition will do their analysis by means of some sort of genetic epistemology, analysing and evaluating pieces of knowledge in terms of the processes which gave rise to them (whether these might be actual historical processes, as in Hegel or Marx, or activities of the transcendental ego, as in Kant). Husserl used neither of these; he used the theory of part and whole, a theory which is known as mereology. His interest in this subject dates from his early period – Investigation III of the *Logical Investigations* is to do with the theory of wholes and parts – and he continued to use it throughout his career; most of his results are formulated in mereological terms.

Set theory and mereology are, it is true, both theories of aggregates, but that is about where the resemblance ends. It is important to bear this in mind, since nowadays set theory dominates Anglo-Saxon philosophical discussion, so that discussions of mereology are quite infrequent, and one tends to assume that problems about part and whole can all be stated, and solved, in purely set-theoretic terms. Whether or not this is true, Husserl stated his results directly in terms of wholes and parts, so it is important to bear in mind some of the characteristic formal properties of mereology.

A whole may consist of parts, just as a set (in a sense) consists of members; however, there is a decisive difference. A set has a determinate number of members (this is built in to the definition of set), but a whole has no determinate number of parts, except in rather special cases. A table, for example, can be divided into the top and four legs, or into the right half and the left half, and so on, and all of these are perfectly valid divisions into parts. Furthermore, the whole-part relation is transitive; a part of a part is a part of the original whole – for example, the left half of the top of the table is still part of the table. This is definitely not true of the set-member relation, except in rather special cases.

Husserl's mereology, then, is a distinct formal subject in its own right; it is motivated by some of the properties of physical wholes and parts, but it has some rather non-intuitive properties which make it suitable for analysing the results of phenomenology. Physical parts can, generally speaking, be separated from each other and can exist independently (although this may require the use of chain saws and such like implements). This is not true in general of Husserl's "parts"; he is quite able to countenance the existence of parts which are incapable of independent existence. Such dependent parts are called moments.

It is in these terms that Husserl discusses philosophical questions such as the problem of universals. What is to be explained here is that sometimes a group of things is seen as being similar, or they are all referred to by the same term; we need some sort of philosophical account of this. Set-theoretically, one would talk of their common membership in a certain set; mereologically, however, one would say that they all had a part in common (although in general this would be a moment, rather than a fully independent part). Thus, Husserl will frequently distinguish between abstract and concrete essences, saying that an abstract essence (being the essence of a moment) is incapable of independent existence, whereas a concrete one is; thus, abstract essences will partially specify the concrete objects that they belong to, but not completely – in general, there will be more than one object containing a moment of that type. Thus, in Husserl's ontology, abstract essences play the same sort of role that abstract concepts play in more familiar philosophies – abstract concepts, too, specify the objects that fall under them partially, but not completely.

These concepts may seem counter-intuitive and unmotivated, but what one should remember is that Husserl's language of parts and wholes is a technical language, and as such it is a wide, and rather metaphorical, extension of our ordinary language of parts and wholes. In a similar way, set theory is a metaphorical extension of our everyday language about collections of objects; and, because both languages are technical, it is not very appropriate to object to either of them on grounds of counter-intuitiveness. They ought to be judged by how well they function in the context of the theories for which they were developed.

With this in mind, many features of Husserl's philosophy become less startling than they seem to be. He has an ontology which, at first sight, appears to postulate a baroque collection of weird entities: noeses, noemata, and the like. However, these are only postulated *within* a technical language which uses the part-whole distinction to talk about structure; if, perhaps, one were to translate Husserl's assertions into set-theoretic terms, they might well have roughly the same content, but seem rather more innocuous. Of course, there remains the question of the ontological commitment of technical languages like mereology or set theory; however, as there is with set theory, there is probably also room for a good deal of argument about the precise ontological commitments of a mereology such as Husserl's.

# Some Phenomenological Concepts

## Noesis and Noema

Let us consider our everyday experience of objects. We generally take it that this experience is of physical objects, external to us (thus we live in what Husserl calls the "natural attitude"). However, we can ignore this everyday ontological commitment, and concentrate on the structure of the experience itself; this is what Husserl calls "bracketing" (the existence of external objects is "put in brackets", or suspended), or *epochē* (using the Greek word). What remains, then, is structured experience, a realm of essences and meanings, and we can consider, within this, two series of continuities. There are, on the one hand, the continuities that come from the experiencing subject – one judges, imagines, speculates, draws conclusions, and so on. On the other hand, there are the continuities that come "from the side of the object" – or rather, that would be considered to come from the side of the object had we not bracketed out the natural attitude, but which can still be considered *as continuities* when we are simply considering experience phenomenologically. When Husserl talks about these continuities in his own technical language, he postulates two corresponding series of entities; an entity coming from a subjective continuity is called a *noesis* (plural *noeses*), and an entity coming from an objective continuity is called a *noema* (plural *noemata*).

The noemata are possibly the more interesting of the two. Let us start with the rough distinction between the things we perceive and what we perceive of them (this has been described, in the philosophical tradition, as a distinction between "things in themselves" and "sense-data", both terms which Husserl would emphatically reject). How are we to describe the distinction phenomenologically? Both factors are clearly noemata – they are given to us in experience, rather than being activities of the experiencing subject – but they behave very differently. Suppose we have an experience as of a green object. This experience could well be illusory: the object might, on closer examination, show itself to be red. And even if it is not illusory, the object will always have other features which go beyond what can be grasped in a single experience (the precise texture of its surface, how it feels, the colour of the other side of it, and so on). The object, then, always has what Husserl calls a *horizon* of possible other experiences; Husserl also calls such objects *transcendent*, meaning that their horizon will always transcend what can be given in any one experience. By contrast, the experience itself is not transcendent: it is given "all at once". An experience as of a green object is, simply, an experience as of a green object, and there is no horizon of hidden possibilities of *that* experience for us to explore. If we subsequently find out that the object is, in fact, red, we will find this out by a different experience, rather than by finding out the true nature of the first experience. So experiences are what Husserl calls *absolute,* or *immanent;* we can thus have indubitable knowledge of them (this is a perpetually recurring Cartesian theme in Husserl).

There are thus these two different sorts of noemata, transcendent and immanent. Husserl has radically changed the traditional meaning of the concept of transcendence; it usually means that something is beyond any possible experience, that it belongs to some sort of metaphysical realm. By contrast, Husserl's transcendent noemata belong to experience (in fact, he emphasises that they *must* belong to experience); their transcendence simply consists in their horizon of as yet unexplored possibilities.

## The Transcendental Ego

So far, we have been discussing the phenomenology of objects of experience or objects of thought; this is what Husserl calls *eidetic* phenomenology, and its phenomenological redescriptions of experience belong to what Husserl calls the *eidetic reduction,* which has been carried out by bracketing out the existence of the world and of objects of perception, and concentrating attention on essences and meanings. We thus discover the realms of noeses and noemata. However, the bracketing can go further: we can bracket out also the noeses and noemata. All of these are particular concepts of experience, which can, in principle, be different; none of these, then, is essential to experience as such. When we formulate this mereologically, we are led to postulate the so-called *transcendental ego*, which Husserl regards as the source of all experience; it is not given directly in experience, but it is rather what relates itself to the contents of every experience, or, alternatively formulated, what constitutes every experience. This transcendental ego may seem at first sight to be rather a startling entity, and Husserl occasionally describes it in almost mystical language; however, the motivation for this doctrine is fairly unproblematic. It is simply the fact that (as Wittgenstein and others point out) our consciousness is not to be identified with any particular content of experience (because all contents of experience can, potentially, be different); we do not experience our consciousness as simply another object in the world, but it is, rather, something which accompanies, and must accompany, all of our concrete experience.

## Reception and Evaluation

Husserl's thought has been extremely influential, in a whole variety of ways; he has influenced people as diverse as Sartre, Heidegger, Dreyfus, and Simons. This diversity is probably not accidental, but is to do with the fact that Husserl's thought is genuinely difficult to interpret or to evaluate. To start with something very superficial: very few other philosophers use a mereological technical language to quite the extent that Husserl does. It is therefore extremely difficult to translate Husserl's assertions into more familiar terms, and there are a good number of important problems (such as the question of the ontological commitment of this mereological language) that have not been extensively worked on. So one faces a dilemma: if one tries to evaluate Husserl in his own terms, one faces the difficulty that the groundwork has simply not been done, and one thereby runs the risk of meaningless repetition of Husserlian technical terms, without either explanation or critical evaluation. On the other hand, if one translates Husserl's work into one's own conceptual scheme (both Heidegger and Dreyfus approach him this way), one can discover quite exciting things, but it is still extremely difficult to justify the precise translation that one makes; again, much of the exegetical groundwork has not been done.

There are other difficulties. When one evaluates or describes the work of a philosopher, there is usually a group of key questions that one would like to answer: questions such as the philosopher's ontological commitments, his or her view of truth, whether he or she is a realist. These questions are extremely difficult to answer in Husserl's case, simply because he does not really discuss them very explicitly, and prefers to talk about problems of the structure of experience and of phenomenological methodology. And quite often when one can find answers to these stock questions, they come from the least interesting part of Husserl's thought. (This is especially true of his views on the nature of scientific and philosophical method.)

However, there are several things which Husserl is responsible for, which are genuinely important and which have been very influential. One of them is his emphasis on structure, and, in particular, on the complexity of the structure of experience. Linked with this is a concentration on the problems of everyday experience and everyday perception; he is one of the first philosophers to find deep problems in our everyday dealings with normal physical objects (his work on this has been enthusiastically taken up by both Heidegger and the cognitive scientists). Finally, his work on the way in which possibility interacts with the structure of perception has been quite prophetic, foreshadowing much recent analytical work on the causal theory of reference.

# Further Reading

Nobody has ever claimed that Husserl wrote well. Volume I of *Ideas* is probably the best place to start, since it is relatively short and contains many of Husserl's characteristic themes. Which of Husserl's works to read next will depend on what one is interested in; *The Crisis of European Sciences* has important material on his concept of the life-world, there is a lot of detailed analysis in the *Logical Investigations* – especially the critique of psychologism in the introduction – and the *Cartesian Meditations* are important for his doctrine of the ego. Most of the secondary literature is jargon-filled and uncritical, although fortunately there are some exceptions: Dreyfus' *Husserl, Intentionality and Cognitive Science* is a stimulating introduction to recent applications of Husserl's doctrine, Smith's *Parts and Moments* has interesting material on mereology, and Smith and Macintyre's *Husserl and Intentionality* is a good treatment of intentionality. Bell's *Husserl* is very clear, although his treatment of intentionality is in some respects contentious.

# Bibliography

D. Bell, *Husserl*, London: Routledge 1990.
H. L. Dreyfus (ed.) *Husserl, Intentionality, and Cognitive Science* Cambridge MA: MIT Press 1982.
E. Husserl, *The Crisis of European Sciences and Transcendental Philosophy*, tr. D. Carr, Evanston: Northwestern University Press 1970.
——*Cartesian Meditations*, tr. D. Cairns, The Hague: Nijhoff 1973.
——*Ideas: A General Introduction to Pure Phenomenology*, tr. W.R. Boyce Gibson, London: Allen and Unwin 1931.
——*Logical Investigations*, tr. J.N. Findlay, London: Routledge 1970.

B. Smith (ed.), *Parts and Moments*, Munich: Philosophia 1982.
D. W. Smith, R. Macintyre, *Husserl and Intentionality*, Dordrecht: Reidel 1982.

# 9 Martin Heidegger
## Graham White

Martin Heidegger was born in 1889 in Messkirch, a village in Baden, south Germany. He studied theology and philosophy at the university of Freiburg from 1909 to 1914, reading a wide variety of both philosophical and non-philosophical texts – Brentano, Husserl, Rickert, Nietzsche, Kierkegaard, Dostoevesky, Rilke, and Trakl. At the time, the three dominant philosophical schools were phenomenology, neo-Kantianism, and neo-Thomism, and Heidegger was, in one way or another, influenced by all of them.

He had a tremendously successful early academic career as a philosopher: he obtained his doctorate in 1913 and his *Habilitation* (the formal qualification to teach in a university) in 1915. From 1916 on, while teaching at the university of Freiburg, he collaborated extensively with the prominent phenomenologist Edmund Husserl. In 1922 he became a professor at Marburg, where he collaborated with the theologian Rudolf Bultmann. *Being and Time*, the most important work of Heidegger's early period, was published in 1927, and dedicated to Husserl. He was beginning to acquire a reputation in the German academic world for being both radical and original, and for continuing Husserl's philosophical initiative in a decisively new way. As well as being a successful academic, he also remained stamped by his south German, rural origins; in 1922 he constructed a cabin in Todtnauberg in the Black Forest, and from then on he would constantly use it to retreat from the academic world.

In 1928 he became a full professor at the university of Freiburg; in 1933 – the year the Nazis came to power – he became the rector of the university, and gave an inaugural speech which was unequivocally pro-Nazi. The extent of his subsequent involvement with Nazism is a matter of some controversy; there seems little doubt that, while he was rector, he was quite seriously involved, and he signed a number of explicitly Nazi proclamations. However, he resigned the rectorate in 1934, and there are signs of greater reserve towards Nazism after this, although he never publicly renounced his involvement with the Nazis. During these years, his philosophical interests changed decisively: his style became less academic, his writings were shorter and more essayistic, and he became much more interested in problems of language, poetry, and art. After the war, he was forbidden to teach by the French occupying powers from 1945 to 1951; he retired to the Black Forest cabin and, although he did not lecture in public, he continued to travel and to publish significant works of his later philosophy. In 1951, the ban having been lifted, he resumed teaching until 1953. He died in 1976.

His writings fall into three main groups: as well as the published works there are extensive series of lectures and also a large amount of unpublished material (both notes and longer, more organised pieces). The unpublished writings, and many of the lectures, are only now being published in the complete works; there is little doubt that when it has been published, a much clearer, and in many ways more comprehensible, picture of Heidegger will emerge.

# The Early Period

Heidegger's philosophical activity falls into two periods, and the most significant work of the early period is *Being and Time*. This is a complex and closely argued book, which sets itself a radical agenda: to overturn the Western philosophical tradition which stretches from Aristotle through Descartes to the present.

## Descartes

It is probably easiest to start our discussion of *Being and Time* with an example: Heidegger's treatment of Descartes. Heidegger considers Descartes to be deeply wrong – not an unusual attitude for a philosopher of the early twentieth century – and he considers him to be wrong because of one basic error – again, not an unusual attitude – but what *is* distinctive is that Heidegger thinks that the basic error is one of *ontology*, rather than of, say, epistemology or philosophical method. This basic error, namely, is that the ontology of the world is described in terms of extension – that is, in terms of Descartes' mathematicised concept of space – and that other concepts – for example, that of substance – are described in terms of spatiality. This leads to quite implausible results; for example, Descartes describes the feeling of hardness in terms of the resistance of the felt object to our touch, thus overlooking the problem of the *perceptual* aspect of hardness and the ontological status of that perception. As Heidegger puts it, Descartes "translates [these phenomena] into the only thing that he knows". And this "only thing" that Descartes knows is based on the mathematicised idea of spatiality, which in turn is based on an ontology of things which are present and which persist through time. Heidegger does not deny that there are such things, but claims instead that they only amount to a particular way for things to be. Descartes' error, then, is one of overgeneralisation: he has ascribed the characteristics of a particular way of being to being as a whole.

This basic error, then, leads Descartes into two related sets of problems. Firstly, he arrives at insurmountable structural difficulties – his ontology falls apart into the three regions of God, the self, and the (external) world, which, once separated, cannot be reconciled. Furthermore, the coherence of the world itself is threatened, and items – such as values – which do not fall easily on one side or the other of the self/world distinction simply get left out, and are impossible to restore on the basis of a Cartesian ontology. This is one side of the problem: it might be called the threat of disintegration.

The other side of the problem is rather more subtle: it is that, with an ontology so conceived, one's explanations stop short before they become interesting. Thus, one simply says, of material substances, that they are extended in space, and thereby closes off the question of what it is for them to be substances – and here Heidegger quotes Descartes saying that the *substantiality* of a substance is inaccessible to us, that the only thing we have access to is its spatial extension.

One thus arrives at two basic errors, which Heidegger thinks have been characteristic of the way that ontology is practiced in the Western philosophical tradition: firstly, the ontology degenerates into a mere catalogue of different beings, or different kinds of being; secondly, one simply says that beings of such and such sorts exist, without being able to say, or otherwise indicate, what it is for them to exist, or to be. Indeed, one characteristically goes further, and attempts to justify this failure by saying that being is an empty concept, or "not a real predicate", or such like.

This critique of Descartes is only an example, and Heidegger claims that these errors have dogged "the Western metaphysical tradition" since its beginning, with Aristotle. One should notice several things about this diagnosis. Firstly, it is a diagnosis of a fundamental and subtle error, not a superficial or obvious one It is an error in the *foundations* of Descartes' thought, or in the thought of other Western metaphysicians; and it is an error concerning things that, as Heidegger puts it, are "fundamentally not discussed". It is an erroneous answer to a question that people have forgotten even to ask. And even though all of Western thought may rest on inadequate foundations, this does not render it completely nugatory – Heidegger talks of what Plato and Aristotle did as an achievement, the results of which lasted until Hegel's time. What Heidegger wants is to *remind* his readers, to show them that it is necessary to ask these ontological questions again. And this necessity is not merely *philosophical*, but also historical: the Western metaphysical tradition has, as it were, become exhausted, with the result that disciplines such as anthropology, psychology, and biology are in need of a new impetus, which can only be given by an *ontological* insight. Ontological insights of this sort – such as were achieved by Plato and Aristotle – are tremendously productive: they map out a region of being, and make it available for investigation by other disciplines. The insights of Plato and Aristotle, although valuable, have thus come to an end, and a new ontological foundation is necessary; and it is in *this* sense that Heidegger can talk of a "destruction" of the previous history of ontology.

## The Way Forward

*Being and Time* is not solely a critical book; there is a large amount of original philosophy in it. The *positive* innovations of *Being and Time* are, basically, twofold: the development of new, more appropriate philosophical language and concepts, and the execution of a research programme based on these concepts.

## Writing

These new concepts and language are one of the reasons for Heidegger's notorious obscurity; he thought that success in philosophy depended crucially on philosophical language, and his writing is (in all periods of his work) tremendously idiosyncratic. It is not only *vocabulary* that is peculiar to Heidegger: he has his own syntax (for example, he often uses constructions borrowed from Aristotle's Greek, or from medieval Latin), he uses (or abuses) word-play to a tremendous extent, and, in the later works, he has his own orthography. Not only does this make Heidegger difficult to read in German, but it makes a successful translation almost impossible. All one can do here is to explain a few of the key terms, and leave it to the reader to puzzle through Heidegger's language with due care.

## Being and Beings

One of the key distinctions is between being (*Sein*) and beings (*Seindes*). In German, *Sein* is an infinitive of the verb to be, while *Seindes* is the neuter singular of the participle of that verb: although it is grammatically singular, it can be used to mean either a single entity, or a group of entities of unspecified number. Unfortunately, in English the relevant participle and infinitive are exactly the same ('being'); most translations get around this by translating *Seindes* as 'beings', although the German in no way implies a plural number. Heidegger uses *Seindes* in both singular and plural senses, and for any sort of entity – not merely substances or physical objects, but also relations, processes, events, and the like. Basically, then, *Seindes* is a place holder for any sort of referential term. *Sein*, on the other hand, is something else; it can be thought of as what one explains when one explains what it is for beings to be beings. Thus, Heidegger has a long section on the ontology of the world – containing, among other things, the critique of Descartes – in which he investigates the being (*Sein*) of the world: that is, what it is for the various beings (*Seindes*) in the world to make up a world. Now the being of the world is not an extra entity beside the beings that make it up; the point is, rather, that when one has adequately explained what it is for the beings of the world to be, then it will be clear what it is for them to make up a world, and thus one will have described both their being and the being of the world. Being, then, is used as a term that distinguishes between deep and shallow explanations.

Roughly corresponding to the difference between being and beings is the difference between the ontological and the ontic. Basically, any of our normal referential language is ontic; it talks about beings, successfully refers to them, and accomplishes such explanations as we need for our non-philosophical concerns (be they academic or not). But for philosophical discourse, we need more than to talk about beings; we need to talk about their being. Language that does that is ontological. This is the basic sense of Heidegger's distinction between ontic and ontological (although he certainly uses the distinction in other senses – occasionally, for example, he uses it to distinguish between theory and world. However, the sense derived from the distinction between being and beings is certainly the basic one.)

## Dasein

One of the German words for existence is *Dasein*, which literally means "being there"; in one of the most notable idiosyncrasies of *Being and Time*, Heidegger uses it to stand for a human being. (Note that Heidegger generally uses the word without an article — he says "Dasein" rather than "a Dasein". The point is probably that humans are to be understood primarily as individuals, rather than as reproducible tokens of the type humanity.) This is motivated by two things: the philosophical tradition, and the syntactical possibilities that the word affords.

The key figure in the tradition, as Heidegger sees it, is Kierkegaard, who, in protest against Hegel, opposed "the existing human individual" to the constructions of Hegel's system. Of course, this involves a polemical contrast between theory and reality, but more than this is at issue: for Kierkegaard, being a human individual is a task which is to be fulfiled by *living* an authentically human life, not by following the instructions of some system. Heidegger takes from this the idea that, for *Dasein*, existence precedes essence: there is no fixed set of concepts from which all of the properties of existing human beings may be deduced, but, rather, the relevant properties must be read off, in each case, from existing human beings.

The other important thing is the syntax of this word. As I have said, it is literally "being there", and Heidegger feels free to substitute a variety of things for "there": not only physical places, but ways of life, relations (to other people or to things – one's house, for example), and even moods. This may seem arbitrary (relying, that is, on the syntactic peculiarities of a particular language), but Heidegger would reply that, although this syntax does belong to a peculiar language, the syntax is part of the implicit grasp of ontology that the language offers its speakers: German just happens to be particularly suited to philosophy, due to this phenomenon and others like it. Arbitrary or not, it does allow Heidegger to give an account of human beings and their world (physical and social) which is relational from the beginning, which does not have the unbridgeable gap between person and world which Descartes' system suffered from.

## Being and Time, *Part I: Starting with* Dasein

Heidegger's analysis of being starts with a particular sort of being: human being, *Dasein*. This has also been the starting point for a good deal of philosophy since the sixteenth century, but in Heidegger's case the reasons are different: he is not starting with human experience for Descartes' reasons – that our knowledge of our minds is more certain than our knowledge of anything else – or for reasons inspired by humanism – that the "human world" should be our proper concern, and anything outside it is a needless distraction. On the one hand, he was never very interested in the problem of certainty; on the other hand, he would have thought that the "human world" – interesting though it may be – is still only *part* of the world, and therefore would not give one access to being.

The reason why Heidegger starts with *Dasein* is, rather, this: that *Dasein*, properly understood, is a complex and subtle being, and that when one has understood *Dasein*, one can then understand other beings. But one must understand *Dasein* in the correct way: it is fatal to do as Descartes did, to reduce *Dasein* to the contents of consciousness, and, in consequence, to divide *Dasein* from the world. This division is only possible because Descartes isolates one particular way that *Dasein* relates to its world, namely, the disinterested contemplative attitude, which corresponds to a view of the mind isolated from the world and of things as isolated substances occupying a mathematical space.

Heidegger does start with *Dasein*, but he starts with a different attitude than the detached contemplative one: he starts, rather, with *Dasein* engaged in the everyday world of work and of manual tasks. In the world of work, things – tools, raw materials, one's workspace – and people – one's co-workers, those whom the work is done for – are not considered in themselves, as isolated substances; rather, they already belong to a complex system of relationships. One makes something *for* someone, using certain tools, out of a particular piece of raw material: Heidegger's ontology starts with things so related to each other, and people thus related to things. And he refuses to consider the world of work as something epiphenomenal, as constructed on the basis of things in themselves by attaching certain subjective valuations; for him, this would be to reverse the order of priority, to make primary what is only derivative, and, ultimately, to pose oneself insuperable ontological problems.

We should notice several things about this analysis. Firstly, it is *phenomenological*: it starts with something that presents itself (that is, the world of work), and it goes on to draw ontological lessons from it. Secondly, its starting point (the world of work) is something that has not usually been thought worthy of *ontological* analysis; and, thirdly, the things that Heidegger interprets ontologically are things that have usually been thought to be merely subjective. These three tendencies are things that Heidegger has in common with his teacher, Husserl, the founder of the phenomenological movement; the final one in particular (the anti-subjective polemic) is one of Husserl's most characteristic innovations.

All three of these themes recur through *Being and Time*, and to some extent the further course of that work can be described in terms of the series of phenomena that Heidegger subjects to ontological analysis. Thus, after the analysis of the world of work (and of the anonymous presence of one's co-workers and clients), there is an extended treatment of moods and of emotions such as fear; these reveal the way that *Dasein* finds itself in a world and already related to it (rather than having to deliberately put itself into a relation with an "external" world). And there remains the problem of the structure of the whole (*Dasein* and the various beings in its world); this is solved by talking about care (*Sorge*), a word which – in German as in English – has a wide spectrum of meanings (to be concerned about, to be in charge of, to be worried, and so on.) This wide spectrum – linking emotions, the interpersonal world, and work – reveals the ways in which beings in the world are related to each other, and in which *Dasein* is related to its world. (Again, Heidegger would argue, this wide spectrum of meanings is neither ambiguity nor imprecision, but is ontologically significant.)

## Being and Time, *Part II: Conscience, Death and Time*

This analysis is, as it stands, far from complete; it corresponds to the first part of *Being and Time*, and we still have to describe the second part. It has shown how a being like *Dasein* can exist and can be related to a world, but it ignores an important aspect of the problem of being: the fact that our understanding of the world is far from fixed, and that it can be changed, often in quite radical ways. One can, of course, change one's mind about individual beings, but one can also change one's conceptual scheme as a whole, change it to admit concepts that might be incommensurable with the concepts that one started with. As we saw, Heidegger thought that the history of philosophy was fundamentally discontinuous: there have been, it is true, periods of stability, but there have also been innovative figures – Parmenides, Aristotle, Descartes – who made radical innovations, who initiated new ontologies that could not be described in terms of the old.

This is more serious than it might appear, since we are not simply describing reconceptualisations of one and the same reality that we are isolated from. Rather, we ourselves are *Dasein*, at once part of this reality and the being that is reconceptualising it and ourselves; and we are reconceptualising ourselves by changing our ontology, our grasp of being, and – according to Heidegger – *Dasein*'s grasp of being is fundamental to the way that *Dasein* is; so, if you change this, you change everything. (This is the basic reason why Heidegger claims that *Dasein's* existence precedes its essence; it is what Heidegger calls the *transcendence* of *Dasein*.) So how can Heidegger describe the unity of *Dasein* in the face of this radical diversity, especially since he has forsworn any attempt to start with a fixed, merely physical or natural part of human nature and then add on such things as mental contents, a cultural situation, and so on?

The answer to this lies again in the ontological reinterpretation of certain human phenomena; these will give us an ontological description of these radical reconceptualisations that *Dasein* is capable of. The phenomena that Heidegger describes in this part are less everyday; they are paradigmatically religious or ethical (they are such things as conscience and the awareness of death). There is a reason for this: Heidegger sees the everyday world as a rather neatly defined structure, in which things fit into a closed system of relationships, and in which one lives in a mood of almost conscious refusal of awareness of anything beyond that. This refusal of awareness can be described as a loss of authenticity, a loss of one's self. The moods in which one breaks through this closed system are, consequently, less everyday ones. It is also characteristic of Heidegger that, in this portion of the work, the authors that he follows were not part of the mainstream academic tradition: rather, they are people such as Luther and Kierkegaard, who saw themselves as outsiders, outsiders who were testifying to the kind of extreme experience that Heidegger is analysing here.

There is another important fact about these phenomena – conscience, dread, awareness of death. Their essential feature, according to Heidegger, is that they do not have an object in the way that everyday moods have objects: for example, dread is carefully distinguished from fear in that fear has an object, whereas dread does not. (This is a distinction which goes back to Kierkegaard.) Conscience, properly understood, says nothing, but calls *Dasein* back to itself, back to its lost authenticity. And awareness of death is, specifically, awareness of *one's own* death, not of the death of others; the awareness of one's own mortality is much harder to assimilate than is the awareness of the mortality of others. (Heidegger relies heavily on Luther for this description of the awareness of death.)

This gives these situations (particularly conscience and the awareness of death) a particularly important place in Heidegger's system. The whole problem with radical reconceptualisation is that afterwards one has an ontology which could not be described in terms of the previous one; consequently, it seems very difficult to describe the change as taking place in a reality-guided way, since before the change one could not have been aware of any of the new features which could have motivated it or made it rational. Kierkegaard (in *The Concept of Dread*) makes this point in the form of a religious parable: before the Fall, how could Adam and Eve even have *understood* God's command, since they did not then have the knowledge of good and evil? The Fall (understood as the acquisition of moral awareness) is here taken to be a paradigm of a radical reconceptualisation, one which changes the being of the people who undergo it. But, when we are thinking about this sort of problem, something like conscience could well offer a clue; it calls, and – if one takes it seriously – it calls in a reality-guided way, but, according to Heidegger, it does not have a definite content: rather, as he puts it, "[t]he call does not say anything, does not give any information about events in the world, has no story to tell."

These, then, are the reasons why phenomena such as death and conscience take up so much space in the second half of *Being and Time*. Although there is no space to do anything more than sketch the development here, what this leads to is a conception of *Dasein*'s being in the world that is fundamentally finite and fundamentally temporal, and, furthermore, a conception that places the finitude and temporality as much on the side of reality as on the side of *Dasein*: it is of the nature of the world, that is, that it can be grasped by finite and temporal beings such as *Dasein*, beings who thus undergo the radical changes involved in ontological reconceptualisation. Ontology – that is, the grasp of the world that beings such as *Dasein* have – is thus fundamentally historical.

It is important to realise that all of this analysis of *Dasein* aims at ontology; it is not just psychology or anthropology or cultural criticism (interesting though it may be when considered in those respects). Rather, these particular phenomena are selected with a view to the ontological information that can be extracted from them, and, as Heidegger repeatedly points out, to consider them *merely* from an anthropological or psychological viewpoint is to trivialise them. And even though Heidegger may depend heavily on people like Luther or Kierkegaard, or on the philosophical tradition, such dependence is not merely a passive assimilation: he is, rather, extracting ontological information from texts that, very often, are not *prima facie* ontological.

# The Later Philosophy.

Heidegger's later philosophy is in many ways quite different from the philosophy of *Being and Time*; the works are much shorter and more impressionistic, and the themes have changed. Where the earlier philosophy was concerned with the ontology of human existence in the world, the later essays investigate such problems as truth, art, and language. However, it is possible to see these works as an accentuation, rather than a negation, of the philosophy of the early period. The phenomena that are investigated may be different – Heidegger may think about poetry, for example, rather than anxiety – but nevertheless the goal is still the same: it is to discover the ontological import of the phenomena in question. Similarly, there may be less about the human subject in the later philosophy, but this should be considered as a continuation of the tendency in *Being and Time* to stress the reality-guided aspect of the human phenomena that Heidegger was investigating. Finally, the historical claims may be different in detail – Heidegger may see the roles of Aristotle, or of the pre-Socratics, rather differently – but the broad historical picture remains the same: ontology is historically variable, this variability occurs by means of sharp discontinuities rather than gradual change, and the current period, which started roughly at the time of Aristotle, is only now coming to an end.

But there are some quite striking accentuations within this broad picture, and one or two new elements. Whereas in *Being and Time* the historical variation of ontology is brought about by human reconceptualisation – albeit in a world-guided way – in the later philosophy, this variation is seen as part of "the history of being", a history which "carries and determines every human condition and situation". So there is a sort of inversion; it is *being* which has the history, and human actions are only derivative to this history of being. Similar inversions abound; we are told that "language is the house of being", and that *we* live in the dwelling that language provides. This inverts what we might think of as the obvious order of dependence; we would like to think that language is dependent on us, rather than vice versa. Even the transitional essay *On the Essence of Truth*, after describing the connection between truth and human freedom (freedom to be truthful or to be in error, but, more importantly, freedom to reconceptualise and thus express previously unexpressed truths) *then* goes on to describe this freedom as the ability to let being be. So the crucial thing is receptivity to being. Metaphors of this sort abound in the later philosophy: metaphors, for example, of being making a space for truth, of being as a clearing, of being as light, as illumination – these are all metaphors which shift the accent onto being, and correspondingly make the human responsibility one of receptivity or sensitivity.

Are these more significant than simply metaphors? To an extent, Heidegger would argue that they *are* metaphors, but that that is what is most important about philosophy anyway; and this is not to trivialise philosophy, but to point to the centrality of metaphor. Normally, of course, we consider non-metaphorical language to be primary, and metaphor to be secondary; Heidegger would not deny that a linguistic theory of the usual sort *can* be useful. However, what it accomplishes is *ontic* explanation; such a theory will be useful *within* a given ontology, and will say how language is related to beings, not to being. But we do more than that with language; in some way, we *can* talk about being, and our use of language transcends any particular ontology – even though we may reconceptualise quite radically, we still continue to be language-users. So what is *ontolog-*

*ically* relevant about our use of language must not depend on a particular ontic theory of language; it must depend, rather, on our freedom to change our language use, to use language receptively and, as Heidegger would put it, in a way that is open to being. And Heidegger would argue that this freedom and openness has a lot more to do with metaphorical than with literal language.

It is probably in this way that much of the later philosophy should be seen. This is not to diminish either its argumentative structure or its scholarship – and there is more of both in the later philosophy than might appear – but Heidegger's views on the primacy of metaphor apply just as much to philosophical language. In fact, very often Heidegger's task seems to be to develop new metaphors for philosophical thinking, metaphors on the basis of which one could go on to develop more detailed theories. From Heidegger's point of view this would only be appropriate: he is interested in ontology, and for him what is ontologically decisive about philosophical language is the metaphorical, rather than the literal part. And this gives rise, quite often, to an odd feeling of frustration when reading Heidegger: one wants *results*, and all he gives one is a new metaphor.

# Assessment

Heidegger is an extremely difficult figure to assess, and this difficulty has as much to do with his politics as with his philosophy.

## Politics

There is very little doubt that Heidegger was culpably involved with Nazism for at least a year or so after 1933. The crucial questions are, firstly, when and whether he ceased to have questionable political sympathies, and, secondly, how much of his philosophy is tied up with this. Both questions are extremely difficult to answer. Heidegger was extremely reclusive, and very rarely revealed anything about his personal opinions; this was accentuated after the war, when he was banned from teaching. At the very least, his subsequent silence about his political involvement is shameful and politically naive, regardless of what sinister political motives might or might not lie behind it.

But how much does this affect his philosophy? There have been a number of political attacks on his philosophy, all of them arguing that, because of certain of his *philosophical* doctrines, his thought is necessarily repressive; these polemics have questioned such things as Heidegger's supposed irrationalism, his sentimental attachment to the world of the peasant and the craftsman, the idea that human history is determined by the history of being, and, finally, the arbitrariness and obscurity of his philosophical language. It must be admitted that Heideggers' own philosophy naturally invites such questioning, precisely because of the way that it links thought and life; one simply cannot respond to these challenges by saying that the man's life was one thing and his thought was another. Probably the best and most constructive response to this very worrying series of questions is to assimilate Heidegger's thought critically and carefully, to look at his doctrines on their merits and to be aware of the possible philosophical implications; this may seem an anodyne response, but yet neither Heidegger's supporters nor his antagonists seem to have been able to manage this sort of critical detachment.

## Philosophy

The philosophy is, likewise, difficult to evaluate, and that in almost all areas, from his historiography onwards.

## History

As we have seen, Heidegger's philosophy is intimately involved with a certain view of history, and he makes some very strong claims about the entire history of Western thought (basically, that it has been dominated by what he calls metaphysics). There are difficulties with a number of these claims. One of the most problematic has to do with his treatment of medieval thought: the problem is that even though he read quite a number of medieval texts, he always tended to interpret them with the conceptual scheme of his conservative Catholic education, and this conceptual scheme seems to be rather questionable in the light of current medieval scholarship. For example, it now appears that Aristotle's *Metaphysics* was not a very important text in the Middle Ages, so that Heidegger's interpretation of medieval thought in terms of structures derived from the *Metaphysics* is rather anachronistic. (Of course, medieval thought may still have been *metaphysical* even though it was not directly influenced by Aristotle's *Metaphysics*, but one would have to argue for this rather more carefully than Heidegger in fact does.) One could generalise this criticism a little: for Heidegger, Western thought seems to have had a fixed *structure* (everything else depends on metaphysics, which in turn depends on ontology, the doctrine of being). However, for a historian, the structure of human thought is a historical variable like any other, and there seems in fact to have been considerable variation – a variation that Heidegger is not very sensitive to.

## Language, Technology, Science

In a similar way, most of Heidegger's weak points are due to the limitations of his educational background. For example, he talks about language a great deal, but he always discusses language in terms of the philology of the late nineteenth century; he never seems to take linguistics into account. Similarly, when he discusses logic, the people he has in mind are the philosophical logicians of the late nineteenth century (Lotze, Sigwart, Mill and so on) and, occasionally, Leibniz; the logic of the twentieth century does not come into the picture. And his rather ambivalent attitude to science and technology is very important, especially for *Being and Time*. However, one could justifiably doubt whether this ambivalence has more to do with the *hauteur* of a humanistically educated German professor, than with genuine insight into the problems.

All that having been said, Heidegger remains one of the few major philosophers of this century, and a thinker who amply repays the considerable effort needed to think along with him. The various criticisms of him that one can make all seem to imply that, if one wants to use him, one has to think; what is dangerous (both politically and philosophically) is slavish imitation – the uncritical repetition of his terminology, the naive use of his historical examples, the mindless assimilation of his cultural prejudices. This is probably the way he himself would have wanted it: for him, philosophy was a serious business, and to be a philosopher meant taking great care about every aspect of one's thought (from the terminology onwards). To do Heidegger justice means taking that concern seriously, it means using his work as a stimulus to think for oneself, rather than as a reservoir of conveniently obscure phraseology.

# Further Reading

Heidegger's major work, *Being and Time*, is the main source for his early work. There is a useful anthology of his later work, *Martin Heidegger: Basic Writings*, edited by David F. Krell. Heidegger has not been well served by the secondary literature, although the recent *Cambridge Companion to Heidegger* is a welcome exception and a very useful reference. Dreyfus' commentary on *Being and Time* can likewise be recommended, as can Haar's *Le chant de la terre*. Neske and Kettering's collection, *Martin Heidegger and National Socialism*, is a good basis for an assessment of Heidegger's political role.

# Bibliography

H.L. Dreyfus, *Being-in-the-World: A Commentary on Heidegger's* Being and Time, *Distinction I* Cambridge, MA: MIT Press. 1991.

C. Guignon (ed.), *The Cambridge Companion to Heidegger*, Cambridge: Cambridge University Press 1993.

M. Haar, *Le chant de la terre*, Paris: L'Herne 1987.

M. Heidegger, *Being and Time*, tr. Macquarrie and Robinson, New York: Harper and Row 1962.

——*Basic Writings*, ed. D.F. Krell, New York: Harper and Row 1977.

G. Neske and E. Kettering (eds.), *Martin Heidegger and National Socialism: Questions and Answers*, tr. L. Harries, New York: Paragon 1990.

# 10  Jean-Paul Sartre
## Jenny Teichman

Jean-Paul Sartre (1905-1980) was a prolific author who, in addition to a comparatively large output of philosophy, also wrote novels, plays, literary criticism and an autobiography. He studied at the École Normale Superieure in Paris, and like many French graduates he taught for a time in high school. In 1933 he went to Berlin, where he came under the influence of Husserl. During the early part of the second world war he read Heidegger's *Being and Time*. His work was influenced by both these philosophers, and by Marx, and Nietzsche, and, negatively, by Freud. Sartre's interest in abstract questions about objective reality is nearly always combined with puzzlings about human freedom and the nature of morality. This comes about because his theory of consciousness, according to which all human beings are "existentially" free to construct their own lives and personalities, clashes with his Marxism, leading to the following dilemma: How, if at all, can one choose between political commitment and existential freedom?

Sartre always uses his works of fiction as vehicles for philosophical ideas. We will begin this chapter with a discussion of one of those works.

## The Roads to Freedom

Consciousness, freedom and political commitment are the themes of Sartre's long book, the three-volume novel *The Roads to Freedom*, published immediately after the end of the second world war. The events of the trilogy take place in 1938-40, the years in which it was finally demonstrated that the policy of appeasing Hitler could not lead to peace. The plot has to do with various kinds of liberty – personal, social, and political – and the characters are shown as existing in different states or stages of freedom and unfreedom. The main protagonists are a philosophy teacher, Matthieu Delarue, his friends Daniel, Gomez, and Brunet, his student Boris, and various women. All these people appear in the first novel, *The Age of Reason*, and most reappear in the two later ones. The second book, *The Reprieve*, introduces new characters, including the national leaders Chamberlain, Halifax, Deladier, Masaryk, and the man with "the face of a human fly" (Hitler). We also meet a pacifist, Phillippe, some cowards, and some paraplegic patients, whose inertia perhaps symbolises that of

120

France. *The Reprieve* is written in an experimental style; it spreads out in space rather than in time, and gives the impression of a kaleidoscope because the scene keeps switching from one place to another with no linking passages. In the third novel, *Iron in the Soul*, Sartre returns to a more conventional form. At the end of the novel Matthieu is called into the army and is killed fighting the Germans.

The struggle for freedom is shown as occurring at several different levels. The characters play out their own anxieties about personal liberty on a stage, as it were, in front of a looming national disaster. Many of them cannot understand what is happening; even Matthieu the professor says that he cannot understand national events, only the events in his own life. Those who seem to comprehend, or at least to care, are depicted as losing liberty in a vain fight to gain it. Thus the communist Brunet and the Spanish republican Gomez abandon their freedom for the sake of a lost cause. The free decisions of these men to make themselves unfree have a certain manliness when compared to the anxieties of the non-political characters, who appear by contrast as petty and selfish. It is difficult to tell whether this effect was intended, for Matthieu, a non-political, is generally taken to be a portrait of the author himself. In picturing Brunet and Gomez, potential members of the Resistance, as in some sense unfree, Sartre might have been attempting unconsciously to exonerate those intellectuals who survived the German occupation by concentrating their attention on abstract questions and private problems.

Many different roads to freedom are sought by the various male characters in this long novel. Sartre also makes some attempt to place the women characters on the same road, but the attempt fails. By the standards of the late twentieth century, Sartre's view of women is more than conservative, it is antiquated, and as a result his female characters, though quite realistic, invariably turn out to be irrational, shallow, weak, tearful, clinging, sticky, and smelly. The hero Matthieu treats women with kindly condescension (in real life Sartre's condescension was not very kindly), while the politicals clearly despise their wives and girl friends. The novel seems to contain a hidden message, hidden perhaps even from the author himself, namely, that women do not really set out on the road to freedom because they are the slaves of their weak bodies and inferior minds. The girl Ivich, for example, cannot free herself from economic dependence on her parents because she is incapable of passing exams and too feeble to hold down a job. Lola is enchained by sexual love and cocaine. Sarah is crippled by her persistent but completely useless kindliness. Marcelle is dominated by the maternal instinct, yet her freedom to have a child is compromised by a passive acceptance of decisions made by other people

– first Matthieu, then Daniel. Even Charles, the paraplegic, is more free than these women because he has an active masculine consciousness. He at least has a conception of freedom. They do not.

Matthieu, the hero of this story, struggles towards freedom by trying to understand its nature. Yet the struggle itself hampers him; he is debilitated by an obsession with a philosophical question and plagued by the perpetual fear of losing his sexual liberty and Bohemian credentials.

Sartre's intention in creating the character Daniel is in some ways obscure. Daniel is a homosexual – he is as it were neither a man nor a woman – and if he had appeared in a modern novel he would perhaps be seen as representing humanity as such. But Sartre is not a modern novelist. Is Daniel supposed to be an existential hero? He certainly looks like the beginnings of one because he makes several attempts to carry out random, gratuitous "existential" acts. On the other hand, he is driven by destructive or self-destructive impulses which it seems he cannot control and which he never gets rid of. When he marries Marcelle his decision is not genuinely free because he has ulterior motives, namely to harm himself *qua* homosexual and to humiliate Matthieu.

This thought brings us to the problem of bad faith. In his philosophical works. Sartre says that bad faith consists in refusing to believe you are free; the story of Daniel, however, points to a different and possibly incompatible theory. Daniel's bad faith consists in the false belief that he is able to get rid of the motivations which determine his actions.

Although *The Roads to Freedom* is a novel of considerable historical interest, Sartre, unfortunately, is no Tolstoy. Tolstoy's discussions about the philosophy of history do not diminish the intensely dramatic character of *War and Peace*. Sartre's philosophy, on the other hand, tends to trivialise his accounts of real (and terrible) external events, first by burying them in jejune and aimless soliloquies ("Who am I? What is freedom? All Frenchmen are swine!", etc.), or by drowning them in tedious lectures on communism.

Sartre was a man of the left, but his hatred of the middle classes did not preserve him from prejudices which are often associated, rightly or wrongly, with the bourgeoisie. Prejudice can be seen in his attitudes to homosexuality, to women, and (perhaps more surprisingly) to blacks and to the working class. Thus the homosexual character is depicted as necessarily hating his own nature, the working class characters are either moronic (like Big Louis and Zezette), or brutal (like the men who attack Maurice and Big Louis). At one point the plot hangs on the "fact" that blacks "all look alike", and the pacifist Phillippe's encounter with his black woman is no advertisement for anti-racism.

Perhaps we need to remember that one of Sartre's most famous slogans is "Hell is other people".

## Object and Subject

Sartre's philosophy proper is often obscure. The following sections will present what is a fairly standard interpretation of these difficult books, but readers must not be surprised if they find different interpretations elsewhere.

We will begin with a discussion of an early work, *The Transcendence of the Ego* (1936), in which Sartre applies a phenomenological or Husserlian reduction to the concept of consciousness. He rejects the idea that consciousness is an entity, arguing that the subject, that is, consciousness, is nothing over and above a collection of experiences and capacities. He thus adopts what the British philosopher P.F. Strawson calls the bundle theory of the mind. Sartre continues to develop the thesis that consciousness is not a thing in *Being and Nothingness* (1943). Once again he insists that consciousness has no properties or capacities, but is itself nothing over and above a bundle of those very items. It is for this reason that he says that consciousness is *nothingness*. The idea of consciousness is the idea of a non-entity. Like many other philosophers, he distinguishes between the world around us, which he calls the given or the world of objects, and consciousness, which he calls the subject or the human subject. The world of objects, he says, exists in-itself, i.e. as self-subsistent, while consciousness, the human subject, exists for-itself, i.e. it exists only in relation to other items. If we think of the for-itself and the in-itself as opposites, and if objects are entities, then consciousnesses, subjects, must be non-entities. Hegel's distinction between objects and subjects allows for a dialectical synthesis of the two. Sartre insists that the "cleavage of being" between subject and object is absolute. On the other hand he also insists that, since consciousness is always consciousness of something, its existence presupposes the existence of objects. Conversely, because there are no objects, or at any rate no facts, without consciousness, the existence of facts presupposes the existence of subjects. The upshot seems to be that subject and object are separate but mutually dependent. It is not easy, though, to understand how a nothing can be either separate from, or dependent on, a something.

The thesis that the human subject is a non-entity, a kind of nothing, has two or three strands. Firstly, as we have already seen, Sartre defines subjects as in some sense the opposite, or negation, of objects. Secondly, he says that, although consciousness is experienced, it is not experienced in the manner in which objects are experienced. Thirdly, he draws from these two considerations the important conclusion that, while the world of objects is governed by causal laws, consciousness is not. Consciousness is free.

How can the word 'consciousness' have any meaning if it refers to a nothing? The answer is that this nothing is actually a kind of something; it is a collection of capacities and activities. Yet we might still ask how we can know anything about this collection, for, after all, we cannot see it or hear it or touch it. Sartre's reply would be that seeing, hearing, touching and so on are not the only ways of being aware. When we perceive physical objects and remember events, we are simultaneously aware of the activities of perceiving and remembering. We can also be aware of evaluation, that is, of comparing, judging and analysing the things we see and hear and touch. And we can be aware of initiation, that is, of willing, and choosing, and planning. Consciousness is made up of these awarenesses, these actions, these capacities. The human subject is not a being, it is a doing.

If consciousness, the subject, is a non-entity consisting of capacities and activities it follows, according to Sartre, that these capacities and activities must themselves be "aspects of negation". He illustrates this idea with examples. Fortunately, the examples indicate that negation, in its subsidiary aspects, is a fairly harmless notion: it is not equivalent to nothingness, but rather to oppositeness. (This weaker conception of negation comes from Hegel.) In one example Sartre describes the experience of seeing a shape against a background. The shape has to be perceive via "negation" because it has to stand out against a background of what it is not. Another example: when we initiate some action, we "negate" what is present by "replacing" it with a chosen future.

## Pure and Impure Reflection

How do we come to hold the common but incorrect opinion that consciousness is a thing? Sartre believes that we experience objects from a point of view or perspective. (Note here that he ignores tactile and auditory perception and concentrates on the visual, and that his reduction of the sensory to the visual is the probable origin of the generalisation that perception is perspectival, for vision, of course, is literally, that is spatially, perspectival.) Do we experience the subject, as well as objects, from a perspective? This seems *prima facie* unlikely. If consciousness were to gain a perspective on itself, would it not have to move outside itself? And moving outside oneself is surely an extremely difficult operation! Yet the human subject's false idea about its own nature has to be explained somehow, and Sartre chooses to explain it by postulating a false awareness *by* consciousness *of* consciousness, which he calls impure reflection. The role in life of impure reflection is to lead the thinker to false conclusions about the nature of consciousness. Having wrongly surmised a dualism between reflecting consciousness (consciousness as subject) and reflected consciousness (consciousness as object), the subject mistakenly takes itself to be that which is reflected, in other words, an object, the ego.

This explanation of how the human subject gets a false picture of itself suggests the need for an explanation of how it comes by a true picture. Here Sartre refers to a movement which he calls pure reflection. Pure reflection is pure because it does not produce the false idea of the subject as object. It leads only to the (supposedly non-dualistic) thought that "the one who is reflecting on me is myself".

## Explicit and Implicit Awareness

If consciousness is not a thing or object but the collection of activities and states which appear to pure reflection, what reason can there be to believe in the *continuity* of consciousness? If consciousness has no continuity how can it have unity? If there is no unity how can it make sense to speak of human subjects? Sartre begins to answer these questions by asking another, namely: What happens when we are not aware of some "mental" activities? Part of the answer is that awareness is sometimes explicit, sometimes implicit. Sartre uses the technical terms 'positional' and 'thetic' to label the explicit, 'non-propositional' and 'non-thetic' to label the merely implicit, but we can stick to ordinary language. We may note in passing that the question 'How is unity of consciousness possible?' comes from Kant, while the distinction between explicit and implicit goes back to Leibniz; we see here evidence of the fact that our author, like most twentieth century philosophers, was also a professor.

Sartre states that explicit consciousness of objects is always accompanied by the implicit consciousness of the state of awareness itself. Yet the implicit need not remain so: it can become explicit, a theory which is defended with examples. Consider reading and memory. When reading a novel, say, one can be completely engrossed with the plot, yet also able immediately afterwards to remember, not only the story, but also one's own apparently non-self-conscious attitudes to it. What one remembers in recollecting these attitudes or evaluations is an earlier state of implicit consciousness of consciousness. More generally, the ability to distinguish genuine memories from imagination shows that implicit consciousness is never absent. The continuity and unity of the subject consists in this never-absent consciousness.

## Sartre Against Freud

Freud's theory of mind postulates an entity made up of three elements: the ego, the id and the superego. Part of the totality, he claimed, is unconscious. This supposed unconscious mind contains forgotten memories, secret desires, and hidden beliefs, which can cause action but which are not themselves subject to any kind of control short of psycho-analysis.

The notion of a Freudian unconsciousness cannot be combined either with the existentialist ontology of subject and object, or with an existentialist ethical system. For Sartre, the mind can have no hidden desires, because he believes that every human subject is implicitly aware of itself and must therefore retain conscious control over the activities which go to make up its identity. It follows from this ontological thesis that we cannot dodge our moral responsibilities by appealing to psychological determinism. Existential ethics presupposes existential ontology, and existential ontology does not allow for the possibility of an uncontrolled or uncontrollable unconscious mind.

Sartre's teaching, therefore, is that neither consciousness nor the Freudian Unconscious is an entity. Freud's unconscious mind does not truly explain the ability to recall past experiences that apparently went by unnoticed at the time. If the unconscious mind exists it would have to be just like the conscious mind; it must be a bundle of experiences and capacities. If there is anything special about this bundle, it can only be that it contains the well-known human ability to recall "unnoticed" events.

## The Nature of Freedom

As we have already seen, Sartre's interest in the nature of consciousness is partly ontological and partly ethical. One of his motives is to refute the philosophical doctrine of determinism, a theory which leads to the conclusion that responsibility is a fiction. Sartre argues that man's freedom is threatened neither by nature nor by nurture. He insists that men create their own actions and can invent their own identities.

It seems undeniable that the characteristics of individual bodies are created by genetic determination and environmental conditioning. However, according to Sartre's ontology, body and environment are simply objects, instances of the given, whereas consciousness, on the other hand, is a negation of the given and therefore a negation of the body and its environment. Consciousness, which is a kind of nothing, cannot possibly be controlled by the conditions which control bodies. Secondly, facts about the environment can only become facts when and if the subject has appeared on the scene (as it were), bringing with it its necessarily perspectival point of view. Because facts exist in perspective the subject is actually the source and origin of facts about objects. The conclusion is that the subject itself cannot be causally affected by those facts. Thirdly, the subject resembles a river: it is a flux, it never remains the same, it is a constant surpassing or transcending or negating of what *is* in favour of what *is not yet*. It cannot even be defined as coinciding with itself, since its definition is "being what it is not and not being what it is". Sartre argues that this definitional move proves that consciousness is free even from itself.

Sartre says we ought to feel suspicious of people who complain that they cannot help what they do, cannot avoid making certain choices, cannot help having certain attitudes and values. Such people believe that consciousness can be affected by causes, and the attempt to assign causes to subjects involves an impossibility. What might, for objects, be causes of movement, must, for subjects, be something quite different, namely, reasons for choices. (Wittgenstein too draws a distinction between reasons and causes, but it seems unlikely that either philosopher borrowed this thought from the other.)

The meaning of Sartre's famous assertion "for man existence precedes essence" is that a man is free to make himself into the person he wants to be. A man is not like a tree because the features of a tree can be explained in terms of its origins and development. A tree cannot choose to change itself.

# Ethics, Authenticity, Anguish, Bad Faith

In place of a materialistic or deterministic view of the mind, Sartre proposes a theory according to which judgements and actions are not caused, but rather motivated by freely chosen plans or projects. He rejects "Hume's Fork" – a dilemma which forces a choice between saying that human behaviour is consistent, and therefore rule-bound, and therefore caused, and so not free, and saying that it is random, and therefore irrational, and so again not free. Sartre claims that consistent behaviour is evidence of freedom. This view, of course, has important implications for morality. These implications are expounded in *Existentialism and Humanism* (1946).

The basic axiom in Sartre's thinking on ethics is the familiar Nietzschean idea that there are no such things as objective moral laws. Morality is a kind of fiction, and moral judgements are merely a matter of personal commitment and personal choice. Sartre tries to combine this nihilistic position with a positive doctrine of personal responsibility, as follows: he claims that if there are no objective ethical laws, then each individual is responsible, both for sticking to his own moral principles, and for deciding what those principles should be.

It can be objected here that Sartre overlooks the fact that responsibility is an ambiguous notion. There is a sense in which inanimate things can be responsible, as when rains and a high tide are responsible for flood damage in a village. This kind of responsibility is a matter of material origins, and human bodies, clearly, like other animal bodies, are the origins of many changes in the physical world. The other sense of responsibility has to do with calling people to account for their choices and actions, and it presupposes that someone or something has the authority to call to account, to blame or praise, to punish and reward. In a developed legal system the law of the land has at least the power, and many would say the authority, to call people to account for some of the things they do. To those, like Kant, who believe in an internalised but objective moral law it is the moral law itself which calls people to account (as it were). But because Sartre denies the possibility of objective moral law, and rejects the norms of his own society, it seems that he cannot give any meaning to this kind of responsibility. It is equally obvious that he cannot accept a definition of responsibility which merely equates it with material causes.

Putting that problem to one side, let us now consider what Sartre means by authenticity and anguish. Authenticity is the recognition of one's own ontological freedom, the recognition that one is wholly responsible for one's own decisions and beliefs and character. The authentic personality, moreover, accepts responsibility for creating the ethical criteria by which his decisions, beliefs and character are to be judged. (By *whom* they are to be judged is a difficult question.) The authentic individual, having realised his responsibility, then begins to suffer "existential anguish". Some people will attempt to flee from their anguish by pretending that their behaviour has been chosen for them by others, or caused by innate drives or external circumstances, and this flight, this pretence, is a manifestation of inauthenticity. Inauthenticity is much the same as bad faith. To act in bad faith is to act as if you believed yourself to be unfree. Either a man accepts freedom, responsibility and anguish, or he turns away from the anguish into bad faith. The harsh conclusion follows that anyone who has a philosophical position about freedom or about ethics which differs from Sartre's must be an inauthentic person.

Some philosophers have suggested that inauthenticity is a Sartrean equivalent of immorality – after all, bad faith is *bad*. Sartre does in fact adopt a lofty and moralising tone when describing instances of bad faith, but he would never have agreed that he was invoking an objective morality because his existentialism has no room for this concept. He should have avoided the lofty tone; after all, if his theory is correct then bad faith is not a sin but an ontological obfuscation.

# Existentialism and Marxism

The fact that Sartre never joined any political party might have had something to do with his ideas about freedom. On the other hand, he was always politically left wing. He expressed dislike, even hatred, of middle class ideas and attitudes, and from time to time he made admiring remarks about the Soviet Union. On the other hand, as an anti-determinist he naturally rejected Marxist-style economic explanations of human behaviour. In *The Critique of Dialectical Reason* (1960), he deals with certain apparent conflicts between Marxism and existentialism and tries to create an overall explanation of human action which combines elements taken from both systems. He argues, indeed, that existential ontology is needed for the proper understanding of Marx. In pursuit of this theme he claims that Marx's analyses of economics and society have been misunderstood and distorted by many left wing intellectuals, especially insofar as these have ignored Marx's slogan "While history makes man, man also makes his own history". Sartre was one of the first philosophers to draw attention to the comparatively humane and humanistic views to be found in Marx's earlier writings. Supported by the authority of this "early Marx", he points out that the influence on events of human consciousness, of human individuals, cannot be removed from the pages of history, in spite of the efforts of communist theoreticians. Existentialist philosophy, he argues, shows that our actions as subjects are not, and could not be, ultimately governed by where and when we were born, or by the economic conditions we then find ourselves in. On the other hand, he finally admits that many choices are likely to reflect external conditions in some ways and to some extent. Yet although he thus retreats a little way from his earlier views about freedom, he does not take up economic or philosophical or any other kind of determinism. His final position is perhaps something like this:

First, consciousness, the human subject, is necessarily free because it is not an object and cannot be caused to do anything.

Second, the original account of existential freedom seemed to suggest that the subject existed a vacuum. This was a mistake because existential freedom does not require a vacuum.

Third, irrationality is not freedom; on the contrary, freedom involves thinking and reason. Rational consideration of contingent circumstances, including economic circumstances, is necessary for an exercise of existential freedom. Reasoned choices are choices which acknowledge the facts, and the more reasonable a choice is the more free it is.

## Further Reading

In addition to the trilogy of novels discussed in this chapter, Sartre published a number of other works of fiction, including two very well known plays, *The Flies* and *Vicious Circle*. The first of these is a reworking of Aeschylus' *Eumenides* and Euripides' *Orestes*. His most important philosophical work is *Being and Nothingness,* an extremely difficult book. Perhaps an easier text to start on would be the first part of *The Critique of Dialectical Reason*, published as *Search for a Method*. Of the secondary literature, Peter Caws' book *Sartre* can be recommended, as can Iris Murdoch's *Sartre: Romantic Rationalist.*

## Bibliography

P. Caws, *Sartre*, London: Routledge 1984.
I. Murdoch, *Sartre: Romantic Rationalist*, Cambridge: Cambridge University Press 1953.
J.-P. Sartre, *Being and Nothingness*, tr. H. Barnes, London: Routledge 1991.
——*Critique of Dialectical Reason,* tr. Q. Hoare, London: Verso 1991.
——*Existentialism and Humanism*, tr. P. Mairet, London 1947.
——*A Problem of Method*, tr. H. Barnes, London: Routledge 1963.
——*A Sketch for a Theory of the Emotions,*

J.-P. Sartre, *The Transcendence of the Ego*, tr. F. Williams and R. Kirkpatrick, New York 1947.

——*In Camera and Other Plays*, tr. S. Gilbert, Harmondsworth: Penguin 1982.

——*The Flies*, in *Altona and Other Plays*, tr. S. Gilbert, Harmondsworth: Penguin 1981.

——*The Roads to Freedom* (3 vols.), tr. E. Sutton and G. Hopkins, Harmondsworth: Penguin 1982.

# 11 Simone de Beauvoir
## Gill Howie

Simone de Beauvoir (1908-...) was a maverick, an icon of a generation, a novelist, and a philosopher; but most importantly she was the life-long lover of Jean-Paul Sartre. Or so orthodoxy would have it. That de Beauvoir was a woman, and a woman whose book *The Second Sex* caused uproar in every circle, including the intellectual left, doubtless has never biased the reading of her philosophy as merely ancillary to key existentialist texts, and has no bearing on the fact that she is seldom considered to be an interesting thinker...

Whatever the reason philosophers and other intellectuals might have for bypassing her philosophy in order to concentrate on the well-known vignettes of Parisian café life, it is clear that they underestimate the crucially significant development of existentialist thought to be found in *The Ethics of Ambiguity* and *The Second Sex*. Simone de Beauvoir placed the free agent of Sartre's book *Being and Nothingness* into social contexts, showing some of the ways in which external constraints can limit action. In doing so, she took existentialism beyond its philosophic confines into the realms of social and cultural analysis. The theoretical tensions in her work should not lead to a dismissal of de Beauvoir as a careless thinker, but should instead be appraised for what they are, the contradictions and deep entanglements to be found within existentialism itself.

The questions addressed by *The Ethics of Ambiguity* and *The Second Sex* are why, and how, essentially free subjects live unfreely, and what should be done about this. Both texts are to some extent influenced by Marxism. The method of analysis is dialectical, with the human subject at the centre. However, the friction between the influences of Kant, Hegel and Marx results in a conflict between freedom taken as a universal, absolute category, and a notion of unfreedom which is derived from the world of experience. It is this friction and the ensuing tensions which I shall be tracing through the *Ethics* and *The Second Sex*.

## The Ethics of Freedom

The project of writing an ethics was conceived by de Beauvoir as a response to critics who claimed existentialism was nihilistic: that if all were free, if there were no universal truths, then there could be no morality. The *Ethics* is an exposition of how a philosophy of freedom can involve commitment, responsibility and social practice. In *Being and Nothingness* Sartre hints that an individual could undergo a "radical conversion", a conversion from bad faith to authenticity. (*Being and Nothingness* p. 412) The *Ethics* is an elaboration of that process.

"Man is a useless passion" proclaimed Sartre, and this is the first principle of the *Ethics*. By this is meant that consciousness is primarily a lack: it contains nothingness within itself, and is forever reaching beyond to something else. The something else, the object, is therefore necessary for consciousness. At the same time, consciousness, at a pre-reflective level, has a desire for wholeness, for there to be no dependence between self and self, self and object. We desire to unite the Sartrean in-itself and for-itself, so that we can be both subject and object, self-caused; in effect, to be God. But, because of the very nature of consciousness, which is forever reaching out beyond itself, distancing itself from itself, this desire is inevitably frustrated. Herein lies the ambiguity of consciousness from which de Beauvoir develops a necessary ethics.

Because of the distance within, conscious choice itself is made possible. Without freedom of choice there could be no morality, since value, to be value, cannot be determined. From this structural or ontological freedom is derived a second principle, the principle that human freedom is the source of all value. The next step is to argue that, if in freedom we choose to value something, then freedom itself should be taken as the primary value.

In this attempt to derive an ethics from an ontology, it might appear that de Beauvoir is guilty of arguing from is to ought, of committing the so-called naturalistic fallacy. For she seems to be saying that, because of the *fact* that we are structurally free, we should choose to *value* freedom as fundamental. But she circumvents this problem by her account of structural freedom. Such freedom is only realisable in action; and the implication of this is that the fact of free choice is inseparable from the making of a choice, i.e. from evaluation.

But here another question arises. If we accept that ethical meaning erupts in the world because human beings can make choices, and that this is why freedom should be valued, does it follow that all free choices have equal moral worth? According to de Beauvoir, the will to freedom is not the freedom to do anything which one wishes, and it is not a Nietzschean will to power concerned only with strength. At root the will to freedom must always point towards "an open future, by seeking to extend itself by means of the freedom of others." (*Ethics of Ambigiuity*, p. 60)

Once we understand that we are the source of all values, we can joyously partake in the richness of life which is essentially creative. This joy is lived by affirming that it is the very distance in consciousness between self and self, self and other, which produces meaning.

De Beauvoir explicitly rejects nihilism, adventurism, and the stance of the merely passionate individual. The nihilist holds that there is no suprahuman ethical code, no Absolute Truth, but denies both the joyous affirmation and the ensuing responsibility. The adventurer asserts her/his freedom yet refuses any content to his or her own free choices, making the affirmation of freedom into a mere affirmation of self-gratification. Both the adventurer and the nihilist refuse to recognise how necessary otherness is for their sense of self, for self-consciousness. Passionate individuals, on the other hand, by projecting themselves onto objects, accept the necessary relation between objects and the constitution of their subjectivity, but for them, unfortunately, these objects are then seen as Absolute, which again undermines the basically dynamic quality of consciousness.

These three ways of living assume freedom but treat other people as objects to be absorbed and used in projects. In rejecting them de Beauvoir emphasises the essential relation between different consciousnesses: "One can reveal the world only on the basis that it is revealed by other human beings". (*Ethics of Ambiguity*, p. 73) Hence we have discovered another principle entailed by our primary valuing of freedom, the principle that we must necessarily value the freedom of others.

It is not enough to merely accept this principle, not enough to indifferently contemplate the world as though one were removed from it. Such a reflective aesthetic attitude fallaciously separates consciousness from the world. So we reach the principle which advocates action. Action is necessary because meaning and freedom can only be brought into the world through *projects*.

What does it mean to value freedom? De Beauvoir responds to this question with a negative definition of liberty, the freedom from oppression. Individuals are oppressed when they are denied the chance to live their projects, when because of interference their projects cannot be realised. When inanimate objects obstruct the fulfilment of a project this can engender creativity, but obstruction by people appropriates the freedom of others. Because oppression originates in the interdependence of all our wills, it is the responsibility of everyone to challenge it through action. People only submit to oppression through ignorance. If one does not want to be a tyrant, then one must "put the oppressed in the presence of his freedom", one must give the oppressed an opportunity to exercise freedom in rebellion, the first step towards transcending the immediate situation.

Yet if we act according to these maxims it soon becomes clear that some freedoms stand against others. The freedom not to be oppressed is in conflict with the freedom to oppress. De Beauvoir says that each conflict must be evaluated on its own merits, always bearing in mind the general aim of universal emancipation. Given the extreme unlikelihood of a general moral conversion of tyrants, we need to see that a few people (the tyrants) will have to be oppressed. The immorality of this act is diluted by the outrageousness of the acts committed previously by those tyrants. According to de Beauvoir, complicity with oppression, even if through ignorance, amounts to tyranny, and during a struggle for liberation violence against the complicitous is justifiable.

It is in the nature of violent struggle that bodies confront bodies and are reduced to the status of things. Interestingly, de Beauvoir does not shy away from this implication, but instead advocates facing the paradox with honesty and integrity, and accepting, but not glorifying, the violence.

A lone voice does not constitute a struggle for emancipation, and so the individual must look elsewhere for support and strength. Yet de Beauvoir disclaims Fascist and Marxist ideologies alike, maintaining that they converge in their contempt for the individual. That individuals are marshalled into submerging their identities into a group ethos is an attempt to once more deny individual freedom, martyring it for an Absolute; and this also leads to oppression. Exclusively promoting the collectivity promotes a belief in an Absolute, and to justify this from the vantage point of historical materialism is to do as much violence to those inside the group as those outside.

De Beauvoir has a further problem with Marxist ideology. According to some interpretations, historical materialism rests on the theoretical cornerstones of linear causality and determinism, which necessarily run counter to fundamental existentialist tenets. For de Beauvoir, revolt itself refutes a deterministic conception of history by disrupting the continuum. This disruption of the continuum is acknowledged in existentialists' emphasis on the present. For existentialist ethics claims that there are no givens, and hence such an ethics can only suggest the framework within which choices of action should be made. Thus it is argued that actions should not be undertaken for the sake of a future utopia. Although the present is informed by the past, and responsibility should be taken for the outcome of any given action, just as human beings should be treated as ends and not means, every choice must still be firmly situated in the present.

We can reformulate the argument: because the individual is structurally free, at a pre-reflective level s/he desires to be God. Reflectively this desire can be overridden with the valuing of freedom itself. It is logically consistent to take freedom as a primary value and then to universalise it for all consciousness. We can see from this that underlying the *Ethics* is a Kantian prescription to universalise judgements, and that where Kant argues that self-respect and respect for others are mutually entailed, and discoverable by reason, de Beauvoir invokes ontology as a basis for this entailment. She writes "man is free but he finds his law in his very freedom". (*Ethics of Ambiguity*, p. 156) It is this law which enables the *Ethics* to be individualistic without being egoistic or solipsistic.

The ontology of the *Ethics* is a development of the existentialist ontology expressed in *Being and Nothingness*. In that work, subject and subject face one another in hostility, each trying to make an object out of the other, each fighting to reclaim their own subjectivity. This position clearly conflicts with the Kantian prescription to universalise judgements. The solution to the dilemma is found in the recognition that both the self and the other are contingent, i.e. are finite and face death. Consequently the self no longer regards the other with hostility.

Although existentialism aspires to work with a materialist dialectics, it in fact remains idealistic because it postulates ontological freedom as a premise, and situates conflict at a primarily phenomenological level in and between consciousnesses. Idealism informs the attempt to make Kantian practical reason truly practical by giving content to an otherwise empty moral law.

Rejecting the Marxist notions of ideology, reification and false consciousness, de Beauvoir introduced in their place the concept of *mystification*, to explain how people could be beguiled into living in bad faith. This concept is problematic, since existentialism insists that self-consciousness is transparent. Moreover, in denying the importance of history and collective action, while at the same time arguing that no individual salvation is possible, the *Ethics* turns out to be somewhat nihilistic. De Beauvoir herself later criticised the idealism which permeates this work (see *Force of Circumstance*, p. 76), but the tension reflects the attempt made by existentialism to reconcile the claims of ontological freedom with a growing acceptance of the view that consciousness is socially constructed.

The unravelling of this problem can be most clearly witnessed in *The Second Sex*. As an enterprise *The Second Sex* aimed to dissipate myths about the "essentially feminine" by examining justifications for the oppression of women drawn from biology, history and psychoanalysis. Arguing that historical materialism did not sufficiently explain the origins of women's oppression, de Beauvoir placed the Hegelian master/slave dialectic into the context of gender theory.

## Sex, Power and the Narcissistic Woman

"Sexuality" writes de Beauvoir, "has never seemed to us to define a destiny, to furnish in itself the key to human behaviour, but to express the totality of a situation that it only helps to define." (*The Second Sex*, p. 726) The ahistorical and genderised principles of psychoanalysis assume certain givens which then define the living-out of one's life and projects. To be consistent an existentialist must challenge all presuppositions which claim to determine choice, since a belief in determinism aids the flight from authenticity and the slippage into bad faith.

De Beauvoir analyses the relation between the penis as a physical appendage and the phallus as a symbol of power and domination. By doing this, she dismantles Freud's Oedipus Complex and the supposed penis envy suffered by girls. De Beauvoir maintains that the girl does not desire the penis as a physical object, but envies the penis in its phallic function as a symbol, the symbol of all the family and social privileges held by boys and denied to girls.

Male castration fear is explained as a complex which emerges firstly from the penis' symbolic function as the ability to project power into the future, and secondly from the fear of the frustration of that project by a paternal authority figure. On the other hand, the boy is able to project his *alter ego* onto his physical penis, thereby retrieving his integrity by being, for himself, both object and empowered subject. (*The Second Sex*, p. 79) Unfortunately, the girl has perhaps only a doll to fulfil this role, and this results in her making an object of her whole self as other. Because she is refused any true, active engagement with the world, the girl makes herself into a project – she must above all else be desirable. Narcissistically she identifies her mirror image with her ego, and in doing so entrenches her own passivity. This identification spirals into a reliance on the gaze of the other to gratify her narcissistically constructed ego. Her ego relies moreover on the other's look from a position of authority, be it male or god, to regain the transcendence otherwise refused. The hope is thwarted because, in desiring the gaze without conflict, the ego is doomed to passivity and an inability to project itself authentically.

Although it has often been claimed that de Beauvoir was hostile to psychoanalysis, it can be seen that her discussion of its position is a creative critique. She condemns the determinism implicit in Freud's "anatomy is destiny", and makes explicit the fact that his ostensibly unbiased theory of sexuality was actually defined via concepts which legitimised male desire by imprisoning female desire in passivity. Similarly, it is sometimes said that her interpretations of Freud and Jung lack subtlety. Even if that were the case – which can certainly be questioned – her critique of the gender bias of Freudian and Jungian theory remains one of the most powerful on offer. The distinction drawn between the phallus and penis was and is vital for any cultural critique that aspires to a socio-historical understanding of concepts.

The penis helps consciousness to experience itself in an authentic manner, i.e. as both subject and object, and thus enables a psychological development which is more balanced than that of a a woman. It also encourages the male to see himself as a future-oriented creator, in a way which will be explained later. The active principle emanating from the penis, embodied in the symbol of the phallus, is further compounded by the fact that a man lives his sexuality through his penis and in this his erotic pleasure is actively directed towards an other. The woman is dependent on the man for her sexual gratification because coitus requires active participation only from the man. (The missionary position is seen by de Beauvoir as an exemplar of woman's passivity and submission.) The suggestion, later to be echoed by Andrea Dworkin, is that in the very act of penetration the male is the taker and the female the taken. Unfortunately, de Beauvoir's biological arguments seem in conflict with her idea that sexuality is socially constructed, and hence with the related possibility of a non-violating, non-alienating penetration. We can see here a tension between an essentialist assumption – that women are pre-determined by their biology – and her general critique of essentialism.

This tension appears again in the search for the historical juncture at which the penis acquired its phallic significance. With the aid of Hegel's master/slave dialectic, de Beauvoir tries to answer the question "why have men adopted the position of subject, the essential, and women allowed themselves to be made the object, the inessential?" (*The Second Sex*, p. 80) Although she accepts Engels' view that the family structure originally springs from the division of labour and the development of private property, she declares that Engels failed to fully explain why history took that particular trajectory.

Before tools were discovered human beings, according to de Beauvoir, lived "subjectively", unable to objectify themselves. She accepts Engels' thesis that it was by working with tools and dominating nature that men learned to project themselves into the future and came to understand themselves as creators and agents. What she adds is an analysis of why it was that men, and not women, manipulated tools.

She argues that while men were able to project and invest themselves into the land and so identify with something outside the self, women remained enslaved to the species. At the mercy of their bodily functions, pregnancy and menstruation, women were dependent on the male hunters. Physically weaker than the male, women were unable to manipulate and dominate the world quite so determinately. This meant that men came to think in a more extended, future-oriented fashion than women, a fashion which could transcend immediately given situations. Because of this the physical penis became the symbol of activity, the phallus. By chancing their lives in the battle for life, men transcended contingencies, by choosing war over cowardice they experienced themselves as value-creating subjects. Women on the other hand did not chance their lives freely for any goal other than the survival of themselves and their offspring. The only battle with death which they encountered was demanded by their biological destiny, childbirth. The phallic man began to see woman from the vantage point of his own project; she came to be viewed as an inessential object to be determined and controlled.

Man's tendency to dominate rather than to cooperate stems ultimately from the imperialistic nature of consciousness. Needing an other's consciousness for a sense of self, imperialistic consciousness faces this other and necessary being with hostility. Ontological hostility makes an oppressive and dominating social formation more likely than cooperative organisation. De Beauvoir explains the historical development away from communally owned property to private ownership in a similar manner, i.e. in terms of ontology. (*The Second Sex*, pp. 87f.) Although attracted to certain features of dialectical materialism, especially its vision of human being as essentially creative and historical, de Beauvoir finally rejects Marxism because of what she regards as its crude economic reductionism. She also rejects the idea that all women can be seen as one class. She argues that class implies a specific economic relation, with the entailed possibility of transcending immediate situations by virtue of productive relations. Woman, reduced to her productive capacity of child bearing, does not have the same opportunity to objectify herself through her labour as a worker or a slave, and consequently does not have their opportunities for revolution. De Beauvoir also rejects the Marxist analysis of ideology because that analysis suggests that the experiences of alienation and hostility are not ontologically necessary but are historical phenomena, deriving from specific socio-economic organisations. Her own gender specific anthropology reinscribes patriarchal prejudices in a feminist critique.

However, as we have already seen, the ontological and historical conceptual frameworks adopted by de Beauvoir in order to explain the particular experiences of women tend to produce tensions in her analysis. One such point of tension lies in her critique of the universal category "woman". This universal category, fabricated by men to bolster their own sense of self was, according to de Beauvoir, a myth operating in the interests of the "ruling class". (*The Second Sex*, p. 285) The content ascribed to the universal concept "woman" began to take form when natural creation in the vegetable world lost its mysterious quality with the advent of agricultural tools. Because women as procreators were believed to be close to nature they would seem to be ideally suited to being perceived as the new and likewise mysterious realm. De Beauvoir first explained this concept of woman as mysterious in terms of ontological and biological necessity, so that her subsequent historical exegesis is compromised. Unaware of this, however, she gives a cogent historical and psychological analysis of the development and ideological function of the concept of "womanhood".

The collective myth of womanhood is most obviously propagated in literature. Since woman is more closely related to nature she is taken to incarnate it. The Romantic connection between nature and the irrational is poeticised into woman as other. Poetically described as restoring peace and harmony, woman is doomed to an immanence masked as privilege. It is through woman, the other, that men discover and fulfil themselves, but the woman's otherness is already defined in terms of inessentiality and passivity. Into the category "woman" men project their fears, because her supposed closeness to nature signifies flesh and mortality. Men's ambivalence towards women emanates from their definition of them as a "fixed image of animal destiny"; in this image men confront their own fragility.

The concept "woman" is thus constructed in terms of artifice, an eroticism at once natural yet constructed for male desire. Woman is both truth and non-truth. Yet the universal category "woman" is applied to real people who have real experiences. Affecting respectability in the public sphere, men assert the sanctity of chastity, enshrining its value in law. In the private sphere men find themselves transgressing their own code, yet expecting women to abide by it: consequently the "moral" man forces women into "immorality". The public anti-abortionist, for example, privately insists that his pregnant mistress aborts. (*The Second Sex*, p. 509) Although women suffer under these values, they rarely confront such contradictions, for not only do they lack the opportunity and education, but their narcissistically constructed egos make them complicitous with the male authority which categorises them as immoral. Men are, of course, aware that women experience these contradictions and inauthenticities, and so they fear women's knowledge. But women, by their passivity, enable immorality to be continually masked as morality, and this means that they have to deny the truth of their own experience, while continuing to feel the contradictions in "wounded flesh". (*The Second Sex*, p. 509)

As in Sartre's dialectic between self and other, such hostility and bad faith is self-defeating. The self requires free recognition from a respected other. Even when she acts inauthentically, a woman cannot completely suppress her subjectivity, and so she is condemned to duplicity. Men demand, however, that women show themselves occasionally to be the free subjects that they in fact are. In oppressing, the oppressors oppress themselves. To justify their sense of self, men need women to be independent.

De Beauvoir herself later criticised the philosophical idealism which pervades *The Second Sex*. (*Force of Circumstance*, p. 202) The presentation of the opposition between self and other as ontological contradicts the view that such conflict is historical and contingent. This difficulty concerning the relationship between ontological and historical explanation infuses existentialism in general. It can be seen very clearly in Sartre's attempt to mesh Marxism with existentialism in his *Critique of Dialectical Reason*.

Extending ontological status both to the categories of self and other, and to the dialectic between them, de Beauvoir then explains these concepts in terms of gender theory, setting up parallels between activity as the masculine principle and passivity as the feminine. Because men have the role of subject, denied to women, authentic actions become imbued with "masculine values". What is valued is not only activity but also a specific style of thinking which gives priority to the "rational" over the "irrational", and to careers over child rearing. This style accepts a public/private distinction and privileges the former over the latter. Moreover, the categorisation is predicated on a basic heterosexism. The lesbian, for instance, identifies with the active principle of masculinity, which results in her preying on a passive female body.

The autonomy of the individual is basic to existentialism, and intrinsic to this is the idea of a freely transcending consciousness. Unfortunately, this leads de Beauvoir to regard the female body, together with menstruation and procreation with some distaste. For she believes that a woman's body somehow impedes the actualisation of a freely transcending consciousness. Her view of the female body stems from the Cartesianism implicit in existentialism: that is, the Cartesian separation of mind from body, which in turn involves the idea that the mind controls and dominates the body. Here we can see how a metaphysics can incorporate uncritical social prejudices.

Another criticism of existentialism that might be applicable to de Beauvoir is that it underestimates the importance of language in the construction of consciousness. The lack of linguistic analysis strikes the reader of the 1990s as a void. De Beauvoir's crucial work on the representation of women in literature, for instance, is incomplete insofar as it lacks any analysis of other cultural imagings such as pornography. Nevertheless the time at which she was writing should be born in mind, and the challenges that *The Second Sex* raised to psychoanalytic and all other genderised theory (much to the chagrin of her contemporaries – see *Force of Circumstance* pp. 196–203) should not be underestimated.

De Beauvoir also deals with the question of how to change the world. She writes "In order to change the face of the world, it is first necessary to be firmly anchored in it, but the women who are firmly rooted in society are those who are in subjection to it." (*The Second Sex*, p. 162) Women are determined according to how their bodies are controlled, this control delimiting their relations with the external world. For a woman to be able to transcend contingent circumstances, she must break free from her particular objectification and, as an authentic subject, project herself into the future. Liberation from controls which hamper projection has to be a collective enterprise, so women need to learn how to cooperate with each other. The early close bonding of girls seen in many societies, including our own, is a bonding of passive objects which is transformed by society into competition for the male gaze. Women, then, need to reassess how they relate to other women.

De Beauvoir emphasises the importance of economics in the social structure, yet also stresses the need to alter the superstructure, i.e. the moral, social, and cultural arena; and here she presents certain "transitional demands". Girls and boys should have the same educational opportunities and so the same horizons. Erotic liberty necessitates voluntary maternity, including abortion on demand, free contraception, pregnancy leave, and the erasing of the stigmas attached to illegitimacy. The marriage contract should be rejected in favour of free arrangements which can be broken at will by those involved. The hope is that, if these conditions were fulfiled, reciprocity between men and women could be based on mutual recognition and an authenticity which would enrich all human relations.

De Beauvoir situates all women as object in the same way, and because of this she tends to ignore the particularity of class and race experiences. Although she acknowledges the benefits of democratic socialism, she does not explore the possible connection between an economic system based on the exchange of objects and the nature of the subject/object interaction. On the other hand, she does discuss the links between the way certain economic and social organisations enable men to dominate nature, and the association of nature with femininity, links which possibly provide a kind of rationale for the domination of women by men.

# Conclusion

In many ways de Beauvoir's concerns prefigure those of today. After Nietzsche's critique of Enlightenment thought, and his heralding of the "death of God", philosophy was left with the problem of explaining value. De Beauvoir's antagonism to certain universal categories such as "totality", "woman", and to the supposedly linear movement of history towards a certain Utopia, are prevalent themes in continental "post-modern" philosophy. Her analysis of the concept of "woman" as illusion, mask and non-truth has been taken up from its Nietzschean roots and reworked by Derrida and Deleuze, who treat it as an indication of a general truth of existence, that of becoming.

The tensions in de Beauvoir's works are those of a non-materialist philosophy attempting to incorporate materialist theses. In the process of attempted incorporation, the underlying theoretical heritage of the work is uncovered. In a way, such tensions are what are most interesting about existentialism itself, for they may explain why existentialism's (patri)lineage prevented it from achieving its political and practical aspirations. These tensions are also permanent nowadays, because modern political philosophy is still desperately seeking a new way to conceive value.

Many feminist critiques have developed out of de Beauvoir's explication of psychoanalysis and her rich and vital cultural analysis. Her analysis of "woman" as constructed, as object to the male subject, and as suffering under passivity, is probably still an accurate description of the general relation between men and women.

Finally, since it is often the case that the tensions within an author's work are its most valuable, most informative aspects, de Beauvoir's philosophy deserves to be "canonised" – even if only in the interests of accurate historiography.

# Further Reading

Simone de Beauvoir wrote an autobiography, several novels, and a memoir of her mother, as well as more academic works. *The Second Sex* is doubtless her most famous book, and perhaps the most philosophically important. However, as has been suggested in this chapter, *The Ethics of Ambiguity* is almost equally significant. The following books about de Beauvoir, and about feminism, can be recommended: Cixous and Clement, *The Newly Born Woman*, Heath, *Simone de Beauvoir*, Forster and Sutton, *Daughters of de Beauvoir,* and Whitmarsh, *Simone de Beauvoir and the Limits of Commitment.*

# Bibliography

H. Cixous and C. Clement, *The Newly Born Woman*, tr. B. Wing, Minneapolis: University of Minnesota Press 1986)

Simone de Beauvoir, *The Ethics of Ambiguity*, tr. B. Frechtman, London: Citadel Press 1976.

—— *The Second Sex*, tr. J. Cape, Picador Classics, 1988.

—— *Force of Circumstance* tr. R. Howard, Harmondsworth: Penguin 1968.

P. Forster and I. Sutton (eds.), *Daughters of de Beauvoir,* London: Women's Press 1989.

J. Heath, *Simone de Beauvoir*, London: Harvester Wheatsheaf 1989.

J.-P. Sartre, *Being and Nothingness*, tr. H. Barnes, New York 1956.

A. Whitmarsh, *Simone de Beauvoir and the Limits of Commitment*, Cambridge: Cambridge University Press 1981.

# 12 Jürgen Habermas
## Nicholas Davey

Born in 1929, Jurgen Habermas has become the most notable and independent-minded successor to the Frankfurt School of philosophy, which attempted to remould Marxism into and incisive ideological and cultural criticism. In 1956 Habermas joined Adorno at Frankfurt University, and, since 1964, has occupied the chair of philosophy there. Over the last twenty years, Habermas has extended his concern with Marxist thought as a critique of ideology into a broad preoccupation with those cultural and political factors which distort and disrupt human communication. His most distinctive contribution to contemporary European philosophy lies in his argument that perfectible structures of reasoning, as well as cumulatively liberating insights into truth, are already within our possession. They are not grounded in, or reflections of, an alleged external reality, but emanate from those socially grounded discourses that constitute our "lifeworld". It is important to note that most of his most important work takes the form of debates with other philosophers. Examples of such debates will be discussed later in this chapter.

## Introduction: A Critical Context

Motivated by a conviction that untruth, whether political or personal, is synonymous with repression, Jürgen Habermas has emerged as one of the late twentieth century's greatest philosophical warriors. Battling and also embattled, he has been involved in many of the formative debates of the current epoch. From the attempts of critical theory to free Marxist thought from stalinist readings, to opposing the nihilistic denunciations of deconstructive thought, Habermas has been instrumental in putting the case for the emancipatory value of truth and the ideal of undistorted communication. For the Anglo-Saxon reader Habermas' thought requires a slight adjustment of expectations. The wide range of his philosophical engagement reflects the passion for public philosophical debate in twentieth century Germany: more importantly, it is an indication of Habermas' opposition to the reductionist thought systems frequently associated with some German philosophy. Habermas acknowledges a great affinity to the Socratic conception of philosophy as open discourse, and so, as with the unexpected conversational twist, his works contain brave changes of

mind. His search for debate, and openness to criticism, express his conviction that intelligent controversy, full of conflict and contradiction,
realises unforeseen potentialities within an argument. Habermas embraces
such controversy because of his belief in the liberating capacities of sound
reasoning.

The following sections consider the various phases of Habermas'
thought, but exegetical convenience must not be mistaken for actuality.
His thinking is not so much marked by distinct transitions as by a bringing forward of one or another of a cluster of related themes that bind his
arguments together. These motifs include a resistance to scientific, political and philosophical attempts to monopolise knowledge and truth, a passionate belief in open and undistorted communication as a means to truth,
and the conviction that vigilant criticism of untruth offers the only route
to an intellectually open and politically non-repressive society.

It is neither an unjust nor an uncommon fate for proponents of modernism (the post-eighteenth century belief in the necessity of achieving a
radical break from the past to enhance the progressive nature of history,
knowledge and truth) to emerge as radical traditionalists. Although
Habermas' early association with Marxist critical theory placed him on
the left wing of the student debates of the 1960's, critical theory represented for many (including Habermas) a link with the nineteenth century
German philosophical and cultural tradition which the Nazi movement
had violently severed. Somewhat paradoxically, the historical scholarship
of the "radical" Habermas has placed the thought of Schelling (1775-
1854) and Fichte (1762-1814) back on the German philosophical agenda.
Furthermore, both his association with critical theory and his public rejection of the thought of Heidegger misleadingly suggest a gulf between
Habermas' own critical stance and that of philosophical hermeneutics, the
philosophy of interpretation. Once the issues which adversarial debate
exaggerates are suspended, certain parallels emerge. Thus, Habermas
shares Heidegger's disquiet about the increasing dominance of technical
reasoning. Both seek an openness to truth, although Habermas regards
this as a function of discourse while Heidegger sees it as a condition of
Being. We are probably too close to these debates to accept the possibility
that the thought of Habermas and Heidegger represent closely related
chords within the polyphony of German philosophical tradition.

# Truth Revealed: Habermas and Critical Theory

Although he warns us not to dwell on his connections with Adorno, critical theory unquestionably nurtured Habermas' convictions concerning the

emancipatory powers of reason. Critical theory (also known as the Frankfurt School) had two historical phases. The first began with the founding of the Institute of Social Research at Frankfurt in 1928, its membership including Horkheimer, Fromm, Loewenthal, Marcuse, and, later, Adorno. All believed in the potential of Marxist thought as a vehicle for genuine social change rather than as an apologetics for social control. The rise of Hitler dispersed the Institute, and it was in American exile that Adorno and Horkheimer were to write the seminal text of critical theory, *The Dialectic of Enlightenment* (1947), a book which was to have a lasting influence upon Habermas.

Marxism is a variant of Hegel's philosophy of identity: a subject (mankind) must become estranged from itself in order to know itself. Marx's teleological framework commences with an abstract notion of mankind as possibility, containing within itself its as yet unrealised creative potential, to be unlocked only by the alienating process of labour. The production of means necessary for survival forces individuals to see their work not as self-expression but as the alienating manufacture of commodities. Only by taking on and overcoming the conflicts of the commodity market can individuals re-possess the products of their labour as the concrete realisations of their inner creative potential. Although the failure the American labour movement and Stalin's perversion of the Russian revolution convinced Adorno and Horkheimer of the political redundancy of Marxist orthodoxy, they retained the Marxist notion of truth as a yet-to-be-realised historical situation in which mankind becomes what it truly is. It provides an ideal norm, facilitating both a critique of deviations from that norm, and critical examination of social and political factors which mask the truth. Since the ability of an individual to realise his creative potential is dependent upon the extent of social emancipation, ideological criticism cannot be dissociated from social and political critique. In its critical and emancipatory capacities, Habermas' ideal of undistorted communication is a child of this Marxist lineage.

In *The Dialectic of Enlightenment*, Adorno and Horkheimer shift the centre of gravity of Marxist criticism from labour to human rationality. Repression is not simply political but a symptom of a certain mode of reasoning. The historical corollary of western rationalism's scientific domination of nature is the suppression of individuality. The realisation of a technically organised society appears to involve the conformity of the individual. *The Dialectic of Enlightenment* offers a nightmare vision of an advanced capitalist society driven by a manic scientific rationalism which tramples on human beings and on the delicate life-worlds of High Amazonia and Baluchistan. One of Habermas' achievements is to shy away from such pessimism and suggest that rational discourse can itself democratise the totalising tendencies of unchecked rationalism.

In the 1960's *The Dialectic of Enlightenment* attained the status of a classic, presaged not only by the return of its authors to Germany but also by the growth of the German student movement, a movement which was furious about how the "German economic miracle" had been used to stifle criticism of the Nazi past. The book was received as an exemplary critique of scientific positivism's hidden authoritarianism. It can also be seen as belonging to a long line of texts dealing with the methodological disputes about and between the natural and human sciences. Horkheimer and Adorno were not concerned to argue for an independent methodology for the humanities (that they assumed), but to defend the humanities against the tendency of technological thinking to universalise itself as the only form of reasoning. Husserl, who had an early influence on Adorno, dealt with parallel themes in his *Crisis of the European Sciences* (1937).

In 1956 Habermas joined Adorno at Frankfurt, and quickly showed his independence by expressing his belief that Adorno's cultural pessimism was itself symptomatic of the estrangement brought about by the cultural dominance of technical thinking. Nevertheless, critical theory undoubtedly provides the navigational framework for Habermas' own philosophical Odyssey. From it he takes the Hegelian equation of reason and freedom, the notion of human discourse as emancipatory, an acute sense of historical detail, and a type of ideological critique. His essay "Between Philosophy and Science: Marxism as Critique" is an apt monument both to his debt to, and to his attempt to surpass, critical theory. In it he argues that, in order to rework Marxist economic theory as a critical theory of history which can "anticipate mankind's elevation to freedom", we must first undertake "to understand Marx better than he understood himself". (*Theory and Practice*, p. 212)

## Positivism and the Rationalisation of Truth

One of the unanswered questions in twentieth century European thought must surely be why the Frankfurt School exhibited such animosity towards Viennese logical positivism, many of whose central spokesmen were close to socialism. The reason probably lies in the fact that logical positivism was wedded to a reductionist materialism, indicative of the repressive universalising tendencies of technical rationality. For Habermas, positivism becomes a philosophical justification for the social powers of "rationalisation". In *Knowledge and Human Interests* he contends that positivism stands and falls with the principle of scientism... The meaning of knowledge is defined by what the sciences do, and can thus be adequately explicated through the methodological analysis of scientific procedures. Any epistemology that transcends the framework of methodology as such now succumbs to the sentence of extravagance and meaninglessness that it once passed on metaphysics. (*Knowledge and Human Interests*, p. 67)

In a seminar held at the University of Tübingen in 1961, Habermas tackled Hans Albert on the grounds that Albert assumed scientific reasoning to be the sole model for all rationality. The basic issue was the question: can reason be tied to questions of social and political freedom? In his papers "The Analytical Theory of Science and Dialectics" (1963) and "A Positivistically Bisected Rationalism" (1964), Habermas argues that positivism is characterised by a methodological monism, that science claims to provide the methodological norm for all other non-scientific disciplines, and that it not only hypostasises "facts" but turns causal explanation into an inviolable given. His ripostes are telling. Like Feyerabend and Kuhn, he disputes both the existence of a single scientific method and the assumption that the paradigm of scientific reasoning serves as the model for all types of questions and answers:

decisions relevant in practical life, whether they consist in the acceptance of principles, in the choice of a life-historical outline or on the choice of an enemy, can never be replaced or rationalised through scientific calculation alone. (Adey and Frisby, *The Positivist Dispute in German Sociology*, p. 146)

The elimination of ethical questions from scientific thinking implies a technological world purged of all thought about purpose, value and meaning. Echoing Husserl's and Heidegger's analyses of cognitive prejudices, those implicit pre-conceptions that shape the manner of our knowing, Habermas argues that the social legitimation of science depends on its translation into languages other than its own: "the advances of the exact sciences rest to a large extent upon translating traditional (scientific) questions into a new language", that is, into the language of the everyday lifeworld. (*The Positivist Dispute in German Sociology*, p. 224) The explanatory procedures and standards of science are not inviolable givens but are open to critical debate. Habermas suggests that an openness to discussion of standards of scientific practice would not only allow for the improvement of such practices, but would widen the franchise of their rational consensus. But as long as science remains positivistically oriented, its view of its own laws as absolute reduces the possibility of rational perfectibility and restricts the attainment of a much wider consensus. It is a closed system, whereas critical discourse is expansive. However, as we shall see, although Habermas uses hermeneutic insights to expose the historical contingency of scientific practice, he is also prepared to criticise hermeneutics for an analogously one-sided manipulation of knowledge.

## Cultural Tradition as a Distorter of Truth: the Critique of Hermeneutics

Habermas insists that not just scientific, but all cultural and historical discourse is underwritten by key theoretical commitments, or what he terms "interests", and claims that the task of criticism is to bring them to light. He endeavours to reveal the extent to which we, as cognitive agents, are implicitly involved in the formation of our knowledge frameworks. "Truth", "reality" and "fact" are not unquestioned givens but human constructions, the product of distinct interests and discourses. Habermas' negative reaction to Gadamer's invocation of the authority of tradition was thus almost inevitable.

When, in 1960, Gadamer published his monumental *Truth and Method*, Habermas was invited to review it, and the resulting exchange of essays has fuelled an intense and long-lasting philosophical debate. By revitalising the philosophical credentials of tradition, Gadamer's argument counters the impact of the Enlightenment on twentieth century thought, directly challenging Habermas whose debt to the Enlightenment is manifest. Though Habermas and others criticised the rationalistic bias against sensuality in the post-Cartesian tradition, they were profoundly indebted to the Enlightenment conviction that either God or nature endowed all humanity with the power to reason clearly. Thus the question arises as to why mankind has manifestly failed to live up to its endowment. For Kant the "perpetual peace" of "men living together" was prevented by historical custom, institutionalised religion and cultural superstition. The Enlightenment provided Critical Theory with the notion of a yet to be realised attainment of a free community of rational beings, which could serve as an evaluative norm for historical and ideological critique. Any invocation of the authority of tradition thus cuts at the modernist, future-oriented roots of Habermas' outlook.

Habermas and Gadamer both agree that there are no truths or validating grounds which stand outside socio-historical circumstance, or which can externally legitimise our various cognitive perspectives. The latter are formed by our "thrownness", that is, by our being placed in a specific cultural-linguistic situation (or "horizon"). The inherited parameters of our cultural placement do not so much determine what we do as serve as the enabling conditions of our enterprises. What concerns Habermas is Gadamer's *acquiescence* to the givenness of tradition, and his failure to offer a critique of the ways in which traditions can distort and limit any discussion of their own norms. In certain respects the difference between the two thinkers is one of degree, for both assert the intrinsic rationality of historical and cultural discourses and oppose any monopolisation of knowledge by technological reasoning. What particularly concerns Gadamer is that the aggrandisement of scientific rationality devalues both the historically transmitted insights of the humanities, and the ethical and legal foundations of our culture. Habermas does not disagree, but he wishes to go further than merely reasserting the presence of traditional wisdoms against the influence of technical rationality. He insists that the claims of tradition be matched against a truth criterion which, once established, will enable us to rationally endorse and extend the tradition that houses them.

Gadamer's insistence that the truth claims of tradition cannot be externally legitimated leaves his philosophy open to the charge that it cannot distinguish between authentic and ideologically distorted traditions. Aware of the way in which German philosophy had been corrupted by Nazism, Habermas is suspicious of historically transmitted material. Thus he argues that if

> the understanding of meaning [in tradition] is not to remain... indifferent towards the idea of truth then we have to anticipate... the concept of a kind of truth which measures itself on an idealised consensus achieved in unlimited communication free from force. ("The Hermeneutic Claim to Universality", p. 206)

"Truth", he contends, "is that characteristic compulsion towards unforced universal recognition; the latter [being] tied to an ideal speech situation, i.e. a form of life which makes possible unforced universal agreement." (HC p. 207) Here Habermas moves towards what will become one of his most powerful suggestions: that which validates the procedures and content of a discourse as truthful is not metaphysically or ontologically distinct from the discourse, but emerges historically from within it. Thus, once questions of the truth claims of a tradition are raised, the participants in that tradition no longer remain passively subject to its received authority, but are invited to rationally reappropriate it, and, through criticism, extend its claims. Reflective critique and the struggle for universal consensus thus become the vehicle through which a cultural tradition might revitalise and cleanse itself of ideological distortion.

In the debates between Gadamer and Habermas, the fundamental point that appears to disturb Habermas is that, through Gadamer's hermeneutics is based on the model of conversational understanding, for Gadamer the revelation of meaning remains essentially a personal experience, despite all its objective preconditions. Habermas is more concerned with the critical legitimation and reincorporation of personal experience into the socially established norms of a discourse. Only then can the participants in discourse rationally determine what distorts its underlying consensus.

## Truth, Knowledge and Human Interests

Habermas' 1968 book *Knowledge and Human Interests* represents a comprehensive consolidation of the primary motifs that governed his critique of both positivism and hermeneutics. The text attempts a thorough historical and analytical account of positivistic undercurrents in European post-Enlightenment philosophy, and then proposes an emancipatory counter-position.

In *Knowledge and Human Interests*, Habermas is concerned to undermine the post-Cartesian philosophy of consciousness, with its emphasis on what falls within the purview of the knowing subject, and also the Kantian notion of the known world being spun out of the activities of a supposedly transcendent subject. Habermas counters this latter idea with the statement that "the achievements of the transcendental subject have their basis in the natural history of the human species". (*Knowledge and Human Interests*, p. 312) The framework of knowledge does not come from a universal capacity that only permits us to think in a certain way, but springs from our concrete circumstances. Yet Habermas does not wed himself to a simple natural determinism of the kind which would suggest that the form our knowledge takes is a survival mechanism. What "may appear as naked survival is always in its roots a historical phenomenon... [subject] to what a society intends for itself as the good life". Not only does this suggest that knowledge has a social origin, but it also displays a manoeuvre characteristic of Habermas: the introduction of the concept of social mediation immediately suggests the possibility of rational discourse, which in turn allows the participants the opportunity to revise the norms and assumptions underwriting any consensus. If discussion about the underwriting assumptions of knowledge is possible, it is also possible to anticipate more comprehensive assumptions. Thus, for Habermas, the anticipation of more adequate and more open foundations for discourse is built into the notion of rational criticism. Such criticism possesses an intrinsic discursive logic, which impels it towards an open and enlightened stance.

Another theme is that knowledge serves certain interests, which transcend the concern for mere self-preservation. (*Knowledge and Human Interests*, p. 313) Three such interests are identified. Firstly, Habermas writes: "Empirical-analytic sciences disclose reality insofar as it appears within the behavioural system of instrumental action... they grasp reality with regard to technical control". (*Knowledge and Human Interests*, p. 195) Secondly, Habermas suggests that, while scientific reasoning is guided by an interest in domination, social and cultural studies, in contrast, are governed by the interest of communicative exchange. This interest, which he also refers to as "practical concern", dwells not on control but on "knowing how to go on" within a given cultural practice. "Whereas empirical-analytic methods aim at disclosing and comprehending reality under the... viewpoint of possible control, hermeneutic methods aim at maintaining the intersubjectivity of mutual understanding." (KI p. 176) There are two assumptions here: one is that cultural studies deal with the existential exchange of life-possibilities, and the other is that these subjects strive to maintain the means to such an end, i.e. the maintenance of "unconstrained consensus and open subjectivity" in which unforced agreement and non-violent recognition in and between cultural communities become possible. The emphasis is both on keeping established channels of communication free from distortion, and on increasing the scope of their rational franchise.

The third interest is that of "self-reflection". This releases the subject from dependence on hypostasised powers, and is determined by an emancipatory cognitive interest; cultural studies share this interest with philosophy. Self-reflection entails an understanding of the process of self-formation, which, according to Habermas, is inseparable from understanding the process of community formation; thus he concludes that understanding self-formation is the same thing as understanding the development of social autonomy and responsibility. It is our mutual social practices which shape us. Habermas argues, moreover, that, insofar as we are socially formed persons, we have a responsibility for the future development of the processes which have shaped us in the past. This emancipatory kind of knowledge not only enables us to return to ourselves as ourselves, but to do so with no motive other than the desire to acquire such knowledge for its own sake.

Habermas thus makes three claims about the interests which constitute knowledge, and, taken together, they have a complex thrust. Unlike positivism, this position emphasises the multi-dimensionality of human knowledge. Like all hermeneutic thinking, Habermas' thought is concerned to prevent one such interest from silencing the others. *Knowledge and Human Interests* reveals Habermas' conviction that the social environment will be dominated by the particular interests of technical reasoning, unless technology is made answerable to questions about its meaning and purpose. Discursive reasoning has a universalising capacity; moreover, every discourse presupposes an ideal of non-coercive, undistorted communication. "Truth is... unforced universal recognition... tied to an ideal speech situation, i.e. a form of life which makes possible unforced universal agreement." (*Knowledge and Human Interests*, p. 206)

The appeal to an undistorted truth principle provides Habermas with a truth criterion characteristic of critical theory. The claim that unconstrained consensus is possible implies the possibility of a non-partisan cognitive interest, and this non-partisan interest will be a norm against which other truth claims can be assessed. However, this appeal is just as close to Kant as it is to critical theory. Just as Kant believed that participation in the disinterested sphere of aesthetic judgements would make people more aware of their implicit communality of feeling, so too Habermas hopes that participation in rational discourse will establish a universalising bond based on understanding.

## The Truth Within: Revealing Communications

In many ways *Knowledge and Human Interests* is an essential prolegomenon to *The Theory of Communicative Action*. This latter book confronts several of the criticisms made against the earlier volume.

Among the problems dealt with are the almost transcendental status attributed to cognitive interests, and the question as to whether Habermas' vision of emancipatory discourse is anything more than his own authoritarian idea about what should count as truth. Habermas energetically resists these charges by building a theory of communicative action. This theory is based partly on a consideration of the nature of the cognitive interests of cultural understanding, and partly on his reflections upon the internal truth presuppositions of linguistic practices.

*The Theory of Communicative Action* marks Habermas' turn towards language. However, rather than following Heidegger and Gadamer, who honour language as "a space through which Being discloses itself", Habermas develops the Anglo-American concept of the speech act. Yet, although he is mainly concerned with the criteria of linguistic competence and with the validity claims which linguistic practices themselves generate, his implicit motives are not dissimilar from Gadamer's. He is preoccupied, not with the functioning of linguistic practices *per se*, but rather with what the well-functioning of such practices facilitates, namely, the emergence of an undistorted form of communication. Revolutionary social change is no longer seen as a product of political economy, but as a realisable potential enabled by the linguistic nature of human beings. This linguistic turn has other, distinct, philosophical advantages.

The examination of linguistic practices reveals that cognitive interests are not transcendental presuppositions, in the Kantian sense, but dispositions which, as language speakers, we are already acquainted with. In other words, we have a "pre-theoretical interest" which underwrites, and is generated by, the languages we speak. Moreover, the linguistic turn, and its unavoidable involvement with the social, offers a riposte to those who criticised Habermas' project as subjective and authoritarian. For his conception of a collectively established validity procedure, occurring within the modes of communicative reasoning, is actually part of his attempt to escape from the tradition of subject-centred philosophy: a tradition which dominated European philosophy from Descartes to Nietzsche and beyond. Habermas is not unsympathetic to the deconstruction of metaphysics as other-worldly wishful thinking, but he resists the nihilistic conclusions of post-Nietzschean thought. Whereas Nietzsche's "will to truth" impales itself on its own premises when it discovers that all truth claims are declarations of perspectival bias, Habermas insists that it is precisely when the universal claims of rationalism are seen to collapse into the subjectivism of a particular interest that new, socially established, parameters for intersubjective truth claims can emerge. For Nietzsche, the discovery of subjective interests destroys the possibility of objective knowledge, but for Habermas it is exactly that discovery, i.e. the recognition that technical and hermeneutic knowledge is only possible on the basis of such interests, which establishes the possibility of objective and reflective knowledge. Nietzsche thinks that truth is a matter of correspondence with reality, and therefore assumes that the absence of such correspondence shows that knowledge claims are nothing but the projection of specific wills to power. For Habermas, on the other hand, truth is not a supposed external to discussion and reasoning, but is produced in and through them; hence he is not embarrassed by the absence of any supposed correspondence.

Habermas' linguistic turn pays handsome dividends. Because it places linguistic and social interaction at the centre of knowledge claims, it can avoid the charge of subjectivism and the nihilist *denouement* of

Nietzsche's thinking. The linguistic foundation of his argument also escapes the criticism that his appeal to emancipatory truth is a modernist fiction created for the sake of his political motivations. This is because objectivity emerges as a consequence of understanding *any* linguistically communicated meaning. Habermas argues that understanding speech is not a matter of two or more interlocutors sharing the same experiences, nor is it a matter of their building the same associations around specific phrases. Grasping the point of what another is saying occurs independently of expressive or biological idiosyncrasies. This argument permits a reformulation of the ideal speech situation. If it is in the nature of discourse to generate intersubjective meanings over and above the biographical idiosyncrasies of particular interlocutors, then it is possible to arrive at an understanding of such meanings by means of sound reasoning. Emancipatory interest is thus intrinsic to, and expands from within, actual discussions.

Habermas' concern with language is not with its semantic or syntactic structure, but with what emerges from communicative action. He wants to disclose the pre-theoretical procedures which enable understanding. It is as if he is probing the conditions which underwrite a speaker's understanding of "how to go on", and trying to grasp the nature of the shared pretheoretical structures which facilitate such "goings on". It is these structures which, according to Habermas, generate of themselves the universalising and consensus-promoting structures of rationality and acceptability in social discourse. Accordingly, he talks a good deal about Chomsky's linguistic theories and Piaget's examination of cognitive development in children. He sees in these researches exemplars of how discourse generates its own consensus-promoting critical norms. Habermas believes that the theory of communicative action proves that emancipatory interest is far from relativistic, since it emerges from the structures of open discourse itself. We are not exactly spoken to by language (as Heidegger and Gadamer contend), but rather we are impelled by it towards an open-ended logic of critique and consensus. Habermas extends Gadamer's conviction that "whoever has language, has the world", the conviction that possession of one's own linguistic horizon gives, through translation, an access to all such horizons. He argues that whoever speaks a language implicitly belongs to, and, in the very act of speaking, aspires to, a universal community grounded on openness, reasonableness and freely attained consensus, in which all will speak as one. The suggestion that this aspiration is neither forced on us, nor the result of happenstance, but springs forth from our actual linguistic practices – that it is something that we actually "talk ourselves into" – is Habermas' profoundest contribution to contemporary European thought.

# Truth Besieged: In Defence of Modernity

It is Habermas' cardinal conviction that "modernity is an unfinished project". (*The Philosophical Discourse of Modernity*, p. ix) Its ideal of an emancipated life-world freed of coercion is something that we can only hope to approximate. Habermas' modernist values, however, come under attack from other contemporary philosophers, notably Foucault.

On one level there is considerable unanimity between them. Like Foucault, Habermas accepts Nietzsche's critique of reason, but he rejects its nihilistic conclusions. For Habermas, post-structuralist thought reveals the extent to which "subjectivity and intentionality are not prior to, but a function of, forms of life and systems of language". (*The Philosophical Discourse of Modernity* p. ix) Thus, the subject does not constitute the world, as in the Kantian tradition, but is an element of a linguistically disclosed world. However, although Habermas uses such criticisms as a prelude to his own project, the postmodernists, in their turn, question the very notions of truth, of reasonable consensus, and of a claim to validity, on which Habermas' philosophy depends. The argument involves a dispute about different interpretations of Kant. Kant's view that the supposed structures of nature are not actual, but are structures of the way we think about the world, gave rise to two streams of thought. On the one hand, Kant was embraced by Marx and by subsequent critical theorists form seemingly proving that knowledge is a human construct; but he was castigated by the same people for accepting the *a priori* nature of thought and ignoring its socio-historical development. Habermas' universal pragmatics follows this stream. Thinkers like Derrida, on the other hand, follow another path. They regard Nietzsche's "second Enlightenment" as having exposed the will to power underlying Kant's notion of *a priori* knowledge. Nietzsche's denunciation of truth as subjective perspectivism is used by Habermas as a basis for his reconstructive turn towards truth. Others, such as Derrida, shun that Nietzschean turning point, and continue the task initiated by Nietzsche of dismantling the objective pretensions of truth and suchlike concepts. Derrida thinks that the notions of authenticity, rationality, and consensus, upon which Habermas' enterprise stands, are humanistic fictions resulting from the impersonal play of language. Foucault contends, on the other hand, that these alleged fictions arise from the power strategies of different social complexes.

Habermas replies to these critics by asking what happens if the critical norms of rationality are renounced? In his recent book *The Philosophical Discourse of Modernity* he argues that Derrida's reduction of philosophy to literature is self-contradictory. The grounds for accepting the reduction can only be rhetorical, and, moreover, if aesthetic preference is to be a norm of philosophy the discredited logic of subjectivity is reinvoked. Any critique of reason which claims to be total, will undermine the rational grounds for its acceptance. If reason is capable of falsity, it is also capable of truth; but Derrida's thought denies this dialectical character of reason.

Habermas sympathises with Foucault's genealogical reduction of humanist ideals to their empirical origins. His own attempt to show how the supposedly transcendental frameworks of human knowledge emerge from the use of language follows a somewhat similar path. Foucault follows Nietzsche in so far as he seems to suppose that exposing the empirical origins of a universal claim is equivalent to refuting it; Habermas, on the other hand, insists that this is not so. The task, for Habermas, is not to reject the ideas of truth and reason, but to reshape both of them.

A difference of political vision separates Foucault and Habermas. For Foucault, human history is a field over which different power strategies have fought and sustained themselves. This vision prompts him to speak for minority groups whose voices are muffled by dominant interests. Foucault's politics are pluralist, in that he recognises many voices, but fatalist in that his pluralism amounts to little more than the statement that history is a war of all against all. Habermas offers a principle of hope, because the theory of communicative action denies that the war of all against all is absolute. If there is strife over an issue, there is at least unanimity over what the issue is, and if that is agreed then the possibility remains of arriving at a consensus as to how differences might be resolved. The notion of emancipatory critique is perhaps the last defence against the murderous selfishness of religious, political and cultural bigotry.

# Truth as Faith: Concluding Reflection

Habermas' philosophical project has attracted considerable criticism. In his book *Modern German Philosophy* (1981), Rudiger Bubner contends that, although we may accept an obvious connection between theoretical reflection and action, there is no guarantee that achieving an understanding of the distorted nature of an individual or political conviction will motivate us to change it. Christopher Norris makes a related point in his

*Contest of Faculties* (1985), suggesting that the force of reason within Habermas' notion of rational consensus has a repressive dimension, which might lead minority parties in a discussion to feel that their views are adjudged deviant. Habermas' position echoes the tendency of utilitarianism to permit the wishes of the greatest number to repress minority views as undemocratic. Paul Ricoeur's criticism moves in an opposite direction: it asks what protects Habermas' notion of the emancipatory itself from distortion? In *Hermeneutics and the Social Sciences* (1987), Ricoeur says that, if the notion of an emancipatory truth is to have any concrete or realisable sense, there must be actual historical incarnations of such an ideal to serve as an exemplar. Yet if such ideals are exemplified, what protects them from distortion by historical transmission or political ideology?

There is, however, a much more pressing difficulty confronting Habermas' enterprise. His philosophy seeks to criticise ideological attempts to define actuality or knowledge – whether it be positivism's efforts at imposing scientistic thinking as the only form of legitimate knowledge, or hermeneutic philosophy's unquestioning acceptance of the norms of tradition. Furthermore, he tries to undercut subject-centred knowledge, and wants to build an intersubjective model of truth and consensus based on the emancipatory ideal latent within communicative action. With the shameful reappearance of nationalist strife within Europe, Habermas' call for emancipatory critique and the expansion of the commonwealth of rationality is now an urgent cry. Against the nihilistic tendencies of our epoch, and the dying authority of ancient political faiths, the notion of the ideal speech situation may seem merely touching. Yet it might just offer the final hope against European culture destroying itself. The problem is: what might make Habermas' convictions persuasive? What vision does it offer? Sound reasoning alone will not do. Kierkegaard rightly argued that, no matter how well built the argument, it will remain unconvincing until it strikes a particular resonance within the individual. The cherishable optimism of Habermas' thought consists in his belief that human beings are not granted understanding by historical destiny or divine intervention. They understand, because understanding is grounded in intersubjective communicative practices. Everyday pretheoretical communicative engagements contain non-distorting and non-coercive procedures, which expand the community of rational consensus. Habermas' argument remains, for the most part, concerned with questions of legitimation and competence, and it is easy to understand why. Elysium, for Habermas, is not what is enabled by the use of language *per se*, but the process of enabling which emerges from it. He does not try to project a specific vision of humanity, but rather to create a situation in which all the hindrances and distortions inhibiting the unfolding of humanity's creative potential might be diminished. His philosophy is not politically prescriptive, but seeks to hold a linguistic ring in which others might speak freely, and, in speaking freely, allow the truly rational human community to expand. But the question remains: how does the single individual incorporate, or even visualise, that objective order as his or her own? How does one overcome the difficulty of grasping such an order in a way which fits it to a personal vision? Unless the individual can endorse the objective orders of communication as meaningful in the realisation of his or her life's ambitions, in the manner that Kierkegaard's dictum implies, Habermas' philosophical project may remain ineffective.

Yet for all his pragmatism, it is perhaps a "leap of faith" that Habermas both makes and offers. When Nietzsche argued that "with one there is never truth, it is only with two that truth begins", philosophers such as Derrida have taken him to mean not so much that truth begins with two, as that it comes to an end with two. Truth and meaning are taken to be impossible, on the grounds of their endless susceptibility to analytic division. Habermas, however, accepts the multiplication of meaning. He sees it, not as revealing endless differences, but as giving rise to a communal understanding that sameness, the sharing of common truths, emerges from the discursive exchange of difference. Whereas post-structuralist thinkers such as Derrida bid us accept that we live in a world where all truth and meaning is, logically speaking, infinitely divisible, Habermas asks us to keep faith in the other logical possibility: that with two, with discourse, the beginning of truth and understanding might indeed arise.

# Further Reading

The main works of Habermas will be found below. Held's *Introduction to Critical Theory* is a good introduction to the Frankfurt School as a whole. Giddens has useful material on positivism, and Arato and Gebhardt is a collection of basic Frankfurt School texts.

# Bibliography

A. Arato and E. Gebhardt, *The Essential Frankfurt School Reader*, Oxford: Blackwell 1978.
A. Giddens (ed.), *Positivism and Sociology*, London: Heinemann 1974.

J. Habermas, *Knowledge and Human Interests*, tr. J. Shapiro, London: Heinemann 1968.

——*Theory and Practice*, tr. J. Viertel, London: Heinemann 1974.

——"The Analytical Theory of Science and Dialectics" and "A Positivistically Bisected Rationalism" in *The Positivist Dispute in German Sociology*, ed. Adey and Frisby, London: Heinemann 1977.

——"The Hermeneutic Claim to Universality", in J. Bleicher (ed.),*Contemporary Hermeneutics: Hermeneutics as Method, Philosophy, and Critique*, London: Routledge 1980.

——*The Theory of Communicative Action and the Rationalisation of Science* vol. I, trans. T. Macarthy, London: Heinemann 1984.

——*The Philosophical Discourse of Modernity*, tr. F. Lawrence, London: Blackwell 1987.

D. Held, *Introduction to Critical Theory: Horkheimer to Habermas*, London: Hutchinson 1980.

# 13 Michel Foucault
## Simon Christmas

Perhaps the most succinct statement of the spirit in which the works of Michel Foucault must be read was made by Foucault himself in an interview in 1984, the year of his death

> The role of an intellectual is not to tell others what they have to do. By what right would he do so?... The work of an intellectual is not to shape others' political will; it is, through the analyses that he carries out in his own field, to question over and over again what is postulated as self-evident, to disturb people's mental habits, the way they do and think things, to dissipate what is familiar and accepted, to re-examine rules and institutions...

This is the role which Foucault attempted to fulfil. His books are not to be seen as a body of work setting out and refining a single theory, but as a succession of analyses in which he challenges what has been taken to be self-evident and, frequently, his own earlier work. His thought never stagnated or became dogmatic – right up to his death he continued changing his mind, unashamedly abandoning his original plan for the massive *History of Sexuality* on which he was working, on the grounds that he had got bored with it.

Taken individually, each of Foucault's books is a new piece of research in its own right; taken as a series they form a remarkable train of thought which this short chapter can only begin to outline.

## Background

To understand the background to Foucault's work, one can turn to his own analysis in his third book, *The Order of Things* (1966), of a hiatus in philosophical thought which divides what he calls the Classical Age from the Age of Man or the Age of Modernity. The watershed between the Classical Age and the Age of Modernity coincides roughly with the life and work of the German philosopher Immanuel Kant (1724-1804).

Foucault argued that thought in the Classical Age had been united by the idea of an ordered universe which could be understood by analysing it into simple elements. The key tool in this analysis had been the representation of the order of the universe by means of signs corresponding to the elements. The problem that arose from this approach was how to include humanity itself in the analysis, since mankind occupies a unique position: it is not only an object of knowledge – that is to say, another entity which can be observed, analysed and represented – but also the subject – it is mankind which is conducting the observation, analysis and representation. The classical system assumed that the subject is able to look upon the objects from outside, from a "position of exteriority". The Age of Modernity began when it was realised, notably by Immanuel Kant, that the knowing subject is not outside the world but wholly involved in it as an object.

The attempts made by philosophy and the human sciences to understand mankind as that which thinks and knows all fall foul of this problem: that humanity is both subject and object of its own knowledge. In addition, human beings have attempted to interpret themselves as the products of their own cultural background (the work of Hegel provides an example of this approach). But such an interpretation is itself conditioned by the very cultural background it purports to treat objectively. To put it another way, the interpretation is "inside" the cultural background which it pretends to view from the "outside", and therefore needs to be reinterpreted itself – and so on *ad infinitum*. This method of successive interpretation has been called *hermeneutics*. Other examples of a hermeneutic approach can be seen in Freud, who interprets men and women in terms of the unconscious mind, and in Marx, who interprets human history in terms of class struggle and progress. Hermeneutics is nevertheless problematic, because in the end it seems to rest on some idea of "the way things really are", or the hermeneutic truth.

Foucault himself took a hermeneutic sort of stance in his first book, *Madness and Civilisation* (1961), in which he investigates the development of psychiatry and the understanding of madness in the seventeenth and eighteenth centuries as if there were something that was "real madness", to which successive understandings aspired but which remained essentially beyond understanding.

# The Method of "Archaeology"

The subtitle of *The Order of Things* is *An Archaeology of the Human Sciences*, and the word 'archaeology' also appears in the subtitle of his previous book, *The Birth of the Clinic: An Archaeology of Medical Perception* (1963), and the title of his next one, *The Archaeology of Knowledge* (1969). 'Archaeology' is the name given by Foucault to the method which he developed after rejecting his own hermeneutic inclinations as manifested in *Madness and Civilisation*.

What is philosophical "archaeology"? Archaeology in the literal sense is a method of studying history which involves digging up the artifacts of the past – cities, fortresses, works of art, mortuaries, pots and pans, and so on. Somewhat analogously, Foucault's philosophical "archaeology" digs up another kind of artefact: past scientific methods, past ideas about knowledge, viewed as human creations. The "archaeologist" aims to step back from asking direct questions about the nature of humanity, and instead studies past systems of understanding, that is, the human sciences and philosophy itself, and the way in which these have developed. For instance, whereas philosophy since Kant has asked the question "How is mankind to speak the truth about itself?", the "archaeologist" asks instead how this question came to be constituted in the way that it has been. How, when, and why did it come to be asked in the first place? We have already seen how, in *The Order of Things*, Foucault traces the emergence of this question from the breakdown of the classical system of thought (what Foucault calls the classical *episteme*), and how the form it took left it essentially unanswerable.

The assumptions behind archaeology are roughly as follows. The statements which make up a particular human science (for instance medicine, with which Foucault deals in *The Birth of the Clinic*) are part of that science, not because of some relationship with some supposed truth about the way things really are, but rather because of the way they relate to the other statements in the science. Thus the question of what was meant by a statement does not arise for the archaeologist. All that matters is whether a statement was seen to be a serious contribution to the science under study at the time it was made. Archaeology proceeds by amassing these serious statements and then investigating the regularities between them – the relationships which lead to them being seen as comprising a particular human science. The archaeologist also investigates the way in which the science develops through time – how the regularities which bind the science together change.

## Archaeology and Structuralism

Philosophical archaeology has much in common with structuralism, which, in its philosophical form, developed as an alternative to hermeneutics and which swept through French intellectual circles in the 1960s.

Structuralism is a multifaceted concept. The word itself, originating in linguistics, has been taken up by anthropologists, literary critics, philosophers, and mathematicians, each giving it a different slant and a rather different meaning. In linguistics, the term 'structuralism' was first used programmatically by the Prague school of Roman Jakobson, drawing on the work of de Saussure. Structuralist grammar suspends the question of the relationship of words to reality, endeavouring merely to set out the structural rules which govern the ways in which it is legitimate to use them.

The main similarity between Foucault's project and structuralism in linguistics is that, having isolated the class of serious statements making up a science, Foucault suspends the question of their meaning in order to investigate the structural regularities that link them.

But there are also differences. Structuralist theories in linguistics deal with possibility, since syntactic theories generally only reveal the combinations of words which are structurally permissible. They do not reveal which sentences will actually be used by real people. Nor do they provide information about pragmatic restrictions – for instance, they do not rule out the possibility that some structurally correct sentences might be so long that they could not be uttered in the space of a human lifetime.

By contrast, Foucault, in *The Archaeology of Knowledge*, is quite clear that the regularities discovered by archaeology are not just the conditions on what it was possible to take seriously at a particular time. Instead these regularities are concerned with what actually was said. Archaeology deals not with possibility but with actuality.

The implications are far reaching. If archaeology were merely a form of structuralist description, then the regularities it revealed, although interesting, would not have the same sort of explanatory power. Foucault claims to have discovered not only descriptive regularities but prescriptive rules – that is, rules which govern the formation of new discourse (new ways of talking and writing) within the human sciences.

Yet it is hard to work out just what these rules are meant to be. Foucault rejects the ideas that they are timeless and universal, or that they are to be found either in people's ways of thinking or in the make up of institutions. But he offers little in the way of positive explanation

## Critique of the Archaeological Method

The method of archaeology becomes very confused at this point. The rules which Foucault suggests are very strange things indeed: rules which supposedly govern the things being said by people within the human sciences without having any obvious means of governing. This odd position stems from Foucault's determination to look only at what he and many other French philosophers call *discursive practices* - roughly, the things people say or write. In *Madness and Civilisation* he had included non-discursive practices – such as the practices of confining the insane – in his investigation of the history of psychiatry, but these are excluded from the subsequent "archaeological" works. As a result he his forced to try to explain the discourse of the human sciences as if the things people say were unconnected with everything else they do.

This apart, the rules which philosophical archaeology purports to uncover have a very dubious status. Archaeologists avoid becoming embroiled in their subject matter by suspending questions about the meaning and truth of the statements which they study. They consider those statements which were taken to be serious in the past without raising the question of whether it was right to have done so. So we can ask archaeologists whether the rules which they themselves produce are serious. If they are serious, then they have to be seen as forming part of the human sciences, and thus as permissible objects of further study. But this is a new form of the old problem of the human sciences: a description which claims to have been made from "outside" what it describes, turns out to be "inside" it. The only alternative for the philosophical archaeologists, however, it to agree that their rules are not to be taken seriously – that is, they are not to be taken as having any serious meaning. This is not a very productive way to conclude one's theorising.

# Genealogy: a New Approach

In his next two works, *Discipline and Punish* (1975) and Volume I of *The History of Sexuality*, Foucault rectifies the two principal mistakes of archaeology. Firstly, he widens his field of investigation to include non-discursive practices. Secondly, the troublesome elements of archaeology, such as the claim to discover rules for the formation of discourse, are jettisoned. But the most important feature of archaeology, the suspension of judgement on the claims of the human sciences to yield truth about humanity, remains as an important tool in Foucault's methodological arsenal. For example, in *The History of Sexuality*, Foucault takes the question "Is sexuality repressed" and asks the archaeological question "How has this question come to be asked and answered in the way it is?"

His aim in doing so is to write what he calls the genealogy of the modern subject. The concept of genealogy in philosophy is derived from Nietzsche, and is another reaction against the search for ultimate truth, fixed essences, and underlying laws in the analysis of history. A twentieth century philosophical "genealogist" will tell a story of how we, as late twentieth century Westerners, have come to understand ourselves as we do, in particular how we have come to be constituted as modern individuals by the interaction of power and knowledge. In setting about this project, Foucault develops a radically new understanding of the workings of power and its relation to knowledge, which remains one of the most challenging aspects of his work, and which will be explored here by a somewhat closer study of Volume I of the *History of Sexuality* (abbreviated to HS henceforth for the purposes of citation).

## The Repressive Hypothesis

In *The History of Sexuality*, Foucault presents his theory of the relationship of power to sexuality by contrasting it with what he calls 'the repressive hypothesis'. The repressive hypothesis was very thoroughly articulated by Freud, particularly in *Civilisation and its Discontents* and in *The Interpretation of Dreams*. The hypothesis rests on two main theoretical assumptions: first, sexuality is seen as a basic truth of one's nature. Second, power is seen as a solely negative force which can operate only through the repression of this drive.

The repressive hypothesis is implicit in the following naïve but common account of history. Having enjoyed relative freedom up to the seventeenth century, sexuality in the ensuing centuries suffered steadily mounting oppression, culminating in the hypocritical prudishness of the Victorian age, which enforced a total censorship upon sex. The effects of this prudishness were so great that they are still present today. Individuals remain repressed, especially those whose sexuality deviates in some way from the restrictive norms imposed during the nineteenth century. In this atmosphere of repression, it is essential to understand and liberate oneself by the discovery and assertion of one's true sexuality, albeit in the face of enormous social pressure to conform.

The whole theory of the repressive hypothesis depends on an implicit acceptance of the two theoretical elements mentioned above, viz.: the assertion of the existence of sexuality as a truth about the nature of the individual, plus the assertion about the existence of a negative power which threatens to crush that sexual nature, a power from which the individual must be liberated.

It is Foucault's contention that, upon closer scrutiny, the historical facts do not tally with the repressive hypothesis. Therefore we need "to examine the case of a society... which speaks verbosely of its own silence".

## Against the Repressive Hypothesis

Foucault observes that, since the end of the sixteenth century,

> the "putting into discourse of sex", far from undergoing a process of restriction... has been subjected to a mechanism of increasing incitement (*History of Sexuality* I, p. 12)

Over this period, the injunction was laid down to fulfil

> the nearly infinite task of telling – telling oneself and another, as often as possible, everything that might concern the interplay of innumerable pleasures, sensations, and thoughts which, through the body and the soul, had some affinity with sex. (*History of Sexuality* I, p. 20)

Foucault says that elaborate ways were developed of talking around sex and surrounding it "at the last moment" with a veil of secrecy.

But underneath these cosmetic measures, there lay a growing obsession with sex. For instance, although "the first in the medical profession" to present case histories of sexual deviancy "stumbled at the moment of speaking"; still, beneath his words lay a "recognised necessity of overcoming this hesitation. One had to speak of sex." (*History of Sexuality* I, p. 24) Foucault probably has in mind Freud's teacher Charcot, the medical hypnotist. As to the stumbling, this refers to a professional tendency to obfuscation in this area.

The nineteenth century obsession with childhood masturbation is one of Foucault's favourite examples. Although the explicit aim of the medical men who formulated the new theories which grew up around this subject was to limit the supposed epidemic threatening the health of the child, and even of the nation, the actual effect of their words was to intensify all the power relationships between children, parents, doctors, and so on. The things they said and wrote about sex encouraged parents to see signs of masturbation in every action of the child, and to incite more and more talk about the problem – talk that would portray "the epidemic of masturbation" as becoming still worse.

The discourse of doctors even offered new forms of pleasure to those involved in certain new practices – viz., the practices of surveillance, voyeurism, and evasion.

Foucault says that he is not claiming that "sex has not been prohibited or barred or masked or misapprehended since the classical age". Nor does he wish, even, to say that sex "suffered these things any less from that period on than before". (*History of Sexuality* I, p. 12) In other words, he remains neutral about the question "Is sexuality repressed" – though he is often misunderstood on this point. His observation is simply that the repressive hypothesis as it stands cannot explain the growing obsession with sex that has marked the modern era.

## Creative Power: The Creation of Sexuality

The key mistake in the repressive hypothesis, according to Foucault, is the characterisation of power as a purely negative force which acts from a position of exteriority to limit and repress the expression of sexuality.

Foucault claims that power pervades all forms of social relationships. He also believes, most importantly, that power does not repress, but *controls*, *incites*, and *creates*. Power is not wielded by one person, or one class, or one institution, over the rest of us. Rather, it forms a situation, or grid, in which all individuals are located.

In Volume I of the *History of Sexuality*, the chief object of the functions of control, incitement, and creation, is presented as discourse, that is, written and spoken discussion targeted on a particular topic – in this case, the topic of sexual behaviour. Foucault argues, very powerfully, that from the Classical Age onwards certain social and historical mechanisms have operated as *incitements* towards the "putting into discourse" of sex. These include mechanisms as varied as the long-known Christian confessional and the modern psychiatrist's couch.

Foucault holds that the incitements have involved not just a quantitative increase in discourse about sex, but also a shift in emphasis from the sexual act to "the insinuations of the flesh: thoughts, desires, voluptuous imaginings, delectations, combined movements of the body and soul". (*History of Sexuality* I, p. 19) This shift in emphasis resulted, eventually, in the creation of sexuality as a focus for the proliferation of various power relationships bearing upon sex and desire, and relationships which, in Foucault's account, provided the means for the greater "penetration of bodies" by desire.

Foucault uses here the example of male homosexuality. Medieval morality had condemned the act of sodomy as sinful, with no concept of an underlying sexual *nature*. By contrast, the "category of homosexuality was constituted from the moment it was characterised... less by a type of sexual relations than by a certain quality of sexual sensibility." (*History of*

*Sexuality* I, p. 43) The "confused category" of sodomy was replaced by the concept of type of person. Moreover, whereas sodomy had attracted extremely severe punishments (although Foucault suggests that it had also been widely tolerated), the homosexual man in the Age of Modernity is not punished, but managed. He became an object of medical and psychiatric investigation, a deviant to be cured, a threat to society and youth, which must be removed, and so on.

It was as a focus for such relationships of management and control that the concept of sexuality as a truth of one's nature developed. Which is not to say that this concept was "invented" for these purposes. Instead the process, as envisaged by Foucault, involves the action of power simultaneously inciting discourse, creating new practices, and providing foci for suppressive action.

## The Repressive Hypothesis as a "Technique" of Power

Central to the operation of power is the "injunction to discourse", that is, the incitement of all and sundry to talk or write about sex. The repressive hypothesis itself is just one means of incitement, a "technique" of power, encouraging people to speak by dangling the carrot of self-understanding and self-liberation in front of them.

> Is it not with the aim of inciting people to speak of sex that it is made to mirror, at the outer limit of every actual discourse, something akin to a secret whose discovery is imperative, a thing abusively reduced to silence, and at the same time difficult and necessary, dangerous and precious to divulge? (*History of Sexuality* I, p. 34)

Foucault is sometimes misinterpreted as saying that the only way to resist power is to stay silent, that those who hope to resist power by speaking the "truth" about themselves are in fact playing straight into power's hands. But this is a simplistic and inaccurate reading of Foucault. There is no way of staying silent, because we are all already situated within power relations. Sexuality is not a truth of human nature, argues Foucault, but he also argues that the idea of a present day individual without a sexuality is nonsensical. For it is with sexualities that we are constituted as individuals at this moment in history.

The way to set up resistance to power is far more complex than staying silent. Indeed the whole question of resistance is one of the most difficult parts of Foucault's characterisation of power.

## Resisting Power

Just because we are all of necessity situated within power relationships, are within the power grid, and cannot resist power from "outside", this does not mean that we are helpless. Power, according to Foucault, already contains "points of resistance" that are "present everywhere in the power network". These points of resistance are an essential part of its operation. Foucault says that the "plurality of resistances" can by definition "only exist in the strategic field of power relations. But this does not mean that they are... doomed to perpetual defeat." There is not just one single power resisted by a "great Refusal". Rather there is a mosaic of different *strategies*, each one comprising a set of objectives and, as it were, struggling against the other strategies to achieve them. (*History of Sexuality* I, pp. 95f.)

Within this mosaic, there are a variety of resources, "tactical elements" which may be used or deployed by different strategies to their different ends. The meaning of this rather enigmatic claim is best illustrated by Foucault's examples, such as the following:

> There is no question that the appearance... of a whole series of discourses on the species and subspecies of homosexuality, inversion, pederasty, and "psychic hermaphrodism" made possible a strong advance of social controls into this area of "perversity"; but it also made possible the formation of a "reverse" discourse: homosexuality began to speak on its own behalf, to demand that its legitimacy or "naturality" be encouraged, often in the same vocabulary, using the same categories by which it was medically disqualified. (*History of Sexuality* I, p. 101)

But despite such examples, Foucault's exposition of this crucial section of his theory of power depends very heavily upon his use of largely unelaborated metaphors – in particular the odd and difficult notion of a strategy. He himself accepted that the analysis of power which he had given in the *History of Sexuality* stood in need of much further work, and in his later years he began to expand and rework his ideas yet again.

We must leave these difficulties to one side, however, to consider the implications of the observations about power made in *The History of Sexuality* beyond the field of sexuality.

## Power, Knowledge, and the Individual

The repressive hypothesis as regards sexuality is just one aspect of a more general repressive hypothesis which regards truth (in this instance the truth of one's nature) as external to and directly in conflict with power. Power has only one function in the repressive hypothesis, to repress the truth. Resistance to power thus takes the form of uncovering the way things really are.

But this project, the project of uncovering the way things really are, is itself a version of the target of Foucault's original critique. That is, it presupposes the validity of the idea of an ultimate truth. Now according to Foucault, all our knowledge of the "truth", including of course all our knowledge of the "truth" of sexuality, is a product of the workings of power. Power and knowledge, whilst not identical (as Foucault is sometimes misread as saying), are inextricably enmeshed. Hence a problem arises for Foucault at this stage similar to the one we encountered in the method of archaeology. On the one hand, he rejects ultimate "truth" as the product of power: on the other hand, he provides what seems to be a theory of the "truth" about power. Surely, then, his theory must explain itself as just one more product of power?

There is something very cogent in this objection, and Foucault himself was deeply aware of it. He does not deny that he speaks and characterises power from a particular place "inside" what he is trying to describe from the "outside". And so there remains an air of the very paradox he tries to escape. Yet in the process of becoming re-entrapped, Foucault's analyses do shed light on other theories. For instance, if he is right then many of the existing models for resistance (such as Marxism and psychoanalysis) turn out to be "empty", in that they base themselves upon an implicit resistance of power by means of the "truth".

So Foucault's work leaves a vacuum which it does not quite seem able to fill again. On the other hand, there is no doubt that he himself believed in the possibility of resisting power: this is borne out by his own involvement in various political and social causes during his life, and by remarks made in interview. But what is the form of this resistance? What are the options left open for the individual when "truth" is so tightly enmeshed with power?

# Conclusion

If anything is to be learned from Michel Foucault, it is perhaps that the spirit of intellectual inquiry is more important than the truth it seeks to uncover. Foucault spoke about himself only rarely, but in an unusually revealing interview in 1983 he hinted at the personal motives behind his work:

> For me intellectual work is related to what you could call aestheticism, mean-
> ing transforming yourself... I know that knowledge can transform us, that truth
> is not only a way of deciphering the world (and maybe what we call truth
> doesn't decipher anything) but that, if I know the truth, I will be changed. And
> maybe I will be saved.

Foucault did not seek truth, he sought change. That is why we should
not hope to emerge from his work with a systematic appraisal of truth, but
only a range of options for further development.

One other thing is very clear about Foucault: he did not offer to think
for other people, or to present them at the end of his deliberations with a
system by which they might understand themselves. Instead, having questioned the self-evident and disturbed our mental habits, he left it for us to
carry on thinking – and changing – ourselves.

# Further Reading

Most of Foucault's writings are very readable, with the possible excep-
tions of *The Order of Things* and *The Archaeology of Knowledge*.
Merquior's commentary on Foucault can be recommended, as can
Dreyfus and Rabinow. There are now two major biographies, of which
Macey concentrates more on the academic career, while Miller is more
speculative.

# Bibliography

H.L. Dreyfus and P. Rabinow, *Michel Foucault: Beyond Structuralism
and Hermeneutics*, Brighton: Harvester 1982.

M. Foucault, *The Archaeology of Knowledge*, tr. A.M. Sheridan, London:
Tavistock 1972.

——*The Birth of the Clinic: An Archaeology of Medical Practice*, tr.
A.M. Sheridan, London: Tavistock 1976.

——*Discipline and Punish: The Birth of the Prison*, tr. A.M. Sheridan,
Harmondsworth: Penguin 1979.

——*The History of Sexuality vol. I: An Introduction*, tr. R. Hurley,
Harmondsworth: Penguin 1981.

——*The History of Sexuality vol. II: The Use of Pleasure*, tr. R. Hurley
London: Penguin 1987.

———*The History of Sexuality vol. III: Care of the Self*, tr. R. Hurley London: Allen Lane 1988.

M. Foucault, *Madness and Civilisation: A History of Insanity in the Age of Reason*, tr. R. Howard, London: Tavistock 1965.

———*The Order of Things: An Archaeology of the Human Sciences*, tr. A.M. Sheridan, London: Tavistock 1970.

D. Macey, *The Lives of Michel Foucault*, London: Hutchinson 1993.

J.G. Merquior, *Foucault*, London: Fontana 1985.

J. Miller, *The Passion of Michel Foucault*, London: Harper Collins 1993.

# 14  1968 and After
## Sadie Plant

## The "Events" of 1968

For 1968 to suddenly appear in a series of chapters on philosophers suggests that something of peculiar significance to European philosophy happened in that year of rioting, barricades, and political turmoil. The
unprecedented wave of discontent which swept much of the world in 1968
was significant wherever it arose, but in France, where it nearly succeeded
in destroying the state, the effects on the cultural and intellectual life of
the country were enormous; so much so that only an impoverished understanding of recent European philosophy is possible without some sense of
the atmosphere and themes of 1968. The debates about humanism and
subjectivity, power and desire which inform the work of writers such as
Foucault, Lyotard, Irigaray, Deleuze and Guattari are intimately entangled
with the events of that year. While there are many other paths through
which the philosophical significance of 1968 could be pursued, the trajectory through poststructuralist and psychoanalytic theory which these
philosophers trace is perhaps the most interesting way of considering the
impact of what is variously referred to as May '68, the May events, or just
*les événements*, the events.

The events, then, involved a three week general strike by some ten mil-
lion workers, mass demonstrations, university and factory occupations
and battles with the police, government threats of military intervention,
and the near-collapse of the state. The sense of frenzied activity with
which people grappled with the possibilities and purpose of such an enormous interruption is unmistakable in the legacy of cultural experiment
and political argument left by the extraordinary variety of voices which
were raised against the social order. For discontent was confined neither
to the students, whose activities had sparked off the wave of occupations
and strikes, nor to the workers in their traditional role of revolutionary
subjects. The hostility to power and authority was exercised in hospitals
and schools, football teams and personal relationships. Revolution was in
the air, but no-one really knew why or how it had arisen. No one seemed
to be in charge, and a cacophony of questions was directed at no one in
particular. People were desperate, but what did they really want? It was
not a question of satisfying material needs; perhaps some other needs, or

desires never before so insistently expressed? People were protesting, but about what, and against whom, were their dissatisfactions raised? They refused to be led, criticised the élitist vanguardism of the organised revolutionary left and demanded to speak for themselves, and challenged every aspect of their lives. To what authority does one complain about everything? This was a situation to which there was no obvious response; it was literally unthinkable, and there are many senses in which the attempt to think it through has shaped subsequent European thought.

That the events caused such confusion and consternation is hardly surprising. With the rest of the advanced industrial world, the France of the 1950s and 1960s was enjoying a period of affluence and stability, and the possibility of revolution or even serious unrest seemed remote. But in a matter of months, small confrontations between students and the university establishment escalated into wholesale challenges to authority and hierarchy, and the students' demands for control over their own lives, from the organisation of halls of residence to the content of courses and lectures, quickly caught on in the factories and across a wide spectrum of French life. Calls for a general strike on May 13th were met with an enthusiasm which brought France to a standstill and outraged managers, ministers, and, significantly, the leaders of the traditional organs of protest: the unions and the French Communist Party. The demands of the activists were beyond the understanding of all these authorities, but there was, of course, a particular irony in the established opposition's response to the uprising. Vehemently opposed to the strikes and occupations, the Party and the union leaders insisted that the students were provocateurs, that the workers would lose the political advantages they had supposedly won by their hitherto disciplined protests, and that the time for revolution was not ripe. The strikes and occupations were wildcat, organised by informal, *ad hoc* committees and with a flagrant disregard for the official organs of union bureaucracy and hierarchy.

Moreover, the demands of the workers were rarely framed in ways that could be easily understood. They were demanding neither pay rises nor changes in working conditions, but asking for nothing in particular and everything in general: a complete change in their ways of life. It was unclear to everyone how the disruption had started, who was to blame, and what the outcome would be.

France is in revolutionary ferment [declared the *Observer* in May 1968]. Who is responsible? Who put the spark to the dead wood? In the permanent disorderly festival of the Sorbonne, drunk on a week's total freedom, all seems confusion and spontaneity.

The events were also far more than a challenge to a particular set of policies. The *Observer* was convinced that the

great upheaval through which France is passing is more than a crisis of the government or even of regime: it is above all a crisis of the State. And not simply of the French State but of the State as it has been conceived in the Western industrial world and its offshoots since the eighteenth century.

It was a crisis of authority in all its forms, and to make matters worse, the general strike caused such disruption that, even though life in France eventually returned to normal, many people had tasted a few weeks of a radically different life.

Without any trains, tubes, cars or work the strikers recaptured the time so sadly lost in factories, on motorways and in front of the TV [wrote one commentator]. People strolled, dreamed, learned how to live. Desires began to become, little by little, reality.

There was a great deal of talk about desire, the imagination, and creativity in 1968, and the long dream of a world constructed on the basis of pleasures rather than necessities seemed possible at last. It was widely recognised that capitalist society had changed in the post-war years, and a by the 1960s a host of terms such as 'post-industrial society' had been used to capture the change from a society based largely on production to one concerned with the consumption of commodities. This was not to suggest, of course, that production was no longer significant to the survival of capitalism, but it did convey the feeling that the ways in which people spent their hours of leisure was increasingly important to an understanding of how society functioned. The accelerated developments of technology, the mass media, advertising, and a whole variety of cultural and social changes which occurred after the way encouraged a variety of new theories about the social world and the principles on which it is sustained and criticised. And by 1968, there had been a number of critiques of consumer capitalism, largely on the grounds that, while it appeared to offer incomparable benefits, freedoms, and luxuries, it remained a fundamentally dissatisfying and alienating social system.

It was merely a happy coincidence that Herbert Marcuse, leapt on by many commentators as "the" philosopher of the activists, happened to be in Paris in 1968. But there was indeed a sense in which his critiques of consumerism and the apparent tolerance of the affluent society resonated with many of the activists' demands. Drawing on other Frankfurt School attempts to develop both Marxism and Freudianism, Marcuse argued that, although some repression of pleasures and desires was necessary for the smooth functioning of a society, there was nevertheless a great deal of room for making social organisation fit our desires, rather than insisting that they should be constrained and repressed for the good of society. The idea that it was necessary to look beyond the obvious material constitution of society to its more cultural, and perhaps even spiritual, problems, meant that critical political theory need no longer confine itself to an interest in the class structure of society, but could look to any and all expressions of discontent, be they from workers, students, gays, the unemployed, women, immigrants, hippies, and any set of people who felt themselves marginalised by the apparently happy and cohesive society in which they found themselves. Marcuse was not alone in arguing that the "one-dimensional society" which capitalism had become could be contested by these groups, as well as by the proletariat, and, in these disparate voices and loose alliances, much revolutionary theory found a new, if rather uncohesive, revolutionary class.

Although this sort of account of the events was radically undermined by the philosophical developments considered in this chapter, there was certainly a sense in which the activists were attacking a society which was still boring and alienating, even though the older reasons for tedious work and unsatisfying ways of life seemed to have disappeared. For example, convinced that the need for material survival was, or at least could easily become, a thing of the past, the Situationists of the late 50's onwards argued that an ethos of struggle and labour was unnecessarily cultivated at a time when people could be enjoying the fruit of centuries of labour with a new spirit of pleasure and play. And in 1968, this was a dominant theme. "Never work", said one piece of graffiti, quoting Rimbaud; "I take my desires for reality because I believe in the reality of my desires", read another. And one famous slogan, referring to the paving stones ripped up by students in their battles with the police, read "Under the cobblestones lies the beach". There are many senses in which this last piece of graffiti encapsulates both the spirit of 1968 and the philosophical debates engendered by the events. That there was thought to be a beach under the cobblestones, a new world waiting to be discovered when the streets of the old one were torn up, was perhaps the most enduring and intriguing of the possibilities raised by May '68. There are, however, several other themes, tactics, slogans and demands from the events which continue to enjoy a philosophical resonance. The hostility to authority, for example, developed into a distrust of theory and the hierarchies of philosophical discourse, and a new respect for the immediacy of the event and the possibility of unmediated forms of communication and expression, which was also encouraged by the legendary use of graffiti in the events. Questions of how and where power is exercised were raised by challenges to every area of life; the activists' resistance to categorisation and conventional forms of organisation led to questions about all types of order and structure, and their emphasis on pleasure and desire reflected an interest in psychoanalytic theory which continues to have a profound philosophical effect.

The events are often remembered as a student rebellion, and France was not alone in facing a dangerous situation, which had indeed been hatched in the universities at least as much as in the factories. But while this aspect of the events is sometimes rather overplayed, the role of the students and intellectuals in 1968 is certainly significant to a consideration of its philosophical effects. The fact that many of those writers whose work is suffused with the themes of the events were politically active at the time, reinforced a long-standing tendency for French intellectuals to play a far more public and political role than their counterparts elsewhere. And for some years prior to 1968, this fusion of philosophy and politics had been intensified by the centrality of Marxism to French intellectual life. Not every post-war French thinker was a Marxist, of course. But there had long been a climate in which even those who were hostile to Marxism still located themselves in relation to it: the questions of whether, how, and to what extent an intellectual should make common cause with a worker was important in the writings of figures such as Sartre and de Beauvoir. And outside the rigours of the French Communist Party, the Marxism which had flourished in France since the war was a humanism, based on a critique of the alienating social relations reproduced in capitalist society, and emphasising the possibility of a revolution which would allow people's true needs, desires, and creative energies to flourish for the first time.

While the May events had a profound effect of subsequent European, and particularly French, philosophy, many of the later theoretical developments were, of course, also based on philosophical positions which had been mapped out in earlier years. In particular, the events and their philosophical fall-out were played against a backdrop of debates about humanism, with structuralist readings of both Marx and Freud undermining earlier understandings of the significance of the human individual as the basic building block of the social world. And although the events acceler-

ated the "crisis of the subject" already precipitated by structuralism, send-
ing it off in a variety of extreme and fascinating directions, the basic
moves of structuralist theory remains of vital significance to poststructuralism, postmodernism, and a number of other philosophical positions
considered in this chapter.

# Re-Thinking Marx

The most interesting and important structuralist argument was that the
world does not come already divided into well-labelled things.
Structuralist theorists raised the possibility that there is no necessary connection between words and things, and that the fact that we are so used to
using certain words – like 'society' and 'individual' – does not mean that
there are natural things which correspond to them. In the 1960s, Louis
Althusser's structuralist readings of Marx used this basic thought to challenge humanist versions of Marxism. Althusser argued that the widely
held belief, that Marxist theory had grown out of feelings of anger about
the injustices of poverty, exploitation, and oppression, was completely
unfounded. Marx, particularly in his later works, was far more concerned
with the fate of capitalism as a system than with individual workers as
people. The proletariat should realise its own strength, not in order to free
itself, but to hasten the collapse of capitalism. And, moreover, the conviction, that each of us is a free thinking, autonomous individual with our
own "true" self, was severely shaken by Althusser's thesis that social and
economic relations do not merely impinge on our lives here and there, but
actually constitute us as subjects. We grow up thinking we are free individuals, but in fact this is merely a story told to us in our contacts with
schools, churches, universities, the media, trade unions, and a host of
other institutions which form our identities. Convinced that the world
revolves around us as human subjects, we never see that what is really
important are the structures and institutions and economic relations in
which we live.

Althusser also challenged earlier Marxist ideas about the nature of
these structures and institutions. Whereas most forms of Marxism had
seen the economic structure of society as exercising some form of definite, or even determining, influence on all the superstructural aspects of
society – culture, education, the media, etc. – Althusser argued that each
of these areas of society operates with "relative autonomy" from the others and from the economic base. Although the economy remains "determining in the last instance", he also insisted that "the lonely hour of the

last instance never comes"; economic crisis is insufficient to the collapse of the entire social structure, and society is made up of all sorts of conflicting and contradictory tendencies, which make the business of social revolution no simple matter. But, while Althusser's analysis was, in some senses, useful to understanding what happened in 1968, his emphasis on the ways in which both individuals and the social world are made up of complex structures and relations meant that there was little sense of how social change actually occurs. Undermining previous conceptions of the autonomous human subject, Althusser left himself with no other place to look for an understanding of how the structures and relations he identified develop and change. In this respect, the events were as incomprehensible to the structuralist Marxist as to a bank manager. What structuralism had allowed, however, was an investigation of the ways in which language shapes our experience and understanding of the world. The possibility that what we experience as reality is merely a series of contingent conventions raised a huge variety of questions concerning how these conventions came to be established, and how the structures within which we live actually operate.

In the aftermath of the events, these were some of the issues taken up by both Michel Foucault and Jean-Francois Lyotard, and while they travelled in very different directions, there are a number of points of common interest in their work. Both were very critical of the dialectical thought presupposed by Marxism, and, beyond this, of the presuppositions and implications of *any* theoretical discourse. Both were concerned to elucidate the extent to which the world is actually constructed by the discourses we tend to assume are merely describing it, and both challenged the negativity inherent in both the Marxist and Freudian world views in and against which they worked, with Foucault developing a positive and productive conception of power, and Lyotard effecting a similar transformation of desire. And both attempted to  combine the ahistoricism of structuralist theory with dynamism and movement.

In part, this last project was fulfiled by a turn to Nietzsche, who sensed that the apparent order of Western civilisation was infected with hidden and denied realms of instability and irrationality. Nietzsche's conception of the world as a whirling "monster of energy", the product of dynamic forces of chaos and order which continually rise against one another, can be read in the work of Foucault, for whom this dynamism is populated by endless networks of power and knowledge, and Lyotard, whose development of a philosophy of multiple and positive desires was shared by Deleuze and Guattari. In their challenges to Hegelian conceptions of rational historical progress, many of the philosophers writing after 1968 tended towards the more Nietzschean view that the events were manifestations of a permanent contest between order and its subversion. Lyotard, for example, in his own rejections of the very idea of a totalising world view such as that offered by Marxism, turned his attention to the ways in which certain hidden points of intensity and desire interrupt both the apparent rigour of the theory and the calm exteriority of social organisation. Thus, in 1968, Lyotard saw the possibilities of a new "philosophy of desire" in the subversive explosion of eroticism, creativity, the sense of immediacy and the spontaneity of what he called the "attitude of here-now". And the idea that the same underlying forces and points of intensity underlie both order and its subversion was also central to Foucault's post-68 writings, in which the structuralism of he early work was developed into a series of analyses which examined the way in which the world we experience is constructed by the discourses with which we think and write about it.

For Foucault, the overriding question thrown up by the failure of the events was how, where, and to what ends power is exercised. If Althusser had extended the scope of this question, Foucault threw it wide open, rejecting Althusser's insistence that the economic structure of society always plays a determining role in both the functioning of, and the critique of, society, and arguing that the economic and class development of societies is merely one aspect of their very chequered and often quite arbitrary histories. That there was no single history, particularly one attached to the class struggle, was one of Foucault's major poststructuralist arguments, and much of his later work was devoted to teasing out the implications of this position. In the wake of the May events, it meant that the failure of the revolution was somehow bound up with the activist's inability to effect a fundamental change to the overriding theory of revolution, Marxism. For Foucault was convinced that Marxist conceptions of history, society, and the subject were fundamentally mistaken, not only in terms of their content and meaning, but also, and most significantly, in terms of the form they assumed, particularly in relation to Marxism's aspirations to a totalising theory about society as a cohesive and unified whole.

While Foucault's post-68 writing facilitated a good deal of fascinating political and philosophical development, Lyotard's active involvement in the 1968 events makes his philosophical reflections particularly interesting. Lyotard had been involved in a left-libertarian politics for some years before his involvement with the *mouvement du 22 Mars*, one of the many groups to spring up in 1968. His own immediate interest in the events was with the extent to which the activists' efforts to assume a position of uncompromising opposition to the existing social order had so clearly failed. For although an extraordinary variety of ways of life, sites of power, and forms of knowledge and communication had been contested, the failure of the events suggested that there remained whole swathes of social and discursive relations as yet unchallenged. While the attempt to run free of all the old world's means of categorisation and control had meant, for example, that the activists' criticisms of the hierarchical and bureaucratic nature of traditional revolutionary organisations spilled into critiques of their theoretical positions as well, there was still a sense in which the basic dialectical assumption – that it is necessary to find a position from which capitalist society as a whole can be challenged – was still maintained. And it was this presupposition, fundamental to Marxism and the Hegelian world view on which it is based, that Lyotard and Foucault challenged in their writings after the events. Looking back on the *mouvement du 22 Mars*, Lyotard observed that, in their struggle to find some "other" to capitalist social relations, the activists with whom he had worked had failed to confront the possibility that this search was itself perfectly acceptable and commensurable with the established order. The activists, he wrote, had been trying to set up an "other", an alternative to the whole of alienated life as they conceived it, but where had the elements of this new future come from? Were they harbouring presuppositions contaminated by, or implicated in, the old world? To what extent did the activists appear to be radical and oppositional, while at the same time being part of what they were contesting? Was it possible that the search for contradictions and positions of negativity might itself be part of the problem rather than the revolutionary cure? These arresting thoughts, which suggested that there was something radically mistaken about the most basic presuppositions of revolutionary politics, marked much subsequent philosophical reflection on the events and led to a devastating critique of dialectical thought and all attempts to find some alternative, better, more authentic form of social organisation.

The suggestion that a position of negativity is itself integral to the established order was clearly pointing to a very different "order" than that presupposed by Marxist critiques of capitalism as a social and economic system. Like Foucault, Lyotard suggested that capitalist society was merely the tip of an infinitely broader, more complex and profound iceberg, a series of orders which runs as deep as the very ways in which we think, feel and write. Moreover, as the activists' critiques of the revolutionary organisations had suggested, Marxism was fatally and unwittingly implicated in these underlying systems of domination. The spontaneous upsurge of a multitude of perspectives, interests, and desires in 1968 suggested that Marxist dreams of a single, unified revolutionary project belied a dangerous tendency to totalitarianism, concealing the real variety of differences and subversive forces which make the revolutionary moment. Dialectical attempts to identify central contradictions in the social world, to reach more rational and coherent theoretical positions, and to see every aspect of social and individual life in terms of a single, unifying perspective, were themselves seen as "deeply rational" and "reformist" activities which are "deeply consistent with the system". The critic, wrote Lyotard, "remains in the sphere of the thing criticised, he belongs to it, he goes beyond one term of the position but doesn't alter the position of terms." There is always a sense in which dialectical criticism is merely reacting to the existing state of affairs, contesting it from a position which is already external to it and not at all expressing any real difference or radical divergence.

From this perspective, Marxism itself becomes an agent of oppression and domination: ultimately, everything has to fit the theory, as the activists discovered in the French Communist Party's insistence that the revolution should not have been happening in the first place. For theories like Marxism also need theorists and leaders, those who can educate the masses and write the manifestos. And they also need to claim some access to the truths of the world; truths which, for Lyotard, were inevitably fictional narratives with no more truth than fairy stories. But Lyotard was not merely writing against capitalism, and neither was this merely a critique of Marxism; indeed, in many senses Marxism was more likely to recognise its presuppositions and histories than other theory. But it was the possibility that dialectical theory might itself be a concealed form of authoritarianism which led Lyotard to argue that all theories are covert systems of domination and control. Theories are merely good stories about the world with truth claims which are themselves merely founded on other stories and beliefs: stories founded on stories, or, as he calls them, *meta-narratives* such as the belief in progress towards the truth, the discovery of the real, or the emancipation of the oppressed. These are stories common to religious, scientific, and philosophical discourses, yet quite insupportable except by an appeal to themselves. Marxism's narrative of liberation, for example, tells stories about the grand march of history, the revolutionary role of the proletariat, and the possibility, even the necessity, of some future liberation from the toils of the capitalist world. It is not difficult to see the ways in which this story resonates with Christianity's tales of the second coming, the chosen few, and the prospect of future reward in a heavenly afterlife, and it was precisely this sort of connection which Lyotard sought to expose. This isn't a revolutionary story, he argued; it's completely in tune with the prevalent world view. Progress and rational direction are the very bedrocks of our civilisation, and not at all the basis of an opposition to it. And if we unthinkingly find ourselves in accordance with it, we will inevitably want to make all the endless difference and specificity of events, experiences and desires fit comfortably and without interruption in our meta-narratives.

But desires and events are not that easily tamed. Their specificity may have been denied and their variety ignored, but they continue to arise and interrupt the well-ordered and cohesive stories we tell about the world, and what was remarkable in 1968 was not at all the sense of common purpose and identity amongst the activists, but the way in which so many disparate voices were raised against such a wide variety of experiences of capitalist society. The tendency to seek out identity and similarity, the desire to order the world and develop a cleanly rational conception of it, has always flourished at the expense of all the wild desires, the untamed experiences, and the disruptive, disorderly events which refuse to take their place in coherent stories. After 1968, the possibility – that the most productive atmosphere in which to think was one which saw the history of capitalist society in terms of a struggle between order and disruption, control and chaos – was developed into a world view which completely undermined all the presuppositions of both revolutionary theory and its wider philosophical context. Difference, singularity, multiplicity, and everything which ran counter to the prevailing tendency to identify, contain, and order the world, was forcibly launched onto the political agenda. It was no longer a question of opposing right and left, the oppressors and the oppressed, but rather a matter of seeking out the concealed and denied elements of disruption which have always cut across our tendencies to order.

If this was one of the most extreme points to which philosophical reflection on the May events led, it was also deeply rooted and widely shared. It was, of course, no wonder that the events had failed if what they had really displayed was a moment of overt hostility between desires for disruption and needs for order. On the other hand, the language of success and failure was quite irrelevant to a world view which refused to give credence to Marxist conceptions of social revolution in the first place. But while Lyotard's work undermined the whole notion of revolution, it was far from suggesting that capitalist society is unchanging and unchangeable, and that there is nothing one can do or say to interrupt or subvert it. Instead, Lyotard's defences of the specificity of events and singularity of dissenting voices were in tune with other moves to displace our obsession with both society and individuals into a molecular view of the world, which looked at how the conceptualisations with which we are so used to working are actually constituted in the first place. To some extent, this had also been Foucault's project: the investigation of the hidden and much smaller circuits which produce all the macropolitical structures and conceptualisations in which we think we live. But for Lyotard, and also for Gilles Deleuze and Felix Guattari, the beach under the cobblestones was a realm of disruptive desires and disorderly chaos, which undermines every attempt at order, be it of the right or left, or in the name of liberation or domination.

# Re-Thinking Freud

This sense of hidden and internal disorder came not only from Nietzsche, but also from psychoanalytic theory. The influence of a variety of early psychoanalytic ideas on the events was clear in both the language of pleasure, desire, and spontaneity with which they were suffused, and also in the upsurge in interest in surrealism and other avant-garde attempts to dig beneath the superficial realities of conscious experience and express the hidden desires of the unconscious mind. Many of these sentiments were couched in the humanism of Marcusean readings of Freud, which insisted that oppression and alienation were based on our repression of the unconscious mind and its drives. Capitalist society prevented the expression of the true self revealed by psychoanalysis, and any successful revolution must result in a society organised for and around this self, rather than against it.

The psychoanalytic theory developed by Jacques Lacan was the product of a structuralist reading of Freud akin to that achieved by Althusser in relation to Marx. Whereas it had once seemed possible that psychoanalysis was primarily a therapy, in some sense, whether socially or individually, operating as a recipe for a more fulfiled and complete life, Lacan argued that we are always and inevitably split from our true selves; alienated in some very fundamental sense, irrespective of specific forms of economic and social organisation.

From the first moment in which we learn to use language in order to recognise and identify our selves and other things in the world, we enter the symbolic order, the entire world of discourses, signs, culture, and meaning. And at the same point, we leave the imaginary, or the undifferentiated and chaotic world in which we lived without this self-awareness and linguistic structure to tell us who and what we are. These terms, the symbolic order and the imaginary, broadly translate into Freud's understanding of the conscious mind and the unconscious, but whereas Freud suggested that analysis could produce some reconciliation between the two, so that we might reach an understanding of our whole selves, Lacan argued that the very existence and nature of this split between the imaginary and the symbolic order are misunderstood. Far from being antithetical to the symbolic, the imaginary can only exist within it, for the symbolic is the realm in which all attempts to conceptualise and express it must invariably take place. Lacan argued that the symbolic realm is one of fathers, laws, prohibitions, and orders; it is the phallus which operates as the symbolic figurehead of this realm, embodying the search for order and identity, beginnings and ends, coherence and sameness, whereas all that is associated with female sexuality – the multiplicity of organs and erogenous zones, the fluidity and diversity of sexual experience – is relegated to the imaginary other. In order to speak at all, therefore, we immediately place ourselves under the authority of the father, the search for identities and ways of organising and conceptualising our experiences.

From this perspective, the experience of alienation, for which capitalist society has long been indicted, is not specific to capitalist social organisation, but has something to do with the very structures of our thought. The ways in which we understand and change the world – conceptualising, naming and identifying it – also determine our relationship to it: the symbolic realm does not even merely distort the reality of the imaginary, for this latter realm is equally the product of our symbolisations and conceptualisations. Thus one can make no sense of any notion of reality, whether material or immaterial, conscious or unconscious, that is not mediated by the symbolic order, by our system of concepts. The beach is always and necessarily overlaid by the cobbled street.

But the beach had nevertheless survived these devastating criticisms of its original conceptualisation. And the fact that it was still possible to speak of an "other" to the existing series of orders meant that many of the philosophies which developed out of Lacan's reading of Freud and structuralism's encounter with Marxism retained a keen sense of political engagement. Luce Irigaray's feminist interpretations of Lacan, for example, suggested that women's position as the "other" in the societies and philosophical traditions of the West placed them outside the symbolic order, and so devoid of a language, history, and all the myths and stories which make up a cultural identity. In a similar manner to Foucault's analysis of discourse, Irigaray argued that the symbolic order is fundamentally patriarchal, and allows no place for women, suggesting both that it is extremely difficult, and not even necessarily desirable, for those whom the symbolic order excludes to enter into it; but her work also opened up new possibilities of subverting and interrupting the orders of discourse and society. The symbolic order is riddled with fissures and possibilities for resistance: we may be trapped within it, but it contains internal tensions which provide the potential for its subversion.

The impact of 1968's refusals of identification and categorisation surfaces not only in Irigaray's writing, but also in the work of Helene Cixous and Julia Kristeva, amongst others. The awareness that conceptualisation and theorising are themselves already implicit in the orders of the world has led to remarkably productive experiments with ways of social and discursive resistance and subversion. Such developments in feminist philosophy in France were particularly influenced by the May events, for in common with much 1960s counter-cultural and revolutionary discourse, the extent to which the events were politically and personally liberating was greatly circumscribed by the atmosphere of sexism and misogyny which suffuses Western political and social traditions. There was very much a feeling that, in 1968, the barricades were "manned" while the women made coffee and bandaged the fallen heroes of the street demonstrations. French feminism flourished in its subsequent efforts to expose the compromised nature of such an impoverished radicalism.

The adventurous radicalism of the philosophical developments considered in this chapter suggests that the identification of hidden structures of power and order has encouraged the desire to interrupt and subvert them. With the publication of Deleuze and Guattari's *Anti-Oedipus* in 1972, this experimentation reached new heights. In tune with Foucault and Lyotard, Deleuze and Guattari developed a micropolitical position which undermined all the traditional conceptions of the human subject, the social world, reason, and history, and suggested that the macropolitical identities and structures in which we think we live are really the products of a multiplicity of elements of disturbing and disordered intensity. In Deleuze and Guattari's work, the beach under the cobblestones is populated not by free individuals or dreams of an other or better world, but by an anarchic and productive chaos of flows and fluxes of energetic desire. All types of social organisation order and code these desires, forcing them into well-mapped territories which they nevertheless continue to exceed and transgress. And so Deleuze and Guattari presented a world of continual play between order and subversion, in which any form of organisation is inevitably subject to the interruption of its own components. But they also argued that this is a process accelerated by the development of capitalist society, for while new territories are mapped and desires coded by giant webs of production and consumption, capitalism's insatiable need to induce a spiralling proliferation of commodities and innovations of every kind exhibits unprecedented tendencies to deterritorialisation. Older forms of political order, moral regulation, and everything which leans towards tight control and prohibition, are swept aside, not by the grand march of the Marxist conception of a history leading to social revolution, but by the very exigencies of capitalism itself. According to Deleuze and Guattari, the brutal irrationality and discontinuity of capitalism should be encouraged, because political radicalism depends not on the development of new forms of theory, order, and codification, but on the *acceleration of capitalism's own tendencies to disorder and deterritorialisation*. Deleuze and Guattari opposed the tactics of the nomad – the one who refuses identification and settlement and sidesteps all attempts at categorialisation and control – to the rigorous discipline of the revolutionary party. Struggle at the molecular, the local, and micropolitical level is preferable to all-encompassing attempts to cast every particular moment or confrontation in terms of a large political project, such as that presupposed by revolutionary theory.

Such ideas do of course offer a radically different perspective on the events – and everything else in philosophy and the world – from that embodied in Marxist theory. If capitalism is already causing its own dissolution, then traditional revolutionary quests for more meaningful ways of living and thinking, and more rational ways of criticising capitalism, are merely reactionary responses which can only hold back and constrain the tendencies to dissolution and instability, of which May '68 was a prime example. It is clear that a context in which struggles between and within orders are replaced by those between order and its subversion has remarkable political potential.

Just as these desiring philosophies were so clearly influenced by the May events, so the political significance of their philosophical challenges has not been lost on those involved in more recent activity. Deleuze and Guattari's nomadic philosophy found a place in the Italian events of the late 1970s, and continues to resonate with attempts to sidestep order and control. In their refusals of categorisation and identification, the terrorists in the Angry Brigade of the 1970s, the travellers of the free festival movement of the 1980s, and the blissed-out party goers of the 1990s motorway service station all embody upsurges of a nomadic force capable of exposing and ridiculing territories, laws, and the entire tendency to authoritarian domination which was itself a ground of the 1968 events.

There are, of course, other directions in which the events encouraged philosophical debate. Some French intellectuals found succour in Maoism, others in the development of a right wing politics. The notions of difference, singularity and writing were vital to the development of deconstruction, which again pursued the structuralist concern with the orders of language and thought to a point at which Derrida, for example, could famously claim that there is "no outside to the text". The idea that, as soon as one posits an all-encompassing symbolic order, there can be no sense of any pre-discursive reality, has also blossomed in post-modern discourse, for which the beach under the cobblestones does indeed finally disappear. The influence of the 1968 events is very clear in Baudrillard's post-modern writings, which assert the impossibility of distinguishing between the real and the discursive, the beach and the street, and suggest that the end of the century world in which we live is homogeneous. Levelled at Baudrillard, the charge of an unproductive and fatal pessimism really does ring true.

More than twenty years on, it is of course impossible to say how different French society would have been without the events. And given that the bases for many of the philosophical developments which followed in their wake had already been established prior to this great eruption of dissent, we cannot be certain that European philosophy would have been radically different either. But the fact that 1968 can be so clearly seen in poststructuralist, psychoanalytic, and feminist theory suggests that this was indeed a year which precipitated a wide range of impassioned challenges to the very foundations of Western philosophy.

## Further Reading

An eye-witness account of the events is in *Paris: May 1968*. Photographs of the graffiti are collected in Walter Lewino, *L'Imagination au Pouvoir*. The bibliography contains a representative selection of texts which either influenced, or were influenced by, the events of May 1968.

## Bibliography

G. Deleuze and F. Guattari, *Anti-Oedipus: Capitalism and Schizophrenia*, London: Athlone 1977.

M. Foucault, *The Archaeology of Knowledge*, tr. A.M. Sheridan, London: Tavistock 1972.

———*The Order of Things: An Archaeology of the Human Sciences*, tr. A.M. Sheridan, London: Tavistock 1970.

———, ed. Colin Gordon, *Power/Knowledge: Selected Interviews and Other Writings 1972-77*, Brighton: Harvester 1986.

W. Lewino, *L'Imagination au Pouvoir* Paris: Le Terrain Vague 1968.

J.-F. Lyotard, *Driftworks* , New York: Semiotext(e) 1984.

H. Marcuse, *One-Dimensional Man: Studies in the Ideology of Advanced Industrial Society*, Boston: Beacon Press 1966.

E. Marks and I. de Courtrivron (eds.), *New French Feminisms*, New York: Schocken 1981.

*Paris: May 1968*, Dark Star and Rebel Press 1986.

R. Vienet, *The Enragés and the Situationists in the Occupation Movement, May-June 1968* New York: Semiotext(e) 1990.

# Index

*a priori* 94
Abraham 58ff.
absolute difference 53
absolute knowledge 21
absolute paradox 54
abstract entities 82
absurd 45
accident 95, 98
act of will 42
action 42, 89, 124, 128
actuality 159, 165
Adorno 36, 145,147f.
advertising 68, 177
Aeschylus 81
aesthetic standpoint 57
Albert 149
alienation 35, 147, 186f.
Althusser 180ff, 186
Amazonia 147
ambiguity 133
analysis 162
Ancient Greece 19, 81, 83
Anglo-Saxon philosophy 4
anguish 128f.
animals 85
anomie 34
anti-Semitism 77
Antigone 20, 57
anxiety 45, 49
appearance 39, 68, 97
archaeology 163f., 166
architecture 45
Aristotle 43, 94f., 98, 107ff., 112ff., 117
arithmetic 92
art 45, 80ff., 105, 114
asceticism 45f.
assumptions 152f.
authenticity 113. 128f., 133, 141f., 157, 183
authoritarianism 148
authority 13, 175ff.
automation 72

autonomy 141, 153, 180
bad faith 122. 127ff., 133
Baluchistan 147
Baudrillard 190
de Beauvoir 11, 78, 179
Being 108f., 146
being 24
beings 108
Bergson 6
Berkeley 39f.
biology 95
blacks 122
Blondel 6
body 18, 25, 41f., 127, 141f., 169
Boole 93ff.
bracketing 102
Brentano 2, 6, 90, 94f., 105
Bubner 158
Buddhism 46
Bultmann 105
bureaucracy 176, 182
capacity 123ff.
capital 63
capitalism 63ff., 70f., 83, 147, 177f., 180, 183f., 187ff.
care 111
categories 21f., 23–28, 95
causality 40, 89, 124, 127, 135, 149
cause 24
censorship 167
certainty 22, 54ff., 83, 94, 110
change 95, 98, 112f., 128, 173
chaos 185
choice 58
Chomsky 155
Christendom 51
Christianity 51, 56, 77, 83f., 89, 184
civic life 50ff., 56ff.
civic morality 59
civil society 31ff., 34, 63, 68f.
Cixous 188

class 138
commitment 119
commodities 65, 147, 176, 189
commodity fetishism 68
communication 179, 182, 184
communicative action 154f., 159
communism 120f., 128f., 135, 175, 178
community 23, 34
computers 72
conceptual revolution 30
conflict 43, 62, 134, 145, 158
conformism 148
conscience 23, 51, 57, 113
consciousness 20ff., 28, 65, 111, 120, 123ff., 126, 130, 132ff., 137, 140f.
consensus 156ff.
constitution 170
construction 164
constructivism 5, 180
consumption 176
contemplation 44
context 132
contingency 141
continuity 100, 124f.
contradiction 25ff., 57, 88, 141, 145
control 153, 168, 184
controversy 146
conversation 152
conversion 132
creation 140
creativity 133, 137, 146, 168, 176, 181
crisis 62, 93, 177
"crisis of the subject" 178
criticism 151, 154
cultural change 25
culture 150
culture criticism 78

Darwin 85
Dasein 109ff.
death 112f., 136, 138
deconstruction 144
Deleuze 142, 174, 181, 186, 187f.
democracy 62
Derrida 1, 6, 9, 143, 156f., 160, 190

Descartes 92, 102, 106ff., 109, 112, 149, 151
desire 32, 168, 174, 176f., 180f.
despair 21
destruction 108
determinism 126, 127f., 133, 135, 138, 144
development 21
deviance 166
dialectic 10ff., 23, 27ff., 31, 36, 129, 146, 180, 183
dichotomy 18, 22, 25f.
Diderot 20
difference 53f., 73, 96, 183f.
discontinuity 112, 114f., 126, 134
discourse 151f., 167f.
discursive practices 165
disruption 184
divine command 58
divine punishment 50
dogmatism 26
domination 139, 183
Don Giovanni 56
Dostoevsky 106
doubt 21
dread 113
Dreyfus 103
Duhem 93
Dummett 4
Dworkin 138

economic cooperation 32
economics 130, 138
effect 24
ego 137
eidetic phenomenology 102
eidetic reduction 102
emancipation 135, 152
emotions 112
empiricism 93f., 97
engaged philosophy 14f., 17
Engels 30, 50, 138
Enlightenment 63, 149f.
epistemology 63f., 73, 79, 82, 86, 99, 107, 148
epoche 101
equality 69
error 79, 125

essence                 23, 67f., 100f.,
                        110, 113, 126
essentialism            5, 17
estrangement            147
eternal recurrence      79, 88
eternity                53f., 60
ethical standpoint      57, 60
ethics                  51, 57f., 86, 113,
                        125ff., 131ff.
European philosophy     4
event                   178
everyday experience     104
evil                    57
evolution               21, 79, 88
exchange value          65, 69
existence               54, 110, 113, 126
existentialism          48, 55, 120, 122,
        127f., 134f., 137, 140ff., 152
experience              25f., 102, 124,
                        132, 137, 151, 155
exploitation            66
expression              178
extension               107
exteriority             162

fact                    148f.
fact-value distinction  133
faith           18, 52, 58f., 145, 160
false consciousness     136
Fascism                 135
fatalism                157
female                  187
feminism                64, 71, 78, 188
Feuerbach               30, 35, 50, 62
Fichte                  145
fiction                 79, 84, 87
finality                54
finite                  26, 54, 56, 59
finiteness              114, 136
flux                    126
folk religion           51
for-itself              123
force                   24
forces                  30
form                    95, 98
form of life            153
Foucault                78f., 158f., 174,
                        180ff., 185ff.
foundationalism         8

foundations             94f., 107
fragmentation           25
Frankfurt school        145, 147, 177
freedom         18, 23, 28, 32f., 36, 62, 89,
        120, 122, 126, 128f., 131ff.,
                        138f., 150, 166
Frege                   iii, 92, 94
French revolution       62
Freud           43, 85, 120, 126, 136f.,
                162, 166, 177f., 180, 185f.
Fromm                   146
future                  137f.

Gadamer                 149ff., 154ff.
gardening               44
gaze                    136
gender bias             141
genealogy               78, 99, 157, 166
generalisation          87
genius                  45
Gilson                  6
God                     26, 55, 83,
                        107, 135, 149, 159
Goethe                  38
good                    57
graffiti                178
Grand Narrative         72
Greek city state        51
Guattari                174, 180, 185, 187f.

Habermas                8, 12
Hegel           5, 8f., 10ff, 38, 49–63,
                99, 109, 110, 124, 131,
                        136f., 146, 180, 182
Hegelians: Young, Old   30
Heidegger               6, 8f., 13f., 95,
                103f., 120, 145, 148, 154f.
hell                    45
hermeneutics    145, 149ff., 158, 165
hierarchy               178, 182
historical materialism  65, 135
history                 13, 113f., 116f.,
                        130, 136, 139f., 145,
                        152, 159, 170, 181
Hölderlin               18f.
homosexuality           122, 169f.
hope                    35, 158
horizon                 102, 151, 156
Horkheimer              146f.
human sciences          148

humanism 11, 111, 127ff., 157, 185
Hume 128
Husserl 6, 11, 13, 106, 111, 123, 147f.

'I' 23
Idea 29
ideal speech situation 155
idealism 136, 140
identity 8, 73, 146, 186
ideology 66f., 77, 83, 136, 154, 175
illusion 39, 41, 46, 88
imaginary 187
imagination 96, 176
immanence 102
immediacy 178, 181
imperialism 137
impure reflection 125
in-itself 123
inauthenticity 141
incarnation 51, 53f.
individual 19, 28, 30, 54, 60, 63, 110, 134f., 140, 166, 170f., 179f.
individualism 31f., 51, 55
individuality 46, 148
industrial revolution 62
infinite 26, 54, 56, 59
initiation 124
injustice 179
innovation 188
instant 58
instinct 23f., 44
institution 183
intellect 18, 40
intellectual, role of 161, 172
intelligence 41
interests 149, 151
interpretation 86
introspection 41
intuition 96, 98
inwardness 55
Irigaray 174, 186f.
irrational 81, 140
is-ought distinction 133

Jakobson 164
Jesus 53
Judaism 77, 84

Judaism 84
judgement 128
Kant 26, 33, 37f., 40, 58, 86, 98f., 125, 128, 132, 137, 150, 152, 153f., 156, 161
Kaufman 77
Kierkegaard 36, 102, 110, 112f., 1582f.
knowledge 89, 145, 151f., 155, 158, 171, 182
Kretzmann 14
Kristeva 188
labour 147
labour theory of value 65f., 71
Lacan 185f.
lack 133
laissez-faire economics 80
Lakoff 12
language 106, 108, 115, 118, 142, 154–160, 185f.
law 32, 35, 68, 136, 187
"laws of thought" 94
Lawvere 14
leap of faith 55
legitimacy 63, 68, 74
legitimation 3, 69, 73
Leibniz 125
lesbian 141
liberalism 31, 33, 62f., 68f., 74
libertarianism 181
liberty 69
life 23, 43f.
life-world 104, 145
linearity 7
linguistics iii, 164
literary criticism 164
literature 140, 157
Locke 40
Loewenthal 146
logic iii, 9, 13, 27, 79, 82, 87, 93ff., 98, 118
logocentrism 9
Lotze 118
Lukasiewicz iii
Luther 113f.
Lyotard 12, 180–6, 188

madness 162
male 187
Maoism 190
Marcel 6
Marcuse 146, 176f., 185
marginalisation 177
market 31ff.
marriage 56f., 142
Marx 11, 18, 31, 36, 51, 78, 99, 120, 128f., 132, 147, 162, 177ff.
Marxism 8, 135, 139, 144f., 146, 178, 180–4, 189
mass media 176
master 85
master-slave dialectic 22f., 138
masturbation 167
materialism 64, 73, 128, 136, 142, 148
mathematics iii, 10, 13, 92, 97f., 164
matter 18, 41, 95, 98
Maya 39, 46
meaning 101, 160, 163, 165, 179
measurement 62, 64, 66
medieval philosophy 9, 118
Mellor 1
memory 124, 126
men 139
mereology 99f.
Merleau-Ponty 18
metaphor 116, 170
metaphysics 4, 9, 24, 26, 51, 118, 142
method 10ff., 147f.
methodology 15f.
Mill 93, 118
mind 30, 126, 128
misogyny 39, 188
modernism 146
modernity 156
Møller 51
moment 100
monopoly capital 71
moral law 60
morality 85, 120
multiplicity 43, 184, 186
music 46
mystification 135
myth 88, 140

naming 186
narcissism 137

narrative 7
nation state 71
nationalism 158
natural attitude 101
natural rights 69
natural sciences 147
nature 29, 43, 64, 140, 150, 167, 169
Nazism 77, 88f., 106, 117, 120, 150
necessity 18, 28, 84, 170, 176, 179
needs 174
negation 124, 127, 132
negative acts 47
neo-Kantianism 6, 106
neo-Thomism 106
Newton 29
Nietzsche 6, 12, 18, 45, 62, 72f., 106, 120, 128, 133, 142, 154–158,162, 166, 182f.
nihilism 132f., 144
noema 100ff.
noesis 100f.
non-existence 47
norm 152, 158
Norris 158
nothingness 123
noumena 40
nous 54
object 9, 122–7, 132f., 135, 137, 162
objective reality 120
objectivity 56, 128, 155
observation 64
ontic 109
ontological 109
ontology 9, 73, 95, 103, 106–9, 112, 113–119, 123, 125f., 129, 133, 136, 138ff.
opposition 182
oppression 133f., 183
optimism 82, 159
order 161, 163, 181, 184, 186f.
ordinary language philosophy 11
other 134, 139f., 182, 186

painting 46
paradox 52, 55f., 88, 135
Parmenides 113
part 95, 98ff.
particular 21, 23, 28f., 31
passion 132f.

passion of faith 56
patriarchy 188
Peano iii
penis 136f., 138
perception 22, 40f., 64, 107, 124
perpetual peace 150
person 32
perspectivism 73, 86, 124
perverse 45
pessimism 38f, 41, 44, 47, 78, 89, 190
phallus 136ff., 187
phenomena 39f., 43
phenomenology 11, 18, 96f., 106, 111, 123, 136
philosophy 24, 178
physics 13
Piaget 155
picture thinking 52
Plato 107f.
play 188
pleasure 168, 176
pluralism 157
plurality 46
poetry 46, 106
Poincaré 94, 98
politics 5, 35, 120
Popper 31
popular culture 68
pornography 142
positivism 4, 5, 148, 158
positivism, logical 4, 10, 148
possibility 96, 98, 102, 104, 146, 152, 154, 164
possible worlds 47
post-Fordism 71f.
post-industrial society 176
postmodernism 156, 179
poststructuralism 179, 181
power 64, 137, 166–72, 180, 182
pragmatics 164
praxis 65, 67, 73, 111, 147
pre-Socratics 115
prejudice 142
prescription 164
production 176
profit 66
progress 180
project 137
protest 175

pseudonyms 50
psychoanalysis 137, 141f.
psychology 93f.
psychology, empirical 30
pure form 46
pure reflection 125
pure thought 55
quality 65
quantity 65
races 85
rational justification 56
rationalism 55, 56, 62, 147, 149
rationality 35, 150, 157, 180, 183
reading 126
realism 5, 17, 103
reality 39, 150
reason 25ff, 39, 42, 81f, 127, 130, 144f, 151f.
reductionism 65, 139, 148
reflection 19, 33, 136, 152, 156
refusal 170
regularities 163
reification 136
relation 180
relations of production 66, 68, 72
relativism 84, 86f.
religion 58, 82ff., 114
religion and philosophy 52
religious metaphors 52
religious standpoint 60
representation 39f., 42, 162
repression 71, 145, 159, 168
repressive hypothesis 166, 169
resistance 170
responsibility 125–8
revolution 174f., 181
Ricardo 63
Rickert 106
Ricoeur 158
rights, abstract 34
Rilke 106
Rimbaud 177
romanticism 45, 58, 140
Rousseau 51
rule 128
Russell 6, 15
Sartre 6, 49, 132f., 136, 141, 178

Saussure                           164
Schelling              9, 18, 50, 145
Schleiermacher                       6
Schopenhauer            81, 85ff, 89f.
Schröder                            94
science            43, 63, 65, 79f., 85,
                    93, 95, 117, 148, 153
scientism                      149, 150
sculpture                           46
self            108, 113, 141, 179, 185
self-consciousness            65, 135
self-deception                      79
self-interest                       33
self-preservation                   44
self-reflection                    153
sense data                      97, 101
sense-certainty                     22
senses                              40
sex                         44, 80, 136
sexism                             188
sexuality                  137, 165–170
signs                              161
Sigwart                         93, 108
silence                            170
Simons                             105
"single narrow door"            42, 44
singularity                        184
Situationists                      177
slave                               85
slavery                         33, 45
social change                      154
social Darwinism                    85
social relations               65f., 73
social structure                    15
social studies                     152
socialism                          148
society                 19, 155, 180f.
Socrates                 9, 79, 82, 96
sodomy                             169
Sophocles                       20, 81
Sorabji                             14
soul                      18, 26, 83f.
space                      40, 107, 154
speech act                         155
Spirit                     18ff., 29, 39
stability                           69
State                 31, 33f., 64, 69
state church                        51
state religion                      53

stories                            183f.
strategy                           170
Strawson                           123
structuralism      156, 163f., 179, 185f.
structure                 98, 100f., 102,
                    118, 133, 155, 179f.
subject          9, 122–7, 133, 136, 138,
                151, 156, 162, 166, 179ff.
subjection                          63
subjectivism                       154
subjectivity                   33, 56ff.
substance            68, 95, 98, 107f.
subversion                     181, 187
suicide                             46
Superman                        79, 88f.
survival                           152
symbolic order                   185ff.
system                          55, 179
syntax                             164

tactics                            170
technical rationality          148, 153
technique                          169
technology         70, 118, 146, 152
teleological suspension of the ethical    59f.
theism                              49
theocracy                           31
theology                            50
theory                 178, 180f. , 183
thing                              135
thing in itself            40, 42, 101
thought                             20
thrownness                         150
time                  40, 54f., 60, 114
tools                              139
totalisation                       181
totalitarianism                    183
trade                               32
trade cycle                         74
tradition                      34, 149f.
tragedy                         46, 80ff.
Trakl                              106
transcendence                 102, 113
transcendental ego             99, 102
Trendelenburg                       95
truth            23, 56, 79, 83, 87f.,
                103, 115, 145, 149ff.,153,
            156, 158, 162, 165, 169, 171f.
Tübingen                            18

ultimate reality 39ff., 43, 46
unconscious 126
understanding 26ff., 155, 159
undistorted communication 154
unity 28, 30, 43, 46, 125f., 183
universal 21, 23f., 28–31, 33, 35, 58ff, 100, 132, 140, 143
universalisability 136, 153
uncertainty 56
use value 66, 70
utilitarianism 85f., 158
utopia 31
utopianism 69, 78

validation 151
value 108, 124, 132f.
"veil of perception" 40
"veil of the intellect" 42
"view from nowhere" 56

violence 135
vulgarity 78

wages 67
Wagner 78, 81f.
wants 33
whole 97, 98ff.
wholeness 132
will 39, 41–43, 47
will of God 58
will of God 59
will to live 44ff.
will to power 79, 84, 88f.
"woman" 140, 143
women 121, 132, 138, 142
work 177
world 26, 108, 134, 151, 158, 184
Wundt 93f.